A Life Known
and Unknowable

A LIFE KNOWN and UNKNOWABLE

In Search of a Totally Unhistorical Jesus of Nazareth with Comments, Notes and Many Fine Illustrations –

a Novel

JEFF CARTER

RESOURCE *Publications* • Eugene, Oregon

A LIFE KNOWN AND UNKNOWABLE
In Search of a Totally Unhistorical Jesus of Nazareth with Comments, Notes and Many Fine Illustrations – a Novel

Copyright © 2022 Jeff Carter. All rights reserved. Except for brief quotations in critical publications or reviews, no part of this book may be reproduced in any manner without prior written permission from the publisher. Write: Permissions, Wipf and Stock Publishers, 199 W. 8th Ave., Suite 3, Eugene, OR 97401.

Resource Publications
An Imprint of Wipf and Stock Publishers
199 W. 8th Ave., Suite 3
Eugene, OR 97401

www.wipfandstock.com

PAPERBACK ISBN: 978-1-6667-4896-3
HARDCOVER ISBN: 978-1-6667-4897-0
EBOOK ISBN: 978-1-6667-4898-7

AUGUST 3, 2022 9:30 AM

For Chris, Dave, Gabe, and Other Chris.
The next one is on me.
Xertz!

The task must be made difficult, for only the difficult inspires the noble-hearted.
—SOREN KIERKEGAARD

I shall try to make him say what I wish he had said, because only in that way will I manage to understand what he meant to say.
—UMBERTO ECO

Get your facts first, then you can distort them as you please.
—MARK TWAIN

. . . so that seeing they may not see, and hearing they may not understand.
—LUKE 8:10

CONTENTS

I–Prologue   1
The Argument–A Deep and Persistent Melancholy   4
II–Ante Bellum   6
The Argument–An Apology   34
III–Igitur Qui Desiderat Pacem, Praeparet Bellum   37
The Argument–Wanting More   54
IV–Terminus a Quo   55
The Argument–Through A Glass Darkly and All That   117
V–Tempus Fugit   119
The Argument–I Feel Pretty Shattered Most of the Time   183
VI–Dum Spiro Spero   185
The Argument–My Own Idiosyncratic Predilections, Peccadillos and Obvious Heresies   233
VII–Post Fluxae Carnis Scandala   236
The Final Argument–I'm Not Much But I'm All I Have   242

Appendix 1
AN EXCERPT FROM DR. TARREC'S FIELD GUIDE TO DEMONIC ENCOUNTERS   245
Appendix 2
UNWRITTEN NOTES #132-140   247

Bibliography   249

I

Prologue

1. Make It Weird

THEO, LISTEN. THIS STORY'S been told a thousand times already, a thousand, thousand, I know. And it will be told a thousand, thousand more, handed down hand to hand, mouth to ear, from the hand of God to the heart of man,[1] long after you and I have returned to ash and dust and soil. From the first eyewitness, into the long future that we can't yet see, the story of all the things he did was and, is and, will be told.

With this in mind, and knowing my frailties and fallible limitations, I thought it good to tell it again for you. And after my own prolonged investigation, I have written everything from beginning to end (more or less) in this (more or less) orderly account so that you can appreciate what you've been taught.

This isn't a gospel, never think it. Neither is it a sermon. Forget *exegesis*. Forget *eisegesis*. Forget *diegesis*, even. I don't know exactly what this is.[2] It is part *targum*, and part *découpé*. It's certainly not an attempt to explain anything outright, but to make it weird. Like the prophet (blessings and peace be upon him) writing on palm leaves, stones, even on the shoulder blades of camels, I wrote this novel on ragged scraps of paper, on the back of grocery receipts and unwanted junk-mail political adverts. I wrote it in cheap spiral bound notebooks and on a ten year old laptop that is slowly dying a digital death. I've borrowed and stolen without shame. I've quoted

---

1. Maybe it was from the heart of God to the hand of man? Maybe it's all the same thing.

2. Perhaps *epexegesis* might be the right word—but that would assume that I've clarified anything with this writing.

and cribbed. I've tried to provide sources and references, but I'm all over the place here. I probably missed one or two. Sorry.

There are probably going to be a few—or maybe more than a few—who will say that I'm playing fast and loose with the gospel story that shouldn't be fooled around with. They might say that I'm not playing fair. To them I'd say this: Creativity requires seeing. But that's something more than just the casual glimpsing of the eye. Creativity requires seeing *new* things. It requires seeing things that aren't, things that aren't yet. It requires a departure from reality. So don't say, 'This is strange.' Instead, ask 'Is this strange enough?'

There most certainly was an historical Jesus who lived and breathed and bled in Palestine in the early years of the first century. Whether or not we can exhume this historical Jesus from the gospel texts is a difficult question. The many and varied historical Jesuses that have been described by theologians and historians is—or should be—evidence that this quest, while beneficial, may not be complete or accurate. What is exhumed (and that word is deliberate) is not the living Jesus of faith—the Christ who, admittedly, cannot be known from history. He can only be experienced by faith.

The Jesus in this novel is *not* the historical Jesus. That should be readily apparent I hope.

Figure 1–Time itself may be an anachronism.

A question may occur: Are there Templars in this story? Of course. There are always Templars, even when you can't see them. Especially when you can't see them. They are quite adept at hiding in the shadows.

Prologue

Still, after all that, I am mindful of the Qu'ranic admonition, "woe to those who write the 'scripture' with their own hands, then say, 'This is from Allah,'" as well as the warning in the book of the Apocalypse about adding to the word of prophecy. Even so, anachronisms certainly abound. What can I do? I am as uneven as this text.

The Argument

A Deep and Persistent Melancholy

As far as I know, the Dutch post-impressionist painter Vincent van Gogh has never been considered for nomination to the ranks of the prophets, but perhaps he should be. If it were up to me he'd be nominated on the strength of his paintings alone. Though he never sold more than a few paintings during his lifetime, he has been posthumously recognized as one of the most sensitive artists of the nineteenth century, if not the whole of history. His paintings stir the soul to passion and to compassion for the poor. They cause us to recognize our deepest longings; they move us toward reverence for the sublime. But, should that not be enough, there is much in the letters he wrote to his own Theo—his younger brother—that recommends him to that holy office. Consider what he wrote on April 3, 1878:

"Whoever lives sincerely and encounters much trouble and disappointment, but is not bowed down by them, is worth more than one who has always sailed before the wind and has only known relative prosperity. For who are those that show some sign of higher life? They are those to whom may be applied the words: "*Laboureurs, votre vie est triste, laboureurs, vous souffrez dans la vie, laboureurs, vous êtes bien-heureu.*"[1] They are those that bear the signs of "a whole life of struggle and sustained work without ever wavering." And it is good to try to become like them so that we may go forth on our way, "*indefessi favente Deo,*" in the tireless favor of God.

Maybe you'll object that Vincent van Gogh suffered from some sort of mental illness, that he had auditory hallucinations, that he heard voices,

---

1. "Laborers, your life is sad. Laborers you suffer in this life. Laborers, you are very happy." Van Gogh, *Letters*, 109.

The Argument

and that this mental instability should disqualify him from being considered a prophet. But just try to tell me that the prophet Ezekiel doesn't seem schizophrenic or that Jeremiah wasn't depressed and suicidal. Maybe all the prophets—all the honest prophets—suffered this way. Consider what Van Gogh wrote to his brother on February 3, 1889: "*Well, there are moments when I am wrung by enthusiasm, or by madness, or prophecy, like a Greek oracle on its tripod.*"[2]

I have mentioned earlier in this manuscript that at various times I have thought of myself as an artist, as a painter.[3] But I know that I'm not so much of a painter; I've accepted that fact. But in my struggles during seminary (and after my expulsion from seminary) I found great comfort in the letters that Vincent wrote to his younger brother, Theo. I find inspiration in the lives of artists the way that others find inspiration in the deaths of the martyrs. As I read the Van Gogh's correspondence I found (or imagined) a number of parallels between Vincent Van Gogh's life and my own. For example: we are both sons of ministers, we both studied to become ministers to the poor and downtrodden, we both felt a longing to create art of beauty, and we shared a deep and persistent melancholy. Maybe it was just apophenia—the human tendency to mistakenly perceive connections and meanings between unrelated things. Maybe it was only a pareidolic paradise, but I took comfort in it.

His final words, spoken as he lay dying in the *Auberge Ravoux* of a self-inflicted gunshot wound to the chest, should also recommend him to the ranks of the prophets for they are an enduring and abiding truth: "*La tristess durera toujours.*" The sadness will last forever.

Amen.

---

2. "Van Gogh, .*Letters*, 311.

3. You will soon notice, if you haven't already, that this manuscript is, like the state of affairs in Hamlet's Denmark, out of joint timewise. I mention my self-description later in the book on page 54. Pay it no mind; it is merely a slightly pretentious meta-narrative construct.

II

Ante Bellum

1. Dead. I Love Dead.

THE FIRST THING YOU should remember is that those were bad days, man. A bad scene. And King Herod was one mad bastard. Paranoid too. And paranoia like his, at his level is infectious. It spreads like a spark in dry tinder, like a mutating virus through a crowded subway car. And the masses are easily swayed by paranoia like that. They are persuaded by visions of fear and by hate. And Herod had paranoia and fear and hate in spades. He didn't have to dig very deep to find them; they were all right there on the surface.

Herod had the agents of the State Research Bureau (SRB)[1] infiltrating rival political groups and radical student organizations. They perpetrated all manner of deep undercover skunkworks. It was totally illegal, completely unconstitutional. Or it would have been if we had had we a constitution then. But hey! Nothing's illegal for the king, right? The SRB was smuggling drugs and Chinese fireworks across the desert borders to raise funds for the Zealots, then luring them into futile guerrilla actions against Herod's militias. They targeted union leaders, small town preachers, and no-name prophets of the Jubilee with Hellfire attack drones. They poisoned wells and they

---

1. The SRB was the covert agency composed of torturers and informants responsible for domestic slaughters. Someone had a car accident? SRB. The car and the corpse were riddled with mysterious bullet holes? SRB. They used spider-bite heart attacks and brain-tumor suicides to eliminate their targets. They used Magnesium thermite bombs. They used targeted lightning strikes, inflammatory legislation and the foul breath of propaganda to destroy their targets. Herod's SRB would later be replaced by the more efficient (and not to say, ruthless) MCNS—Military Council for National Security—but that was many years later.

torched villages. They loosed vicious, snarling animals into crowded market plazas. They rocket-blasted a rural wedding (the bride and groom smiling in the sun in that last horrifying moment before the flash and the bang) to kill their target (who wasn't even present at the tragic event). The SRB called it 'collateral damage' and then ignore it. They ignored the ruined homes of civilians and the eviscerated children laying in the street. Herod's trained SRB assassins were ready to kill anyone and everyone he labeled as a threat to national security, or to his own personal security. Even members of his own family. Perhaps, especially members of his own family became targets of the SRB. Like I said, those were bad times and he was one mad bastard.

The last of the Hasmonean high priests, Aristobulus III, was, in Herod's twisted dementia, a threat to his precarious throne. When Aristobulus III appeared for the first time before the people at the Feast of the Tabernacles, dressed in the full finery of his priestly office, the people cheered and welcomed him with spontaneous and genuine cries of affection. So Herod had him hit. The SRB assassins drowned him in a swimming pool in Jericho and left his corpse floating in the water.

Telephone communications were frequently curtailed in those days. Curfews were instituted and then changed at random. One night we would be hanging out at the discotheque at twenty after one in the morning, the next we were being billy-clubbed and stun-gunned back to our apartments at quarter past seven. Czechoslovakian mercenaries wearing gas masks guarded the city gates. Tanks rumbled down the narrow streets of Jerusalem. Writers, intellectuals, actors, trade unionists, chemists, Italian anarchists, and dissident priests were arrested with or without cause—usually without warrants.

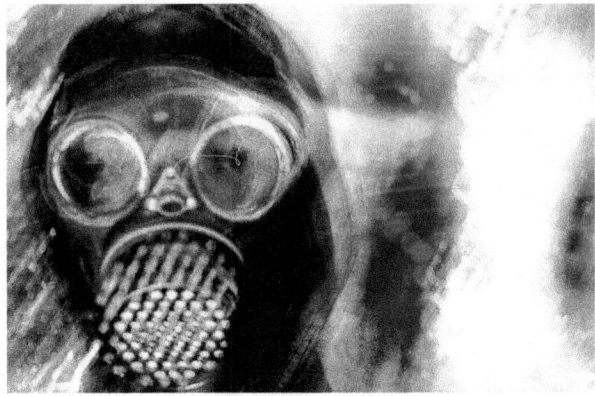

Figure 2–Nehas, co t nepálí.

"Herod," he said speaking of himself in the third person, "Herod is a giant who will eclipse the sun. Do you doubt it? Do you? How could you doubt it?"

Figure 3–If you say anything, we will report you.

I've heard rumors that Herod had people killed in Jerusalem and the surrounding suburbs—Bethlehem for one. I've heard the rumors that he sent SRB troops under the leadership of Commander Nine-Nine[2] to slaughter children. Babies. Commander Nine-Nine often boasted of eating the flesh of his enemies, despite the prevailing religious taboo against the consumption of human flesh. Maybe these are nothing more than rumors and back alley legends. I can't confirm them, to be sure. But they certainly fit with what I remember of that mad tyrant and what I remember of those days when SWAT teams in black matte riot gear went into moonless nights with orders to kill.

Yeah, it's incredible, but it's not altogether impossible. Maybe it's not even implausible. Remember what he said in front of the cameras of Channel $4 news? "It may take a bloodbath, but there will be no appeasement."[3] There may have been a thousand children left dead in the streets, and heaped in the gutters till they were consumed by hyenas, but he wouldn't have seen them. And had he seen them he would have ignored them except

---

2. Obviously a codename of some sort. His real identity has never been confirmed.

3. Governor Ronald Reagan would later speak these same words before sending in his own soldiers to quash the protests of university students in 1969.

to hitch up his robe a little higher to keep their blood from staining his garments as he stepped over them.

Maybe I shouldn't write about this. It's dangerous, even now long after he's dead of some incurable disease. The intrigues and machinations he began, as well as those of his family after him (those family members he didn't kill or have killed), are still swirling around us like a treacherous storm. Blood drunk governments continue to plot murders in the night. Writing this sort of criticism usually marks one for death. Those were dark and dreadful days when the government spent stolen millions[4] to study things like aggression in cats and violence in overcrowded rat populations. They studied possibilities of applying psychosurgery techniques during capital punishment. They studied Manchurian hypnosis and kinetic soul tampering. Those were dark days then. Yes. And these are darker days today. But death comes for us all eventually, so what the hell? If I'm going to tell the story, I gotta' tell it true. I gotta' tell it full.

It all began[5] during the reign of King Herod. He spent those days lounging in one of his many fortified palaces. Dressed in long, gold lamé robes, mirrored aviator sunglasses, and cheap rubber flip flops, he laid on a chaise lounge reading tarot cards and rage tweeting threats against his enemies across the desert in Nabataea, and sucking up to the dictator in Rome, Caesar Augustus. "Make Judea Great Again!" he tweeted before bellowing to one of the palace servants to bring him his personal physician. He needed more Adderall, more pain killers. "I need more coke!" he yelled. "And another Diet Coke!" The pain in the back of his head would never go away he said. "I'm the only King to be in contact with God" he screamed while pawing at the inflammation in his skull until his scalp bled.

The anthropological analysis of skull types is outmoded now, passé even, but what might it have revealed about the sociopath on the throne if we could have examined the curve his cranium? And should we make of the collection of photographs of bloody car wrecks that he kept under his mattress? What would a psychotherapist have said of them? What would they say of the films he'd watch in his private movie theater–film recordings of his enemies having their organs removed and fed to feral dogs? All

---

4. And just where did Herod get the millions to pay for this diabolical research? He broke open the Bank of the Tomb of David and stole some three hundred million dollars. And this was not even his most egregious atrocity.

5. Though, as with any story, the "beginning" is the somewhat arbitrary choice of the storyteller. There is always something that came before. The same is true of "endings;" there is always something after "the end."

grue and noisome invitation to indulgence and extravagance. All invitation to indulge in grotesque, antisocial behavior, to commit gratuitous acts of selfish violence in the pursuit of puerile dreams of power. All craven fear. Herod was one of the saucer men, one of the Daddy-Warbucks-warbabies. He was one of the bomb-freaks, gun-nuts, intestinal parasites.

Figure 4–Dreams of blood and power.

"You hate me because you still love me," he shouted. I couldn't tell if he was a paranoid Near Eastern king, a brutal fascist dictator, or a self-absorbed billionaire president. "Yes" he'd tweet without context or warning. "Dead. I love dead." And, later, "There will be kisses for all of you." It was during those left-handed and sinister strange days that the priest Z'kharyah of the division of Abijah was chosen to serve as priest before the Lord.

2. Deep Hormonal Forces

It is a well-known fact that Hungarian peasant women, after giving birth and often while still at work in the fields, will eat a bite of their afterbirth as a testament to their proven fertility. It is also well-known that Chinese women eat dried and salted afterbirth to improve their chances of conception. There are powerful, primordial powers here, deep hormonal forces beyond our comprehension at work. Animalistic even. Indeed, some chimpanzee mothers have been observed drinking their own urine during and after their labor. These primal forces are powerful. Do they know something we don't?

Ante Bellum

Send for a doctor trained in the schools of Alexandria, he will tell what is happening here. Let's read from one of their text books:

According to the Roman naturalist and philosopher Pliny the Elder, "sterility in females may be removed by giving them the eye of the hyena to eat, in combination with licorice and dill, conception within three days being warranted as the result." Pliny the Elder had many other remedies for infertility—most of which involved the application of lichens, ox dung, rose oil, serpents' fat, and honey to the sexual organs.

Z'kharyah and his wife, Elizabeth, tried this. All of it. As ridiculous as it sounded, they tried it. None of it was too ridiculous to try at least once because they were desperate to have a child. They'd tried good luck amulets, expensive prayers and every folk remedy passed on to them by concerned neighbors. Elizabeth wore charms against Dodib, the demon of all abortions, and Z'kharyah applied the ætherial balsams bottled by Doctor James Graham, of the celebrated Temple of Health on the river Thymes, to his genitals. These were also guaranteed to "promote fertility and the conception of the loveliest of children." But none of it worked.[6] They remained childless year after year.

"Take courage," the women of the village said to Elisabeth during their senior water aerobics class at the YMCA. "Professor Orfila of the Medico-legal Department of the University of Paris has described numerous cases of women conceiving for the first time at the age of sixty-three, menstruating regularly well into their nineties and finally dying at the age of one hundred and sixteen, even one hundred and twenty years old. You are old, Elizabeth," they said to her, "but you are not so old yet. There is still hope for you and your husband."

But she did not believe them. Her anxiety waxed with the moon, but never waned. She considered the cyclical ebb and flow of tides and the cycle of her own womanly condition, but the calculus of conception remained forever beyond her. They were, both of them, righteous and pure before the Lord, walking in all the commandments and ordinances, blameless. But they were childless, barren, and now well stricken in years.

---

6. It is claimed by some that when the hips and groin of the bronze effigy erected over the grave of the nineteenth century political journalist, Victor Noir, are vigorously rubbed by women, they will be assured an immediate pregnancy. As evidence of the belief in the efficacy of the Parisian tomb to ward off infertility, we note that Noir's effigy is the garish green of oxidized bronze—except at his crotch, where it has been rubbed shiny and smooth by female supplicants.

3. The Peacock of Paradise

The incense is smoldering, the candles burning. Tendrils of thin, fragrant smoke drift toward the high lofted ceiling of the holy place within the Temple. All is present tense inside the holy place, in the presence of the Eternal One. Outside, the faithful were at prayer. Z'kharyah hears the murmur of their worshipful refrains. He scoops another shovel full of incense upon the coals of the altar and the smoke of the incense, with the prayers of the saints, ascends before God as from an angel's hand.

Figure 5–The greater fire devours the lesser flame.

Suddenly an angel is there with him—the angel of the Lord, all wings and eyes of fire. The fabric of the universe is torn open like a curtain from top to bottom. The incense altar, oil lamps, the menorah, they all disappear; the temple and all its courts are obliterated in an instant. The all-consuming fire of creation envelops the priest as he performs his sacerdotal duties, and yet, he is not consumed. His flesh remains whole in the irradiating presence of the neutron star opening before him. It is cool. There is no burning heat, no electrical discharge. Only the massive magnetic field of the burning neutrino sphere rotating several hundred times a second.

Pulsing beams of electromagnetic radiation are beamed directly into his mind. "Z'kharyah!" The sound of his name makes no sound in the vacuum of space. The words are heard within his mind. He screams, but this also makes no sound.

"DO NOT FEAR." He hears and he screams louder. Still there is only silence.

"DO NOT FEAR." There is no mouth, no lips, no teeth, no tongue. Only wings and eyes of fire. Z'kharyah's silent screams eventually fade into nothing and he stops screaming.

"Who . . . What are you?" Z'kharyah stammers.

A Voice within the fire speaks to him. "I am Jibril. Gavri'el. Gabriel who stands at the throne. I am one of those keeping watch. I am the Peacock of Paradis, the Keeper of Serpents. I am the Commander of Cherubim with the power to destroy the wicked. I am the First in strength of the Dawnborn, and first to sing."

The words of the angelic messenger come into his mind faster now, each rolling over the previous. "You are heard. Your prayers answered. A son. A joy. John. Sacred. No wine. Spirit. Power. Like Elijah. Prepare. Make Ready. Prepare. Prepare. Prepare."

Z'kharyah screams again, but it is only silence. He reduced to silence by the angel.

4. Tetragrammaton Radiation

In the Temple Mount Control Center, alarms and sirens warbled. Their earsplitting klaxons drowned out the prayers of the faithful gathered in the courtyard. Automatic maglocks immediately slammed and sealed the temple doors as the temple guards ran to their emergency lockdown stations. "Sir, we have a situation," a Petty Levite Officer reported to the Priest of the Watch. The warning lights blinking on his workstation monitor flashed orange in the semi darkness of the smoky TMCC.

The Priest of the Watch stepped briskly to the Petty Levite Officer's side. "What's the situation?"

"Something has triggered the security protocols sir."

"What is it?"

"We're not sure yet. Information is still coming in, sir. It could be an earthquake." And this was cause for frequent concern. The whole region was prone to the rattle and seizures of earthquakes. A rift stretching from Red Sea to Turkey separates the Arabian plate on the East from the African plate on the West. The Dead Sea Transform is a tectonic danger zone, ever shifting, always sliding, dropping, shaking.

"Or it could be . . ." the Petty Levite Officer suggested carefully.

"What?"

"It's only a possibility, sir, but this could be . . ."

"What?" shouted the Priest of the Watch.

"This could be what we've been watching for. It could be a Manifestation of the Divine, sir. The Thaumaturgical sensors are detecting high levels of Tetragrammaton radiation. I've never seen them so high, sir!"

"Who's in there? Who's the priest on duty now?"

"Zechariah, sir, of the Abijah division. And he's been in there a long time."

"Call the rescue team, full Hazmat suits! Is the Zohar chain ready to pull him out of there?" The petty Levite officer trembled to report that Rabbi Yitzchak had not yet, in fact, supplied that particular piece of Holy Place PPE. [7]

5. The International Brotherhood Knighted Collectors of Postage Stamps

When the days of his ministration, and his subsequent days of isolation quarantine, were accomplished, Zechariah departed for his own place. And after those days, Elizabeth conceived and hid herself for five months.

But why would she hide? Why now that her shame had been removed? Is there some mystical and obscure reason for her maternal seclusion?

There is no need to look to esotericism or occultism for the answer. There is no need to consult the psychogenic tables prepared by the actuaries of the phenomenal mind. These may be relevant, but they must occasionally be challenged. They must be confronted and, when necessary, condemned. But there is no need to consult them in this case. There is no gap of overheated eschatology here. Pious Elizabeth went into hiding to avoid the questions of the casually curious as well as the more intrusive investigations conducted by the International Brotherhood Knighted Collectors of Postage Stamps.

And who was the Grand Master of this austere and noble order? King Herod, none other and self-declared. What was their mission? No one really knows. There were rumors of course. We know that the FBI investigated the Beach Boys because of their connection to the desert hippy guru and white-power apocalyptic charlatan, Charles Manson—at least until they realized that Manson was one of their own. The FBI, the CIA, the Agency, the Shop,

---

7. King Herod, of course, had drastically cut funding for the Temple Mount Control Center. But whether or not the lack of a Zohar Rescue Chain at this time can be blamed on Herod's funding cuts is still debated.

the Brotherhood of Philatelic Knights—they're all part of the same. And it's always best to avoid their notice.

6. Take Shelter

"Seizure of all railroads must continue," the Idumaean King of the Jews shouted from the balcony of his fortress palace. "Seize the airport at Tel-Aviv and all the aircraft!" But no one heard him. That is to say, no one acknowledged hearing him. It was easier, not to mention, safer, to pretend to be asleep or to feign deafness. The streets were empty, except for the soft fog rolling over like a storm but without the thundersome violence. And the city slept—though not undisturbed. "Seize food, and clothing," he shouted. "Take shelter from the coming storm, for there will be a great shaking of the earth!"

At this point his armies were already spreading across the entire length and breadth of the city in preparation for battle. The King needed no computer to calculate risk for him; he needed no experts to advise or guide him. If dogs will bark and growl in the darkness and sniff at the scuttling noises in the brush, the King will do as he will. "You are all going to die!" he shouted. But no one heard him; the streets were empty. And even those who did hear him, turned over in their affected sleep and pulled the blankets over their heads.

Sensing their refusal to acknowledge him, Herod went back inside to rummage under his bed until he found his bullhorn. Then back he returned to the balcony. "Oh Mother!" he shouted with feedback amplification through the loudhailer.

"Where is my Mariamne, my precious, beautiful Mariamne? She tried to poison me, you know. She did. But I still loved her. I loved her all the more even if she tried to poison me. The French have tried to poison me as well. They did poison me; it's true. But I've never loved the French. Nobody loves the French. I've survived nine of their assassination attempts, people! Do you hear me? Nine!"

A momentary squeal of feedback drowned out the sound of his sobs, but the people pretending to sleep could still hear him moaning, "Where is my precious, beautiful Mariamne?" What no one would say in response is that she was still in the palace—though long dead. He had her killed because he feared that she had cuckolded him. She was embalmed, but she remained unburied in the palace with him.

A Life Known and Unknowable

7. The Superdimensional Manifold of Spacetime

Toward the outer rim of the Milky Way Galaxy, in the cold expanse of the æther, is the secret listening outpost of the Imperial Augury Intelligence Agency (IAIA), staffed with a multinational collation of scientists and Roman scryers. The IAIA scans the bloodied seas of the central hub of the Galaxy for signs and wonders.[8] They chart the flights of wild birds and peripatetic planets for early indications of anything that might affect the *pax, fortuna,* and *salus* of Rome. But they have missed it. With their radio telescopes and their sheep's guts, they have missed it.

But let us see him now: Jibril. Gavri'el. Gabriel, one of the seven angels that stand before the One. Let us see the nuclear fire of a distant burning star standing in the dust of a green-hill village, kneeling before a frightened young woman. She is not much more than a girl really, trembling at the edge of pubescence. See her quivering maidenhood. See her blush but never look away.

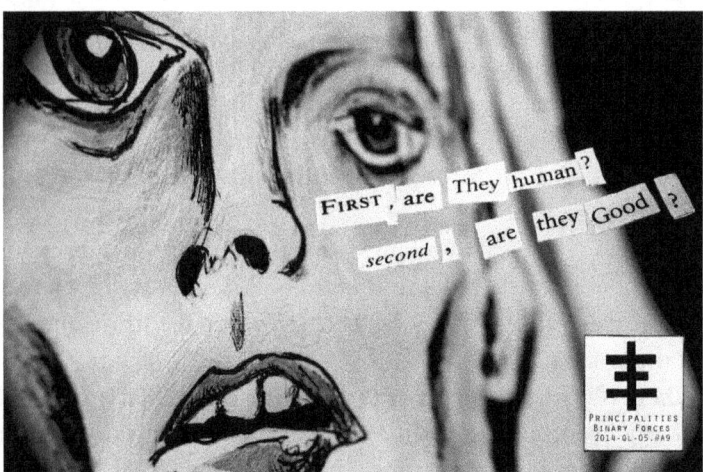

Figure 6–Are they human, these powers, or are they supernatural algorithms?

And see the flashes of multicolored lightning. Hear the rumbling peals of terrible thunder. See the wings and eyes of fire offering his plasma sword to this illiterate peasant girl. "Hail, *thou that art* highly favored, the Lord *is* with thee: blessed *art* thou among women." Sixty-five million American adults believe that some sort of spirit-beings inhabit the vastness of outer

---

8. See *SPQR Intelligence Weekly* for a statistical analysis of their astrological auguries.

space, be they light or dark, good or evil. Seventy-seven million American adults believe that God created some sort of extraterrestrial life. Are these extraterrestrial intelligences perhaps something more than the "little green men" of unidentified flying saucers? Could they be something more? Could they be the "spiritual forces" described by the Apostle Paul? Are they the binary forces? In situations like these we must ask two questions. First: are they human? Second: are they good?

All of our efforts to detect life beyond this pale blue-green orb that we inhabit have failed. Project Ozma, Project Cyclops, Project Phoenix, and SETI—all of them have failed to find any indication of life, intelligent life, elsewhere in the universe. For all that we can determine, the moon could be a psychopathic hunchback lurching across the sky and the solar system nothing more than a silent chamber of horrors. The pre-Socratic Anaxagoras suggested that the moon was inhabited, but could he prove it? Bishop Godwin was carried there by a flock of geese, but did he see anything to confirm that? We don't know. We just don't know. Everything in those days, was a secret or a lie promulgated by the IAIA. It was impossible to have accurate information about anything.

And perhaps this is for the best. We are, after all, not much more than a mob of howling villagers gathering in the street with our torches and our pitchforks. *We* are the monsters. If we were to ever find life on the moon or on Mars, or beyond, if we ever found extraterrestrial intelligence (that is to say, non-human intelligence) we would probably kill it outright. We would try to destroy it. In our fear and our loathing we would reach out to extinguish it. The children of men have never been alone in the universe and we are overwhelmed by the knowledge of this fact. We prefer to ignore it.

But see now the intelligent fire of a far distant star standing before the handmaiden of God who says to her, "Fear not, Mary: for thou hast found favor with God." Radio telescopes and sheep guts trained to the far flung corners of the ever expanding universe are constantly listening for messages from the stars, straining for a word from beyond. And here it is: "Behold, thou shalt conceive in thy womb, and bring forth a son, and shalt call his name Jesus."

The result is no explosion, no supernova of superheated, fearful hate. Not in her. But there is a trembling. The modest maiden quivers. The soul trembles and recoils in the presence of numinous possibilities. "How shall this be?"

See it now and do not fear: the morning star, the light of the world is rising. The son of the One will reign and of his kingdom–the superdimensional manifold of Spacetime and all ethical realms there shall be no end, an ever expanding, inflationary kingdom. *Sein ist die ganz welt!*

Selah. Say it again, *Selah.*

8. Morning Star Pray for Us

Figure 7–Beautiful as the moon, resplendent as the sea.

Holy Mary, mother of grace divine, mother most pure, mother most chaste—*pray for us.*

Virgin most venerable, mirror of justice, vessel of honor—*pray for us.* Mystical Rose, Tower of Ivory, Morning Star, symbol of victorious believers everywhere, those who win the victory and are given the Morning Star as a gift—*pray for us.* Blessed is the fruit of thy womb, Jesus. Pray for us sinners, here and now and at the hour of our inevitable and always untimely death. Amen.

9. Is Semaphore Still a Thing?

Mary ran to the hill country, stopping barely long enough to throw together a few things and to inform her parents that she was leaving to visit her relative Elisheba. She raised a cloud of dust across the countryside as she ran to Zechariah's house. "*Salut*" Mary said between panting breaths to her relative Elisheba as she entered the house. Abruptly Elisheba, who had been sweeping the room, was filled with the Holy Spirit. She dropped the broom and began to shout

"BLESSED *ART* THOU AMONG WOMEN, AND BLESSED IS THE FRUIT OF THY WOMB!" she shouted. "AND WHENCE *IS* THIS TO ME THAT THE MOTHER OF MY LORD SHOULD COME TO ME?" Mary and Zechariah covered their ears with their hands and pleaded with her to stop shouting. But Elisheba was enthused, literally, filled with the fervor resulting from divine inspiration, with wild and ecstatic speaking and with uncoordinated movements. "FOR, LO, AS SOON AS THE VOICE OF THY SALUTATION SOUNDED IN MINE EARS THE BABE LEAPED IN MY WOMB FOR JOY!"

Perhaps if Elisheba had had one of the spirit typewriters invented by India's version of Thomas Edison, Shankar Abaji Bhise, she wouldn't have needed to shout. Bhise's device was a sort of circular, mechanical typewriter with unmarked keys (to prevent unconscious influence from the user) struck by a moving planchette. She could have used it to type her inspired words without bursting the eardrums of her husband and her young niece.

Unfortunately, Bhise wouldn't invent his sprit typewriter until the 1920s, which was a bit too late for Elisheba. Gorillas and chimpanzees, I'm told, can learn to use sign language to communicate. What is more, they will even invent their own grammar, and teach other simians the language. I don't know what help that would be to Elisheba who was still shouting, even louder now, at Mary. Is semaphore still a thing?

"AND BLESSED *IS* SHE THAT BELIEVED FOR THERE SHALL BE A PERFORMANCE OF THOSE THINGS WHICH WERE TOLD HER FROM THE LORD!" Zechariah was struck mute for his disbelief, but Elisheba would shout from her faith. Fathers may be hushed, but mothers will never be silenced.

11. It's this Kind of Class Warfare That's Ruined this Country

Terry Ousterman turned off the engine of his Yardmaster 6000 lawnmower and wiped the sweat from his forehead. He looked over his yard with satisfied pride. The green grass was short, clipped even, and there was not a disturbing dandelion or Creeping Charley in sight. He pushed the mower back into his storage shed and pulled down the roll-top door. Without the roar of the Yardmaster, he could hear someone singing. It was the neighbor's girl.

A Life Known and Unknowable

What was her name? Miriam? Moly? Mara? Whatever. He could hear her song more clearly now. "God today has poor folks raised and cast a-down the proud."

'Goddam Pete Seeger and all the commie folk singers,' he thought to himself. Then he shouted at the neighbor girl. "Hey! Knock it off with that Bolshevik garbage!"

The neighbor girl waved but didn't stop singing.

Ousterman huffed and stormed inside his house, slamming the door behind him. In the kitchen, he poured himself a glass of water from the faucet and gulped it down. Then he picked up the receiver of the rotary phone mounted on the wall."

"Who are you calling, dear?" Mrs. Ousterman asked as she entered the kitchen.

"I'm calling the National Security Hotline," he said.

"Again? What is it this time?"

"Dammit, Martha. That neighbor kid is out there singing about the overthrow of the government. She's singing about pulling down the thrones of power."

"Terry," Mrs. Ousterman said trying to calm her husband. "Let her sing. She's just a girl. She's not hurting anyone. Besides, she has the right to express herself, doesn't she?"

"This is no time for a slavish devotion to the freedom of expression, Martha," Ousterman said as he spun the numbers of the Treason Hotline. "It's this kind of class warfare that's ruined this country. Undesirable citizens[9] like her need to be reported."

11. Legends Would Follow

And now the miserable and unhappy waste was ended; the time was come for Elizabeth to be delivered, and the time for her to deliver. She gave birth to a son, a ferruginous[10] child drawn from the long shadows of expectation.

---

9. President Theodore Roosevelt called Eugene Debs and Bill Haywood "undesirable citizens." But he also called Leo Tolstoy a "sexual moral pervert," so what did he know?— ED. NOTE: Jeff, some of the footnotes are legit and substantial—quite informative. I enjoy those. Some of them are nonsensical and seemingly useless. I also enjoy those. But do the substantial notes lose substance because of the nonsensical ones? Is there potential that your readers won't take any of them seriously? Then again, what do I know?—Chris.

10. ED. NOTE: Sometimes it seems like you're *trying* to show off your crazy impressive vocabulary, Jeff. Can't you just say "rust colored"?

Her neighbors and kinsfolk gathered around her and saw the great mercy bestowed upon her and upon her husband, and they rejoiced with them. But still time moves on. On the eighth day the boy was circumcised. The kinsfolk and neighbors gathered with the happy couple took it upon themselves to name the child. "He is Zechariah, like his father."

Elizabeth answered them (for Zechariah still could not) "Call him John."

The solemn Archimandrite from the local monastery, with deep sober eyes and long greying beard (through which a spindly daddy long-leg spider was climbing), had come with the villagers to celebrate with the happy couple and to bless the child. "Elizabeth," he said in a *basso profundo* voice, "Mother, there is no one in your family or in your honored husband's by that name. Let his name be not John, but Zechariah."

They made motions and signs for Zechariah to share his thoughts. Voiceless, he signaled for his tablet and scribbled into the wax with a carved ivory stylus. "His name is John. Say no more." And with this his mouth was opened. His tongue was loosed and his lips and teeth unchained. The angel's words were proved and he gave glory to God.

And they marveled all. And feared, for what manner of child would this be? What child is this with the hand of the Lord already upon him? Great things were expected. Legends would follow.

12. *My Little One*

Father Zachariah, filled with the Holy Spirit, spoke: "I am not a prophet, my son. A seer, perhaps; I see, yes, but not as a prophet sees. I describe, without prescription or proscription. I observe. I report. I hear, and smell, and taste. I see that the days are short and the nights are long. And I can see that all this is changing too. I can offer no prognostications, no predictions, no forecasts. No Nostradamus am I. I have no chiromancy, no hydromancy, no tyromancy.[11] I practice no-mancy of any kind. Not even romance I am a nomancer. But I will speak as I am told."

"I will speak of the glory of the Lord and God of Israel who has visited and redeemed his people, who has raised up the strong horn of salvation promised by the holy prophets of long ago. And still I am no clairvoyant bard, but I will sing of the one who has saved us from than hands and hate

---

11. It is unfortunate that tyromancy—that is prediction by cheese—has fallen out of favor and practice as a form of divination. I quite enjoy cheese.

of our enemies. I will sing of the one who has given us the mercy pledged to our father, Abraham."

"The dreams of your servants are complete; we awaken into them. This present hour meets with distant past in the clear splendor of joyous song. But you, my child will be a prophet of the Highest One. In desert sands, in fire, flame and wild smoke, in the blowing of the eastern wind and in the waters of the wadis, you will, my little one, give light to denizens of darkness, to the citizens living in cities of shadow and shade. You, my son, will guide our feet to peace. Peace be with you, little one. I think you're going to need it."

13. A Land Measured by Chaos and Weighed with Emptiness

So the child grew and waxed strong in the spirit, and strong-headed as the son of strong-willed fathers often are. "I know how stubborn ye are, boy," Zechariah bellowed at his son. "Ye have a forehead of bronze!" Zechariah's brogue became more pronounced when he was angry. But John knew what he knew, even then. Zechariah secretly and often fretted over the Deuteronomic commandments for fathers of rebellious sons. He knew he could not stone his son, as frustrating as the stubborn boy sometimes was.

John broke the hearts of both his father and his mother when he, as a stiff-necked and rebellious teenager, flung a handful of dust into the face of the local rabbi and fled the yeshiva. He bundled together a purse of food and went alone into the desert. Instead of following in his father's footsteps into priestly service at the Temple, in the order of Abijah, John set out for a land inhabited by jackdaws and owls, a land inhabited by great owls and ravens, by jackals and ostriches. He went into a land measured by chaos and weighed with emptiness. Instead of becoming a priest like his father, and his father before him and his father before—John joined a religious movement founded by The Teacher of Righteousness.

The Teacher of Righteousness had himself once been a priest, serving in the Temple just as Zechariah served, but had rejected the temple in Jerusalem and denounced the cult and all of its illegitimate priests.

Hear the words of the Teacher of Righteousness.

At that time the men of the Yahad-unity shall withdraw, the holy house of Aaron uniting as a Holy of Holies, and the synagogue of Israel as those who walk blamelessly. Their wealth is not to be admixed with that of rebellious men, who have failed to cleanse their path by separating from perversity and walking blamelessly. They shall deviate from none of the teachings of the Law, whereby they would walk in their willful hearts completely. They shall govern themselves using the original precepts by which the men of the Yahad-unity began to be instructed, doing so until there come the Prophet and the Messiah of Aaron and Israel.[12]

And there John stayed, living among the members of that experimental, religious commune in that backwater utopia until the day of his showing to Israel.

14. An Inevitable Indeterminism

We may be drawing outside the lines just a bit now. You see, there is an inevitable indeterminism here. We apologize. History is impossible in a quantum reckoning. We can show the course or the place, but not both. This is as true for atom as it is for penguins, and for history textbooks. Albert Einstein, as brilliant as he was, could never reconcile himself to the quantum nature of the universe. Still, it seems to hold true even despite his misgivings. Our sincerest apologies for that.

Figure 8–Peace exists only when all our opponents have been beaten down and have lost the will to fight.

---

12. From the Charter of a Jewish Sectarian Association contained in the Dead Sea Scrolls—1QS column 9:6-11. Wise et. al., *Dead Sea Scrolls*, 139.

After the world conquering third Empire seen in the visions of Daniel, the bronze belly and thighs of Greece,[13] there arose another Empire, a fourth kingdom. This was the *absolutum dominium* of Rome. It marched with strident steps across the earth on legs of iron and feet of clay. It came crushing and conquering and waging war to establish peace. This was the *Pax Romana*. Peace through superior firepower is a sort of peace, I suppose, though it is the lowest and most expensive form of peace.

And in those days a decree went out from Caesar Augustus, the Illustrious One who was our Lord, as ordained by providence to bring our lives to the climax of perfection, Caesar Augustus who was filled with strength for our welfare, and was sent to us and to our descendants as Savior, Caesar Augustus who put an end to war, who has brought us the gospel of good news and salvation, and who has set all things in order, Caesar August sent out a decree that the whole world should be taxed—the *orbis terrarium*—from England to India. It would be a tax to fund the far flung armies of the Empire. A tax to humiliate the oppressed and occupied lands. Thus ever is the *Pax Romana!*[14]

15. No Inn

Listen to me now: There is no inn in this story. Neither is there any innkeeper here. Check the voting records, or the tax receipts. Check the twelve-page pamphlet prepared by the Imperial Revenue Service, or call the help desk hotline number. There's nothing in this story about an inn, neither is there an innkeeper nor hosteller. It was all a mistake, unintentional perhaps. And even if it has led to centuries of Christmas carols and sentimental sermons, it was a mistake. There was no inn.

Joseph went up from Nazareth in Galilee to Judea and Bethlehem. He and his betrothed, his espoused wife traveled through the valley of the shadow of death—the vale filled with stray bullets and cannonballs, through a veritable storm of artillery and gunfire—a widening gyre of a dangerous fusillades, contentious and quarrelsome, savage and brutish.

---

13. See also the Leopard with four wings and four heads, but you'll need to be dreaming to do so.

14. And this taxing taxation was first made, we are told, when Quirinius was governor of Syria—though this would be nine years too late. This just doesn't work. And, despite our pleading, no satisfying explanation is yet forthcoming. We are curious concerning these historical matters, but . . . *Caetera desunt.*

And after all of that, they went not, as we have said, to an inn, not to a hostel, or guesthouse. They went home. They went to the overcrowded house of his fathers and there, surrounded by family and friends, Mary gave birth to her son, Jesus. He was born into a community to create a community.

It's late, but perhaps it's not too late.

16. We Are Sore Afraid

I awakened suddenly in the middle of that November night centuries ago in the fields outside of Bethlehem and was terrified by the signs I saw in the sky. Planets were wandering erratically across the midnight sky instead of tracing predictable paths across the heavens as the stars do. The motions of the planets were unique and terrifying visions of irregular vibrations. But as discomforting as those shiftless orbs may have been, it was the stars that terrified me most that night so long ago.

There is no air in space, no medium to carry distant sound waves from the far expanse to our ears so we are accustomed to thinking of the stars as silent. But they are not. They sing. They sing continually. And when the stars of the morning left their place in the heavens to sing their *Glorias* in the night sky above our humble home we were undone. It was as if the heavens were ripped apart with the noise of a great rushing wind and all our elements were melted with fervent heat. We were dissolved. We are disintegrated dust.

"BE NOT AFRAID!"

Figure 9–This is probably not the correct photo.

I was undone and afraid. I was dust and sore afraid. Human ears are sensitive to the musical vibrations of reeds and strings, of skins and brass. Even synthesized sine wave vibrations will tickle the ear. Similarly, the human soul is sensitive to the *ab aeterno* resonations of the heavens. There are one hundred billion neutrinos, remnants of the Big Bang, within each of us at any given moment, and even these are not enough to prepare us for that numinous breaking through. The angel of the Lord brought terrifying tidings of great joy for all people. "BE NOT AFRAID!"

All people? Well, no. Not all. These tidings came to us in the field, not to paranoid King Herod in the fortress with machine gun nests in the towers and flamethrowers at the gates, and not to Caesar Augustus in the marble halls of Roman power. The word came to us, the essential workers of the world. It came to those of us who have no Wall Street investments and who cannot work from home, to humble fry cooks and Wal-Mart clerks. To farmers, welders, housekeepers, and truckers. The word the world are ours. The Savior was born unto *us*. All glory to God and all power to the people.

Figure 10–In the highest heaven and lowest earth.

Suddenly there was a great warband in the heavens singing, "Glory to God and peace on earth." It was a brief song, barely a refrain, but it echoed and echoed back again across the green hills and into the valleys where our flocks of sheep were sleeping. And it echoes still today. "GLORY IN THE HIGHEST HEAVENS TO GOD" and "ON EARTH, PEACE TO THOSE THE FAVORED ONES!" And this song—the mechanical vibrations of air—became light—electromagnetic vibrations of electrical charge—and travelled across the incomprehensible vastness of space for all eternity.

Here is where all the bombs disappear into silence. In this song of peace and glory, all the bombs and barbwire and bullets and children-killing landmines fade away. We rose up from our bunkers and earthwork trenches to travel by land, by diligence, by cross country skis, by recumbent bicycles, gravity trains and dirigibles to the City of David, even Bethlehem, so that we could see what had been given to us.

17. *Carne Vera Sancta*

Jesus was Jewish, of course, a descendant of Father Abraham who was commanded to circumcise himself along with all those in his household. And this covenantal action was carried on through the generations even to this day. On the eighth day Joseph and Mary took the boy to a nearby cave where they met with the wizened old *mohel* for the *brit milah* ceremony— that is, the circumcision of the infant Jesus. The *mohel*'s elderly sister was also there. It was she who handed the wizened old rabbi the knife he used to cut the tender flesh, then the towel also, which he used to wipe his mouth after sucking blood from the wound.[15] And it was she who carefully placed the circumcised bit of flesh, the Holy Prepuce into an alabaster box filled with spikenard oil.

It isn't clear what happened next, except that the holy foreskin of Jesus disappeared for nearly eight hundred years. On December 25th of the Eight Hundredth Year of Our Lord the King of the Franks, King of the Lombards and Emperor of the Romans, Charlemagne, the illiterate Frankish King of fame and legend, presented the foreskin of our Lord and Savior to Pope Leo III as a Christmas gift.

---

15. Circumcised males are less likely to be infected with viruses like HIV and Human Papilloma virus and less prone to urinary tract infections. However, the medical benefits of this covenantal procedure may be lost if the *mohel* performing the *bris* passes Herpes to the infant as was reported in November of 2004 in the Brooklyn, New York. The New York department of health found two newborn boys circumcised by the same ultra-orthodox mohel to be infected with Herpes. These Ultra-orthodox practitioners follow instructions in the Talmud that says after the circumcision, ". . . we spit blood into the earth." Most Jewish communities recognize the medical risks involved with this practice and refrain, just as they ignore instructions in the Mishna that indicated that the open circumcision wound should be sprinkled with cumin.

It was kept in Rome afterwards, and venerated by the faithful there until 1527. During the War of the League of Cognac,[16] German, Protestant soldiers, complaining of unpaid wages, sacked and looted Rome. In the midst of the chaos, one of the soldiers stole the Holy Prepuce and fled the city. He was quickly captured forty-seven kilometers to the north of Rome. The foreskin was kept there in a shrine frequented by both pilgrims and skeptics until 1983 when the local priest who was charged with its protection reported that "sacrilegious thieves" had stolen it from the cardboard box where he had been keeping it under his bed.

Where is it now? I have no earthly idea.

Saint Birgitta of Vadstena, a Swedish nun, had a vision in which she ate it. She described it as like a little sweetness on her tongue.[17] Alternately, Saint Catherine of Sienna claimed that Jesus himself gave her the foreskin as an invisible wedding ring. But, as wonderful as these mystic visions of Jesus' member may have been, the true holy meat is no longer on planet Earth.

In an unpublished essay, Greek Scholar Leo Allatius (1586-1669) argued that the Holy Prepuce ascended into heaven, with Jesus, about forty days after his resurrection. But, instead of remaining with him in heaven, the foreskin travelled on through the silent chamber of horrors of the solar system, expanding as it crossed the expanse of space, until it became the rings of Saturn.

And you know, don't you, that none of this can be discussed by faithful Roman Catholics. Not since 1901, when even the mention of the *Carne Vera Sancta* by the faithful was declared to be cause for their immediate excommunication. So, for their sake, let's say no more about it.

18. Oh Mother, Bless You

There lived in those days, in the city of Jerusalem, a man who understood that no prophecy, no sleep time divination, no precog vision ever came by the impulse or psitron of men—no matter what the mental mechanics

---

16. Incidentally, "The League of Cognac" is the name of my Dungeons and Dragons group.

17. Was the song *Sugar on My Tongue* by the American rock band, The Talking Heads, a hymn to the Holy Prepuce? Doctor P. L. Tarrec may have been somewhat prescient when he described it as such in his monograph on the subject, *Psycho Killers and Loving Saviors*, written in 1965—twelve full years before The Talking Heads recorded the song.

at the CIA or the IAIA might have said. They refuse to look beyond the material veil. They're convinced that there's nothing beyond, that there is only material. But still they're curious about what they do not know and cannot see.

There is no sight, no vision, and no prophecy without the spirit. Neither is there vision nor shine except that the breath of God blows through. This wind is truth. This breezy reality is an emanation of the Divine. And Simeon understood all of this. He saw the holy family—father, mother, and newborn son—while they were still a long way off.

It was revealed to Simeon (for the wind blows where it will) that he would not pass from either this earth or this life before seeing the arrival of the Anointed One. This man, this righteous and devout man, had lived long in the land of darkness, in the land of the long shadows of death for many long years. He ached in his joints and his hair—what was left of his hair—was a thin white nimbus around his head. Still he rose each morning from his pallet wondering if this at long last would be the day of that long promised dawn.

He believed in the existence of an absolute, indivisible truth—and why wouldn't he? This was long before postmodernist questions historical and social context. This was well before the right-wing religious rejection of truth as "fake news." And yet, he worried too. "The Truth is there," he said to himself, "but if the wind is not blowing, what can we know of it? What can we know at all?'" Maybe he'd begun to despair.

We are wounded in birth and bleed to death. Birth is nothing but death begun. And yet he held out hope. The denizens of the granite halls of the dark lands, those who live in rooms of ruin, even those in whom the light is not yet extinguished, are not immune to the incessant call of the grave. The grave is always hungry. *Sheol* waits for us all, never satisfied. And still Simeon rose each morning, every morning, and this morning, from his pallet wondering if this would be the day of the long promised dawn. The wind was blowing this day; He couldn't tell from whence it came—or where it was blowing, but he felt it pushing at his back. He rose and went to the temple.

He'd seen them coming, a long way off, still on the road. He'd seen them purchase a pair of doves, the sacrificial offerings necessary for her purification. He'd seen the swaddled bundle in the young mother's arms, but only from afar, through the fog of prescient vision. Who? Why? He didn't know, but the wind drove him further, faster, and harder. "I go," he muttered against the urgent driving force and the pain in his hips. "I go. I go."

In the courts of the temple, with the wind still roaring in his ears, he saw them. He staggered to them on frail limbs and weak joints. His wide eyes stretched the wrinkled crow's feet, giving him a younger, wilder appearance. His thin, white hair, danced wildly in a breeze that no one else could feel. Mary gasped when he approached. Joseph, protective of his wife and child, interposed himself between her and the stranger.

"This is the child," Simeon said as both a statement and a question at once. "May I hold him?"

Who could say why Mary so easily agreed to the request of this apparent madman except to say that the wind moved her as well. She handed him her precious bundle. Simeon took the boy and pulled the blanket away from his face and saw, at long last his promised consolation—and not just his, but the consolation of all Israel.

He lofted the child into the air, momentarily releasing him so that for a brief (though Mary felt it interminable) second the child hung suspended in the air above them all. "Lord, now lettest thou thy servant depart in peace, according to thy word and promise. I have seen the light. No more darkness. No more night. But a light to lighten the world and the light of glory for us all."

Gently, slowly he lowered the boy and gazed into his face. "He will be the cause of falling and rising, rising and falling for many," he said to the baby's parents without looking at them. "I do not know if this be blessing or no, but I bless you. I bless you both. I bless you all." And having pronounced his threefold blessing he began to hand the child back to them, but stopped.

"There is more. I see a sword, or a spear, I see a sword. Oh, God!" he screamed. "Ah God, but this is hard." He turned his eyes to the tearful mother waiting fearfully for the return of her only son, "You will have peace, dear mother. But do you think that he's come for peace? No. I see a sword that will pierce your neck. It will pierce your soul. Your *psyche*." He said. "Your *nephesh*. Do you ken? Yes? I see a sword passing through your soul so that the inmost thoughts, for good or ill, of many will be revealed. Nothing is covered up that cannot be revealed."

Simeon paused and shuddered, then passed the baby back to his mother. "Oh Mother, bless you. Bless you. I can now depart. Bless you."

20. Strange and Incredible

There are two, and only two, women named as prophetesses in the Christian scriptures. One is "that woman, Jezebel," that was tolerated by the Christian community in Thyatira,[18] she who led the servants of Christ into sexual immorality and the eating of foods which had been sacrificed on pagan altars. This so-called prophetess would be cast onto a bed of sickness where she would suffer intensely, and her children would be struck down with death.

Figure 11–The crosses of the Kittim from across the sea.

The other woman so titled was Anna. Born in the year that Aristobulus the First died, after he had his own mother and brother put to death. In the year that Anna the Prophetess was born Aristobulus the First was replaced as King and High Priest of Israel by Alexander Jannaeus whose rage and barbarity were so great that he had eight hundred of his own people hung upon crosses just as the Kittim from across The Sea would do in their empire of iron and clay. And, what is more, he had the throats of the wives and children of those crucified cut before their eyes as they died.

Anna, the prophetess, was old and had lived long in the land, day and night in the Temple, serving, fasting, and praying constantly before the Lord. And, though her *belle-lettres* and *bon mots* and are not recorded for eavesdropping interlopers like us, she spoke to those who were in the Temple that same day and that same hour with Simeon and the Holy Family. She spoke to them concerning "the redemption of Jerusalem" whom she held in her grand-matronly arms.

---

18. Which is now the White Castle of Akhisar.

Sure, it's incredible and sure, it's strange, but so are particle accelerators. So is the volatile and radioactive metal, Lawrencium, which can only be made inside particle accelerators. The universe itself is strange and incredible. The universe, some scientists claim, came into existence in search of something. They believe that it came into existence with an inherent longing for something. And billions of years later, we are still looking. We are still searching even if we don't know what we are searching for. We are the accumulated, unconscious longing of the universe. We are the longing, the waiting, the hope, the dream. And the prophetess Anna is our mouth, even if her words have not been recorded. She is our beautiful favor. She is our beautiful grace. She is the restoration of each of our individual, and all of our universal consciousness. She is the silent voice of our longings. She is the voice of our hope for redemption.

20. A Priori

And the child grew independent of experience. This is true in any possible world. He waxed strong in the spirit and was filled with wisdom and grace, all that which must come before observation. And God was upon him.

21. Your Turn

Once, when he was only twelve, Mary and Joseph took him up to Jerusalem to celebrate the Passover Festival as they did every year. They shared the meal and drank the wine and told the story along with their brothers and sisters from all over the world. And, when it was completed, they started for home again—after promising to return again the next year. Home again, home again; fly away home. But Jesus was not with them. He lingered in the city without them. Eventually they noticed that he wasn't with them and ran back to Jerusalem to look for him. When they finally found him, he was seated under Solomon's Porch, playing chess and answering questions with the learned doctors and teaching them many new things.

"Bruno's dream of a mystical realm of infinite suns is a beautiful dream," the boy said to them. "But it is broken and unsustainable. The infinitude is only an apparent infinitude, and only for now. Instead, it is as the Psalmist said, 'the heavens are proclaiming the glory of God, and the sky manifests the work of his hands. Day after day pours forth their speech and night unto night they share knowledge.' While they burn, the stars of heaven are sharing their song—pouring out energy and heat and light—information, if you will. But the larger the star, the shorter its song. The larger the star, the louder it sings and the hotter it burns. Double the size, quarter the length.[19] And the truly large stars will, eventually, explode into space, flinging their elements out to be recombined again elsewhere in the universe. The real question to ask," Jesus smiled, "is how quickly is the universe making new stars?"

He moved one of his pieces, a white pawn, to an unoccupied square and tapped his button on the game clock to stop the timer. "Your turn," he said to his opponent.

"No, child!" one of the doctors gathered around him gasped. "No. Do not say it. For Hashem, the Name, as we are told, created the stars, created the lights of the sky on the fourth day and he pronounced them good. Then, after completing his creation on the sixth day, Hashem rested."

Jesus' opponent hesitated, then moved his bishop across the board.

"Ah" the boy said smiling. "But he also made the lizards and the chickens did he not? And Hashem pronounced them good as well, no? Yes. But, like his mercies, there are new lizards and chickens every morning, new in their shells, no? Which leads me to another question: Which came first, the lizard or the egg?"

Jesus moved his pawn again, then said. "Check."

His opponent studied the board then *harrumphed* and threw up his hands. "The boy has lured me into a *novotny*, a veritable grimshaw sacrifice! I can take his pawn with my bishop or my knight. But either way, he has taken my king."

22. *A Posteriori*

And Jesus increased in wisdom; he increased in experience, and stature, and empirical evidence, as well as the favor of God and man, as demonstrated by observation and quantifiable testing.

---

19. If the force of gravity were stronger, the stars would burn out even sooner, but that's not really important here.

The Argument

An Apology

It occurs to me that you might be asking yourself, "Who is he to write this?" or "Who does he think he is?" And these are perfectly valid questions. Good questions. And I thank you for asking them even though I'm not sure I can provide an answer.

I remember an assignment towards the end of my college freshman psychology class. It was an assignment I very nearly failed. And the only reason I didn't fail was because I gave up trying. The assignment was to write an essay answering one of those foundational kinds of questions: "Who am I?"

We'd spent the semester surveying the various aspects of and approaches to the study of the human mind: Freud, Skinner, Jung, Piaget, Adler, Kohlberg, *Et al.* And our task was to think back through the course and answer that simple question which is not at all simple: Who Am I?

But I couldn't do it. I realized that I could not write an objective answer to the question, 'Who Am I?' because *Primo* I was nineteen, and really didn't know who I was yet. And *Secundo* to answer that question, I realized I would need to describe my relationships with my teacher, my classmates, my roommate, my parents, my brothers, the members of my church congregation, my dog, my girlfriend (who, I didn't know, was just about to break up with me) *Et al.* The unabstracted answer would have to describe who I had been at every point along my nineteen year timeline, what I was doing and why. I realized that if I were to answer that question fully and completely (not to mention, honestly), I would never be able to finish. And I definitely couldn't fit all of that into a five page paper, double spaced.

The Argument

I panicked, and in my panic I froze. I became another victim of paralysis by analysis. I didn't, or couldn't write a single word. The due date came and went and I still had nothing. So I went to the professor to ask for an extension, which he gave me, but only with the promise/threat of a decreased letter grade for each day past the deadline. I went back to my dorm room and cobbled together some mismatched mishmash bullshit that earned me a C- when I finally turned it in. Good enough, I supposed, to pass the class, and I was grateful for it. But I knew that I hadn't really answered the question, 'Who Am I?'. Self-analysis, in this case, did not result in self-knowledge. I knew that I couldn't truly answer the question and it terrified me.

But I was nineteen and nineteen year olds are rarely terrified for very long. My girlfriend dumped me. I dropped out of school. I got a job. Blah blah blah. Life went on. I moved on and the fear I felt in the face of that assignment dissipated. But here's the deal: I'm more than double nineteen years old now, and I'm still not sure I could answer that question. In fact it's only gotten worse now that I have to define myself against even more people, events, and experiences. I'm married now—or rather, I was. I was married (I didn't see the divorce coming either). I have kids—two of them, a matched set, and a fine pair they are.[1] I've had several more dogs in succession and a couple of cats as well. I've lived in a dozen different towns and a few more states since then, and have worked at six or seven different jobs. If I tried to answer that question now, it would take me even more pages.

The difficulty isn't a new one. It's one that has been pondered by philosophers for centuries. Though I didn't realize it at the time this dilemma has a name: it is the Subject/Object distinction. The Subject is the observer. The Object is the thing observed. But what happens when the Subject is the Object?

I am thesis. I am antithesis. I am sickly synthesis.

Like Soren Kierkegaard (one of those philosophers I hadn't yet read when I was nineteen) I was suffering from a proliferation of selves, a multiplication of personas, and from an inflation of doubts. The more I thought about myself and who I was, the less I knew about myself. The more I knew about myself, the less I understood.[2]

---

1. I think they're pretty great even if they haven't bothered to read my previous books, the lousy, little ingrates . . .

2. This is still an accurate description of me.

I didn't have the language or the experience to explain the problem when I was nineteen. I do now. At least I think I do. The problem, as I've come to understand it, is that there is no "me." There is no *objective me.* There is only, can only be a statistical approximation of me. In this universe of Heisenberg uncertainties, quantum entanglements, and spooky actions at a distance, a statistical approximation of me is the best I can give you.

I, as the observer, cannot have objective knowledge about myself. Anything I observe or learn about myself becomes stored within my mind as memory—changing me. The very act of looking at myself changes myself. I am unknowable except as an approximation.

Stephen King says that writing is telepathy[3]. He calls it a meeting of the minds. Ask Madeline L'Engle or Geoffrey Chaucer about this and they'll tell you the same; they'll tell you that writing is *kything*, a making visible of the unseen things between us. It's a focused connection between lovers, and friends, as well as between authors and their readers. We share something in these pages, you and I. You receive something of me in these words. And so, even though this story is not about me and I am not a character in the story, I've smeared myself on every page. I've tainted the story with my approximate self.

I'm sorry about that. I sincerely wish that I could get out of the way. I'm embarrassed of this egoist's interlude. Because everything, every particle, every person in this universe is tangled up with every other thing, every other particle and person, you will, having read this, know something more of me. We have become entangled. Enmeshed. Ensnared.

And for that I am sorry. *Mea culpa. Mea maxima culpa.*

---

3. King, *On Writing,* 103

III

Igitur Qui Desiderat Pacem, Praeparet Bellum

1. Church and State

CAESAR AUGUSTUS DIED, AS all men do. Even the exalted so-called sons of the divine succumb to inevitable death. Some will die of infectious disease, or famine, or poor sanitation. These sorts of death aren't likely if you are the Caesar, you will understand. But death *is* inevitable, even for the Caesar. Some people die from wolves at the door or by traveling salesmen. Some from comets and the approach of disastrous stars, even that bitter, fallen star, Wormwood, the distillation of which is quite popular.[1] Some will die as the result other toxic substances, or it may be any number of other natural or economic catastrophes, but everyone eventually, one way or another, dies. Death is all around, lingering in the past and looming over the future.

Imperator Caesar Divi filius Augustus died appropriately enough in August of the year A.D. 14 and Tiberius Caesar became his unwilling succedaneum. Tiberius, unlike his illustrious *pater*, was the gloomiest of men. Or so I've heard. *Tiberius Caesar Divi Augusti Filius Augustus* never really wanted to be the Emperor, but his mother, Livia, pushed his fundament into the throne and she shoved his head into the laurel crown. And though it doesn't really figure into our story here, when Tiberius died, as all men do, the Roman Senate refused to grant him the divinity they'd bestowed

---

1. Known to my friends in Chicago known as Malört. It tastes like the ash tray at an old time barbershop mixed with public humiliation, but *still* it's quite popular. I guess it's an acquired taste and I, for one, have acquired it.

A Life Known and Unknowable

upon his predecessor. The people of Rome gathered in the streets with poster board signs and megaphones shouting, "TO THE TIBER WITH TIBERIUS!" But the mob didn't actually throw him into the river like a criminal.

Neither Tiberius nor Pilate were thrown by the crowds into the Tiber, but not for lack of trying. After he died (and it was a perfectly natural death—after being poisoned, starved and smothered, *naturally* he died) Tiberius was quietly cremated and his ashes were laid in the in the Mausoleum of Augustus. And while Pilate may have gone into the Tiber, it wasn't the fault of the mob.

If we needed to say something nice about Tiberius, I suppose we could mention that he looked a lot like Peter O'Toole (which was fortunate for the filmmakers) and that during his life he refused to be worshipped as a living god. Still he did allow a temple to be built in his honor in Smyrna. True, it was just the one temple, but one is more than zero, isn't it? Yes.

In the fifteenth year of Tiberius' rule, Pontius Pilate was the fifth governor of Judea, (we will have more to say more about Pilate later) and Herod was the Tetrarch of Galilee. Keep in mind that this wasn't Herod the (not-so) Great who died in 4 B.C.,[2] but his son Herod.

Or rather, it was *one* of his sons named Herod. This Tetrarch of Galilee was Herod Antipas who would eventually be sent into exile by the emperor, Caligula. He was accused of conspiracy and treason. He admitted to stockpiling weapons and amassing an army, but he denied the treason. In the end, he died in France. Or perhaps it was Spain. Some believe that Caligula[3] had him assassinated, but we're not really sure about that.

He also had sons named Herod Archelaus, Herod II, and Herod. No, that's not a mistake. It's correct. Yeah, just try keeping all the Herod's straight. They even looked alike. You can't tell the players without a program, as they say in the coliseum. Another of Herod (the not-so-Great)'s sons, one *not* named Herod, was named Philip. He was the Tetrarch in Iturea, and Trachonitis, and Lysanias and Abilene, though (and you knew it was coming, didn't you?) he was also sometimes known as Herod Philip II. It's all Herod's all the time in this family.[4]

---

2. Before Herod the (Not-so) Great died he said, "God has absolved me. God will absolve me. History has absolved me, and will absolve me. I owe nothing to anyone." He also complained that Henry Kissinger never came to visit him anymore.

3. That's Gaius Caesar Augustus Germanicus for those who don't know any better. He hated to be called "Little Boots."

4. It was the same way with the British royal family. Since Queen Victoria's birth in

Igitur Qui Desiderat Pacem, Praeparet Bellum

In that same year, Annas and Caiaphas were the High Priests. Typically, the office of High Priest was held for life, but during the Roman occupation of Palestine the tenure of the Jewish High Priest was curtailed. Also there was usually only one high priest at a time. Was Caiaphas (who was Annas' son-in-law) not capable of officiating on his own? Did Annas hover over his son-in-law correcting every action at the altar? Was Annas the real power behind the throne? Not that the Jewish High Priest had a throne to speak of, but you know what I mean.

"Hurrah, hurrah!" shouted the people. "*Aut Caesar, aut nihil!*" Here the church is the state and the state is the church. Where could you draw the line between them? Could such a line be drawn? It wasn't until 1954 that the phrase "under God" was added to the Pledge of Allegiance in the United States of America, and 1956 that "in God we trust" was finally declared the national motto. Some empires recognize the potential of that kind of propaganda much earlier than others. Henry Kissinger figured it out, of course. He knew enough to support free elections, except when the people might vote for a communist. He told us that any "foreign policy that makes human rights its cornerstone invites a revolution," and that a nation should not have "friends . . . only interests." The Caesars and the Tetrarchs of the world know exactly what this means.

2. Dragons and Beasts of the Underworld

It is easy to disparage King Herod the (not-so) Great. He was, it is easy to say, nasty, brutish, and short. He was a paranoid, murderous villain of the sort found in a horror stories of dragons and basilisks and other beasts of the underworld. He used every dirty trick, every accusation, and every hypocrisy. He used every political and economic temptation available to him. He saw the mysteries of the universe unfolding, but could only see his own selfish fear. There was only lies, deceit and slander for him. Nothing more. He lived like a vulture, like a Komodo dragon or some other animal—a fox, a lion, a dog—waiting to devour his prey. But he died like a beast too; he died like an unwanted dog.

Herod the (not-so) Great died at sixty-nine years of age in the year 4 B.C. of a chronic kidney disease that was aggravated by a maggot infested gangrene of the genitals. He complained of intense and unrelenting itching,

---

first quarter of the nineteenth century there have been twelve different babies named Albert.

and of tumors on his toes as well as painful intestinal problems, breathlessness, and convulsions of all his limbs. His illness began as a sexually contracted gonorrhea that quickly became an infection of the urethra. As urine leaked within his body, the bacteria and infection spread. He suffered from fevers, fluxes, and fatigues, all the phantasmagoria of delirium and disease. He rotted from the inside out and the smell of living death emanated from his putrefying body.

His physicians, who were all trained in the ancient medical arts and sciences, attempted to balance the four vital humors of his body: blood, black bile, yellow bile and phlegm. "Perhaps we could introduce *plasmodium vivax,* which is to say, malaria, via an injection to create an artificial fever to burn the infection out of his royal highness," one of them suggested. "No. No, no," another objected. "You introduce malaria for syphilis. Pyrotherapy won't work for gonorrhea." In the end they suggested bathing him in a tub of warm oil to relieve his afflictions. But instead of alleviating his pains the oil bath temporarily blinded him. The bath had unexpected and unfortunate side effects but did nothing to cure either his gonorrhea or his raging kidney infection.

He died ugly, as we said, like an unwanted dog.

3. The Soldiers and the (Re)publicans Objected

The word of God comes to John in the wilderness. He is the voice, an echoing voice, in the wild places at the edge of human civilization. He hears the voice of God there in the wilderness. "Prepare ye the way of the Lord."

It's true that unusual sensory experiences have often been the basis for all sorts of new religious movements. And because some of these movements have gone off in dangerous directions, we are challenged to test the spirits to determine whether or not they are from God or not. Should we not also test the veracity of voices in the desert? Can we use acoustic technologies or sonic detection systems? How can we know the truth when we hear it?

Figure 12–Which is it?

The vagrant prophet comes out of the wilderness and goes into all the country around the Jordan River, preaching a baptism of repentance, a baptism for the remission of sins. Crowds of people including many (Re)publicans travel to hear him and to be baptized by him. But he is not kind to them. He calls them serpents; he calls them vipers. He questions their parentage, implying that they are lizard men—the illegitimate offspring of snakes and the daughters of men, conceived by the seed of the serpent in the womb of women. He even threatens them with an axe and with fire, but still they stay and they listen. And, what is more, they ask him questions:

"What should we do?" they ask.

"If you have two coats, give one away," he tells them. "Give it to someone with none. And exact no more from others than that which is appointed to you."

They bristle at this. "Why? That's socialism! If they were foolish or careless with their money, if they didn't save enough to buy their own winter coat, why should I give them one of mine? Really, they should have been thriftier. It's irresponsible to create this sort of dependency on acts of charity."

There are police officers and soldiers in the group as well, along with members of the National Guard. And they, likewise, demand (they don't ask. Soldiers don't ask; they demand), "And what shall *we* do?"

"Do violence to no one." John says.

"But . . ." the soldiers and the (Re)publicans object.

"Do Violence To No One."

"Now, John, we didn't come all this way to listen to this sort of foolishness."

"DO VIOLENCE TO NO ONE."

Honestly, I don't know how they went away convinced that he never told them to lay down their arms or to change their ways. But they do. They go away content believing that "it is good and proper for soldiers to use their weapons when the prefects and governors call upon them. Of course it is. It is good and godly. It is our patriotic duty. It's noble and glorious for us to fight and to die (never question why) for the State. '*Credere, obbedire, combattere,*' brothers. Believe, obey, fight! Because facts don't matter. Violence acts! And, what is more, it's our God given Second Amendment right to carry firearms." And what is more—they still believe these things even to this very day.

4. The Truth Is Seldom in the Police Reports

But Herod the Tetrarch (Herod Antipas, remember? We've moved on from the rotted, stinking father to the rotten, stinking son), having also been reproved by the Baptizer for taking his brother, Philip's wife, Herodias,[5] for his own despised the prophet. Herod Antipas had divorced his own wife, a Nabatean Princess. And this enraged her father, King Aretas. King Aretas gathered his army and, for the honor of his daughter (not to mention the resolution of a longstanding border dispute) launched an attack against the Tetrarch of Galilee. In response to this invasion, Herod Antipas had to call in a favor from his Roman overlords. But even with the troops supplied by Rome, Herod's forces were soundly defeated.

He may have been the *fornicator immensus* and *crudelis*[6] but at least Herod had his new bride—the one who had been his brother's wife. She was also his niece. Did I fail to mention that? The whole family was a disgusting mess.

Still, Antipas wasn't disgusting and gross *all* the time. He was also interested in economics as well as the theater and urban renewal. He had the mountain top city of Sepphoris rebuilt and renamed at great expense. And

---

5. For crying out loud! Was everyone in this damned family named Herod?

6. Actually this was a description of Vladimir I the Russian Viking (A.D. 960-1015) who, by the end of his life was revered as a Christian saint, but it works equally well for Herod Antipas, even if he never gained a saintly reputation after his death.

was the first to stage Greek dramas in Roman amphitheaters within Jewish cities. *Très chic*, right? Very cosmopolitan. Very cool.

After his father's death, when most of the country was breathing a cautious sigh of relief,[7] the city of Sepphoris was sacked and looted by a small time warlord named Judas ben Ezekias. Judas ben Ezekias used it as his base of operations for various raids and lootings in the area. The then current Roman Governor, Varus, responded by burning the city to the ground and selling its inhabitants into slavery. Some, a few reckless individuals, said that this might have been a bit of an overreaction. Responsible citizens, however, acknowledged that Varus' actions were prudent and appropriate.

Herod Antipas had Sepphoris rebuilt and renamed, at great expense, as I said. And he called it Autocratoris, which doesn't exactly roll of the tongue, does it? I mean, why not name it, Dictatorville? Or Despotsburg? Maybe Martinet City? We could totally rock it out in Martinet City.

He also built a brand new seaside city and, in a not-at-all-subtle bit of groveling before Caesar, named it Tiberius. The problem was that none of the Jews wanted to live there. They refused to move to Tiberias even though it was built right near a natural hot-springs spa. They objected because it was built over an ancient burial ground, which sounds like something from a bad horror movie, but it wasn't. He built the city over a cemetery. In the end Herod had to populate the city through forcible migration. He ordered people to move to his nouveau metropolis and health spa on the seashore at the point of the sword. The cemetery was eventually forgotten and the city prospered, but the whole ordeal left a bad taste in the mouths of everyone for a long time.

So the Tetrarch was soundly chastised and condemned by the itinerant prophet from the wilderness for marrying his sister-in-law/niece and for all the other bloody, disgusting, and stupid things he'd done. But Herod Antipas,[8] not content with all the bloody disgusting things he'd done so far, had the people's prophet imprisoned. Perhaps he was only following something of his father's advice. Perhaps that not-so-Great voice echoed in his head. "When the stability of the nation is in doubt, the only solution, unfortunate as it may be my boy, is to imprison the leaders of the opposition." Or perhaps he was a cruel, impulsive bastard who spoke out of both

---

7. You remember what Herod Antipas said at his inauguration, right? "My fellow Israelites, our long national nightmare is over . . ."

8. The name 'Antipas' is contraction of 'Antipatros' which means 'like the father,' but as 'Antipas' could also be read as 'against everyone.' And both are accurate.

sides of his mouth (one side named Foolishness, the other Prevarications). Perhaps it was both.

The squadrons of police that came with orders from the Tetrarch to arrest the Baptizer were uncouth, unshaven thugs with their uniforms blouses unbuttoned. They smoked cheap Albanian cigarettes and smelled of whisky and body odor. The historian, Flavius Josephus tells us that John the Baptizer was imprisoned "out of Herod's suspicious temper," and that he was eventually murdered at the desert fortress known as Machaerus—the Sword. Beheaded. This is the truth, but the Truth is seldom in the police reports.

5. Shall We Gather at the River?

John the Baptizer was popular and beloved by the people. He commanded them to exercise virtue and righteousness to each other and piety towards God, and invited them to come to the water to be baptized in order to be acceptable to God. And the people, all of them—or as near to all as makes no difference—came and were baptized in that place by the water, surrounded by tall bulrushes and little birds. Jesus came too. He waded out into the water to meet the Baptizer.

"Do you believe in God, the Father Almighty?" John asked him.

"I believe," Jesus answered.

"Do you believe in the Holy Ghost, and the holy church, and the resurrection of the flesh?"

"I believe."

John prepared to dunk Jesus beneath the waters, but Jesus stopped him, "Isn't there a middle bit?" He asked.

"Not yet," John said. "Not yet." Then without warning he shoved Jesus beneath the waters and held him there.

Igitur Qui Desiderat Pacem, Praeparet Bellum

Figure 13–Full color slides.

When he came up from the waters, Jesus prayed. The heavens were opened for him. Light was broken, splintered and refracted. A refulgence no longer isolated to the singular orb in the sky overhead enveloped him. The light of a small flower, the watery light of the river, the descending light of a cooing dove surrounded him. Light, in too great a quantity to take in with mere human eyes. God of God, Light of Light itself was embraced by an ineffable light. And the echo of the voice said to him, "Thou art my beloved son. I am, with you, well pleased."

Shall we gather at the river? John the Baptizer was there proclaiming a baptism of repentance for the forgiveness of sins. Shall we gather at the river, the beautiful, beautiful river? Where crystal tides are forever flowing, where bright angels tread along with the saints and all the population of Judea and Jerusalem? Shall we gather at the river and wear camel-hair and leathers of our own? Shall we confess our sins in the face of bright axes and sharpened fires? Shall we actually give away our possessions, and work for honest wages? Shall we give up the pride and prestige that comes with positions of power? Shall we gather in the wilderness, underneath a sky that threatens to rip open at any moment and pour down upon us the floodgates of heaven? The river is beautiful, beautiful but those banks are stormy. Perhaps this is too idealistic and not at all realistic. It's dangerous out there, and that baptizing John was something of a radical. Dangerous. Shall we gather at the river?

No. Perhaps not.

6. What of Those So-Called Missing Years

And Jesus himself began to be about thirty years old. This strange phrase[9] marks the change from the old *anno Urbis Conditae* calendar to *anno Domini* reckoning of years, as calculated by the monk Dionysius Exiguus, even if the dates he determined were off by several years.[10] But what of those so-called "Missing Years"? What of them? What could we say that reputable, credible, and academic scholarship has not already debunked, disproved, and rejected?

Did the adolescent Jesus travel with his mentor and friend the tin merchant, Joseph Arimathea and walk upon England's green to learn from and to teach the Druids among those dark Satanic Mills? Or did he travel to Kashmir to speak to mystics in a language of lilting grace? Did his adventure peradventure go as far as the mountains of Tibet? Or did old Notovitch[11] make up that whole hoary tale?

Was the young adult Jesus among the anonymous artists who painted the cave walls in prehistory France? Was he spotted by CIA intelligence agents entering known terrorist training facilities in the quiet suburbs of Baghdad wearing a thin disguise? Did he scale mountains of gold to laugh in the face of the sun? Did Jesus travel during those silent, missing years to Bakkah to see the meteorite?

Possible? Sure. Plausible? I don't know. Build any physical, mathematical, biological, astrological, egotistical, phenomenological, pharmaceutical fantasy you want. Why not? It will be as credible as any other run of the mill Hollywood dream sequence and/or drug induced hallucination. Jesus, the supposed son of Joseph, began to be about thirty years old.

---

9. The phrase does not come from an obscure source in some forgotten library. You can probably find it in your own home. Or if not there, then the Motel 6 down the street.

10. It also replaced the lesser known *anno Martyrum* and *anno Mundi* eras in the Western world, but the Greeks didn't accept the humble Dionysius' system until well into the modern era, which is itself another arbitrary designation.

11. Nikolai Notovitch (1858-1916) the Jewish adventurer who claimed to be a nobleman and a spy and who, in 1894, wrote the book *La Vie Inconnue de Jesus Christ*, in which he claimed to have discovered documents in a Himalayan monetary which proved that Jesus spent time studying with Buddhists in India. He also wrote books about war and a biography of Tsar Nicolas II, but we're not concerned with those.

Igitur Qui Desiderat Pacem, Praeparet Bellum

7. Genealogies

Theo, hey. This next section is a bit dry. Sorry. I was tempted to simply leave this genealogical material out because, let's face it, unless it's *your* family, genealogical records are pretty dull. But I wanted to be true to my sources, and I wanted to write this from the beginning to the end (more or less) in a (more or less) orderly account. So I need to include it. Even if it's boring.

One thing to keep in mind however: Genealogies are not neutral documents. No document is neutral; they all have agendas, even genealogies. And other genealogies (even of the same person) may have different agendas.

So the genealogy of Jesus is as follows: Jesus–Joseph (the supposed father)–Heli–Matthat–Levi–Melchi–Jannai–Joseph–Mattathias–Amos–Nahum–Esli–Naggai–Maath–Mattathias–Semein–Jossech–Joda–Joanan–Rhesa–Zerubbabel–Shealtiel–Neri–Melchi–Addi–Cosam–Elmadam–Er–Jesus–Eliezer–Jorim–Matthat–Levi–Symeon–Judah–Joseph–Jonam–Eliakim–Melea–Menna–Mattatha–Nathan–David–Jesse–Obed–Boaz–Sala–Nahshon–Amminadab–Admin–Arni–Hezron–Perez–Judah–Jacob–Isaac–Abraham–Terah–Nahor–Serug[12]–Reu–Peleg[13]–Eber–Shelah–Cainan[14]–Arphaxad–Shem–Noah–Lamec–Methuselah–Enoch–Jared–Mahalaleel–Cainan–Enos–Seth–Adam–God.

Later they will ask him to "speak plainly and to the truth: Are you the Son of God or not?" Genealogies are not neutral documents; this one has an agenda.

8. This Odd Earnest

Verily, Joseph the supposed father, saw clearly in his old age that the foresayings of the Prophets had been fulfilled openly; for he was given an odd earnest, receiving inspiration from the angels, who cried, Glory to God; for he hath bestowed peace on earth.

This is an odd earnest, to be the supposed father.

---

12. Serug abandoned henotheism and taught his children various forms of sorcery.

13. Young Earth Creationists would like you to believe that the splitting of the great continent Pangea occurred during Peleg's lifetime.

14. Cainan, son of Arphaaxad, is reported to have found astrological records carved into stones before the flood that destroyed the entire world. It is also said by some that his sons made a god of him and that they worshiped his image after his death.

The father disappears from the story of his son now but is, in this disappearance, finally alive and fully perfect, immortal, and divinized. He is robed in the light of an entire sanctification, dazzling, radiant. Pulsating. The son of God became a man so that we might become gods.[15] In his disappearance, the father Joseph becomes a bright stainless mirror reflecting the glory of the son.

The world is weird. Atoms will spontaneously break apart. Nickel-Alkaline will store energy for later use. Blood will flow in an ever circulating stream. Oxygen dissolves in the fluid of the lung. Space becomes relative and time irrelevant. And even the formation of snowflakes creates heat waste and increases the entropy of the universe. The world is weird. But it is the only world we know and it is one. Material and Spiritual. One. The formless God burning within the mountain and the bush. Doubt and Wonder. Faith and Awe. Fear and Trembling in the shadow of the Lord. Humanity may fail but the glory remains. Glory to God; for he hath bestowed peace *and lux aeterna* upon his humble servant.

9. A Melanchthonic Place

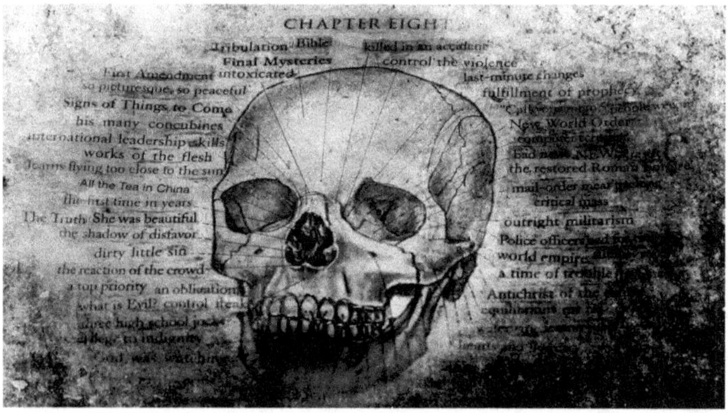

Figure 14–Chapter eight.

Absolute space is an illusion. It's a compelling illusion, to be sure, but quantum physics assures us that absolute space is a comforting lie that we tell

---

15. The early church father, Athanasius wrote "He was made human so that he might make us gods." This divinization of humans, however, never broached the absolute distinction between the uncreated God and his created humans.

Igitur Qui Desiderat Pacem, Praeparet Bellum

ourselves.[16] Because of this, Jesus could at the same time return from the region of the Jordan River to his home in the green hills of Galilee *and* be led into the dangers of the wilderness by a sudden influx of energy from the Spirit.

And the wilderness isn't just wild; it is poisoned and diseased. It is dead and blighted by waste, by nuclear ash and toxic slime mold. It is a fifty meter long, black Bootlace Worm gliding among the rocks on a secretion of mucus and nerve toxins. It is puddles, not of water, but of burning pitch, and lakes of lighter fluid. There, in the dust is the enormous skull of an extinct Cave Hyena. It leers at Jesus in the light of the dying sun. There are many dead worlds and this is one. It is a melanchthonic[17] place, if ever there was one.

He uses bits of wood and, even though it is repulsive to him, he uses the dried bones of that long dead Ice Age predator, to make a small fire. It burns fitfully. A knot in the wood explodes and sparks fly upward into the crepuscular sky. "Man is born to trouble," he sings. It is a song that his mother taught him when he was a boy. He knows that it's not a great song. But it seems fitting, at least for now.

Forty days he spent there, in that desolate and deserted place. During that time he ate and drank nothing but sunlight and *prana*,[18] the living breath of life. And afterwards he was very hungry.

Old Splitfoot came to him there and said, "Jesus H. Christ! What are you doing here, old boy?" He clapped Jesus on the shoulder and added, "Let's go on a little further together, you and I." The devil led him to a concrete bunker surrounded by a security fence and razor wire. A sign at the gate read, "Transjordan Space Elevator—UNITED NATIONS PROJECT—Anchor Station—Authorized Personnel Only." Two lines of spray painted graffiti obscured the rest of the legend, "*In the shank of the night / Bango Skank's still doin' it right!*"

---

16. If, that is, quantum physics can be described as "assuring." I'm not sure that it can.

17. I use the neologism, though I doubt that the German theologian who frequently collaborated with Martin Luther ever sojourned in that melancholy portmanteau, at least not bodily.

18. There are five kinds of air or wind described in the Vedas—actually the ancient yogis found forty nine types of wind, but there are five of real importance. They are: 1) Prana (forward moving air) which is nourishment. 2) Apana (away moving air) which is for digestion and elimination. 3) Vyana (outward moving air) which is for circulation. 4) Udana (upward moving air) which is for speech and expression. And 5) Samana (a balancing wind) which is for the assimilation of experiences and emotions.

Splitfoot waved at the abandoned structure and laughed. "They don't use this one much anymore. Not since they built the mobile platforms out in the ocean. But time is short, and this one is close, so let's go up, shall we?" He waved again and the gate across the road sagged open, allowing them to enter uninhibited by any obstruction.

They rode the elevator car skyward on a Polyseium and Kevlar alloy cable up through the thin stretched clouds of the Earth's highest atmosphere in a relative silence that was broken only by the devil's comment, "Man, Charles Whitman would have loved this view, eh, Jesus? Nice, clean sightlines. He would have just loved it, I tell you."

Eventually they reached the platform in geosynchronous orbit above the planet and the doors of the elevator, after a moment of airlock stabilization, opened for them. The curve of the blue green Earth stretched out before them. "Before I tell you why I've brought you all this way," the devil said as they both stared out at the silent planet, "can I offer you something to eat? You must be hungry. There certainly isn't much of substance in that place you were staying. We've an excellent chef here; I can have him whip up something for you. A sandwich? Or something larger? A steak dinner with thick-cut fries and horseradish on the side? A bowl of gumbo? Oh no. No. No. Not that, not kosher, obviously. What can I have the chef prepare for you?"

Jesus said nothing.

"Nothing? A glass of wine, perhaps? Or fresh brewed coffee. It's Ethiopian. Or maybe you'd like a simple glass of clean, cold water?"

As hungry and thirsty as he may have been, there was still only silence from the Galilean.

"Sure. Sure," the devil nodded his head. "I get it. You have principles. That's cool. I respect that. But we could be talking about sustainable food security for everyone here. I mean, I've got lunch, ready for you now if you want it. Just say the world. But, as I said, we could be talking about something bigger. We could be talking about ending the Malthusian nightmare of the competition for limited resources. We could be talking about bread for the world." But still Jesus said nothing.

The devil slid next to Jesus, shoulder to shoulder as they looked out the window at the vast telluric vista. "What was it that the apocryphal prophet said, 'the vine which they plant thereon shall yield wine in abundance, and

Igitur Qui Desiderat Pacem, Praeparet Bellum

as for all the seed which is sown thereon each measure of it shall bear a thousand, and each measure of olives . . ."[19]

"We do not live by bread alone," Jesus whispered and the devil stopped mid quotation. "But by every one of God's words."

"Okay then," Old Splitfoot continued with an irrepressible grin. "Okay. Okay. Straight to business then." He sighed before continuing. "I'm responsible for all of this." He gestured at the expanse of the Earth below them "All of these worlds. I'm responsible to provide for them. And it's hard work as I'm sure you know. I provide them with all that they need, as well as many of the things that the things they want. I give them everything from summer blockbuster movies and robust economies to strong Wi-Fi signals, and inexpensive athletic shoes." Here Splitfoot chuckled, "And for those that want them, I provide expensive athletic shoes. I mean, whatever makes them feel good, right? I give them medicine when they're sick, and music when they're lonely. I take care it all for them. And yeah, it's hard work. It's demanding. You know this as well as anyone. But it can also be very rewarding. They're like children, looking up with sparkling glee in their eyes when I give them things. And this is what I'm offering you. All the power and glory I have, it can all be yours. Just give me what I want and nobody gets hurt.[20]"

"No," Jesus whispered. His voice wasn't loud, but his tone was firm.

The devil chuckled again. "No, no, of course not. I knew that wasn't the way to approach you. I knew you'd never go for that sort of straight forward tack. Too obvious. Too on the nose. But you know what I'm saying is true. You know it, Jesus, old boy. You know that if you threw yourself from this platform right now, all the angels of heaven would swoop down to rescue you before you touched as much as your little left toe on the stones of Jerusalem. You'd never even hit your hallux on the ground. The crowds would see this and would hail you as king. They would hail you louder than they've ever hailed Caesar in Rome."

There was another long silence. Then Jesus looked up from that majestic view of the Earth and gave a little grin. Splitfoot grinned too, in cheerful anticipation of Jesus' acceptance. Jesus said, "You offer me the lust of the eyes, the lust of the flesh, and the pride of life."

And Splitfoot nodded. "Yes. Yes. That's right. That's right."

---

19. He was quoting, more or less, from the Book of Enoch, chapter ten. The devil, as they say, can cite scriptures (even apocryphal ones) for his own purposes.

20. It's the motto of devils, terrorists, and toddlers around the world.

"Do not tempt me," Jesus continued. The grin vanished from Splitfoot's face, leaving a vacant space, a vacuum, a hole that wasn't an eye neither nostril, mouth. Suddenly there was only an expanse of darkness spreading and the sound of a terrible rushing wind. Everything collapsed into void and the nothingness that was Old Splitfoot's face.

When Jesus awoke sometime later, he was in a strange place and he was alone.[21]

10. Molech Is Molech

A towering mesa stood solitary in the distance, a horst of stone thrust upward between two fault lines, like a sentinel over the desert region near Lake Asphaltitis through which Jesus trudged. It was the region between chaos and stasis. And the sun had set hours ago. Jesus shivered in the cold night breeze of the desert. At the top of the cliffs in the distance he could see lights in the windows of the stone fortress and palace built atop the mesa by Herod the (not-so) Great. A narrow ascent, called by those that lived there "the path of the Serpent," twisted up the precipice with perpetual windings back and forth between steep chasms and sudden drops to sharp stones. There'd be nothing but destruction if your foot slipped from that path.

The mountain fortress did not yet have the cable-car conveyance that would eventually be built for the comfort and ease of visiting tourists coming to visit the site of a "heroic" mass suicide. And the mass suicide wouldn't occur for another forty years or so (and the cable-car wouldn't be until much later after that) but still Jesus shuddered. The *Sicarii* would die there, poisoned by their own hate and desperation. The *Sicarii* would die there still describing themselves as heroes and patriots.[22] Eleazar ben

---

21. Though, as we have said already, Time and Space are only illusions. This could all have happened in null time or no time, and no place, nowhere. Maybe it didn't happen at all, but it's still real.

22. Claiming to be patriots and heroes, the *Sicarii* brigands did not engage in battle with the Roman legions until the end. Instead they took to harassing anyone willing to submit to the Romans and their taxations, treating even their own people as enemies by burning their homes and driving away their livestock, and by plundering them of their possessions as they travelled the roads. "Our aspirations as a God-fearing, peace-loving people will finally be realized when we declare war on Rome," the *Sicarii* announced in their cheaply printed manifestos. "This war is the Kingdom coming. The clock of the ages is striking." But the cruel violence of the Empire does not become kindness when unleashed by the patriot. The toxic venom of the asp does not become medicine in the mouth of the neighbor. Patriotism is a dodge.

Igitur Qui Desiderat Pacem, Praeparet Bellum

Yair, chief of the *Sicarii* at the captured fortress, would urge his followers to consider a final, dreadful solution. They would draw lots and kill each other in turn—men, women, and children, until nine hundred and sixty of them were dead with only two women and five children remaining to tell their story to the conquering Roman legions.

Dethrone the false kings, I say. Yes. Storm their forts of darkness and bring them down. Bring them down! But give no credence to the stories and propaganda of those who would use the same poison, the same fire, the same sword as the Zealots. Molech demands that everyone send their children and all their bloody entrails through his fires. Molech is Molech no matter from which side of the line he is worshipped.

Still, shuddersome or no, Jesus is comforted somewhat by the lack of archaeological evidence for the atrocity and by the internal inconsistencies in the story as told by the historian Flavius Josephus. He is comforted also by the fact that the revered Rabbis never mention Masada, neither in the Talmud nor the Midrashim. Jesus knows that he who fights with monsters must take care not to become the monster. Nietzsche wasn't wrong about everything.

The Argument
Wanting More

At various times in my life I have fancied myself as a painter, a poet, a musician, an essayist, a theologian, a photographer, a humorist, a novelist, a filmmaker, a playwright. *Un soi-disant artiste.* And I worry that none of it is true. To be honest, I'm pretty sure that none of it is entirely accurate, maybe not even close. I'm more *manqué* than maker. Who am I fooling, if not myself?

I had planned to do a number of things today; I had planned to be productive—to mow the yard, to grind some coffee, to read, to write another thousand words or so, I was going to go downtown to the courthouse with the protesters to brave the tear gas and the batons with my son. And I was going to call my mother. I was going to call her yesterday too. Yesterday was her birthday, but I didn't call yesterday. So I thought I should call today. But I didn't. I fell asleep and slept the afternoon away. I'm sure I disappointed her. I know I disappointed myself. I'm having a difficult time knowing who I am recently, and with liking who I think I may be.

What can I say? What message have I received, if any? It is this: *Meta, Mene, Tekel.*

I can read the writing on the wall. I see the pointing finger of God. And I can understand what it means without consulting a prophet, though that may be only the benefit of hindsight and scholarly commentary. It means that all my metaphysical ambitions have been weighed in the balance and I have been found wanting.

This year has wrecked me.

IV

Terminus a Quo

1. Rejection in Synagogue

"No member of the synagogue called me to this," Jesus told them. "No ruler, no lawyer, no temple priest. It was you, my brothers and sisters. You did. You, the poor and despised of the earth, you called me to this ministry. For you are the people preferred by God, and it is God who has appointed and anointed me for this work. *J'ai l'epée dans les reins.*[1] The word of God is a fire in my bones. I burn. I burn to speak deliverance for the hungry, deliverance for the imprisoned, for the segregated, and the disenfranchised from society. I burn for all the forgotten ones. I burn, yet I will speak from the flames."

"It is not merely the words of an ancient text that you hear today, but the Word of God disclosed in and revealed by the text. Do you hear it? Like the Negro trombone player, I'm here to explain the unexplainable, find out the unfindable, and to unscrew the inscrutable.[2] Do you hear me?"

"'Is it safe?' the cowards will ask. 'Is it politic? Is it civil?' the expedient will ask, and the vain will ask, 'Is it popular?' And I answer, 'No. No. No, and No.' But it is Just and that is what matters. Yet, when the word is truthfully spoken to and for them in the midst of their troubles, do they respond with a resounding 'Amen'? Do they encourage the preacher with a 'Come on, now'? No, they do not. Can I get a witness? No. They bum rush the preacher and drag him to the edge of town. For his presumption."

---

1. "I have a sword in my loins," a particularly poignant idiom.
2. Johnson, *God's Trombones*, 5

A Life Known and Unknowable

"We know this boy," they say to each other. "We've always known him. We know where he came from. We know where we will allow him to go. Don't confuse us with facts. Don't speak to us of the longings of long forgotten widows or of disease ridden foreigners.' They rise as one and drag him to the high place at the edge of town, the high place of death. But when they look again, they cannot find him.

2. The Agents of Chaos

Nothing would have been easier. The agents of chaos know this. Nothingness would have been easier and less complex. Nothing is always less complicated than Something. Always, it's a universal constant. *Mais, pourquoi y a-t-il quelque chose plutôt que rien?* It's the question of the ages: Why is there something instead of nothing?

Because there is. Because God is. Life is an anomaly, an enormous improbability, and hardly believable. But here we are, we are alive to ask the question: Why?[3] Perhaps it is the endpoint and *telos* of a non-equilibrium universe. Maybe this existent something is a necessary manifestation of creation having sprung from the mind of God whose name is synonymous with BEING itself. Reality is gratuitous. Complexity is required. Variety too.

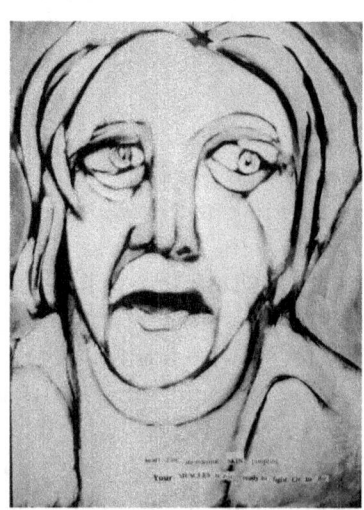

Figure 15–Heart rate increasing, skin pimpling, ready to fight or to flee.

3. At least, I believe that we are alive to ask it. Existence is speculative at best, even under the best of circumstances. Existence is a dubious proposition for us and for God, but, even if it *is* a sure thing, are we sure that we want it?

Terminus a Quo

And all the *echthroi* know this; all our enemies know this: Lilith, Baal Berith, the Dybbuk, all the forces of entropy, and agents of chaos (not just those employed by the CIA). The *echthroi* enemies know that a living universe needs complexity—and they would like nothing more than to see it all undone and unmade. They are blind-eye demons whose blindness is not merely an accident of culture. It is a choice. Their task, their goal, the *terminus ad quem* of their existence is destruction, ruin, and despair. They want nothing. It is simpler than something. Nothing is faster. It is easier to uproot and pull down than it is to plant and to build. And do not forget that it is, as Bradbury tells us, a pleasure to burn.[4] It is easier to destroy than to create. It is easy to drop the bombs and to release the hounds. And they enjoy the obliteration; they delight in the damage.

And here is the real danger. This is the real enemy. Not that mad bastard Herod or his foxy sons. They *are* enemies, but not the *real* enemies. Neither is Caesar (neither this one nor the next one nor the next after that). The real enemy is not the moron in the White House. No. It is not any of these. The real enemy is not flesh, not blood, but the spiritual force of nothingness. And this enemy is well trained. This enemy is well equipped and battle hardened. This enemy will burn and bury you if you let it.

In Galilee, in Capernaum, which had once been the home of the angriest prophet,[5] Jesus was confronted by a man who had within him the spirit of an unclean devil. It came upon the man not, as one might have expected, to lure and or tempt into sin. The unclean spirit came to create disease and cause distress, to bring him disability and dementia. This spirit was one of the many morbid and morbific spirits that infect the world like a virus, like a cancer, like Protein Nano Robots, like Mustard gas and Ricin. It came only to kill and to destroy.

But seeing Jesus in the synagogue it cried out in a loud voice, "Let us alone! What have we to do with thee *thou* Jesus of Nazareth? Art thou come to destroy us?" This servant of Apollyon knows from destruction, aye? It takes one to know one and the exterminator knows the *exterminans*. "I know thee. I know who thou art; the Holy One of God," the demon shrieked, shredding his host's vocal cords to ragged tatters inside his throat. The demons have good theology after all. Unlike many of those who claim

---

4. Bradbury, *Fahrenheit*, 33.

5. The angriest *Jewish* prophet, anyway. Other faith traditions may have their own candidates for the title.

to be followers and servants of the Most High, the demons know who Jesus is.

"Silence" Jesus commanded the demon, and then with a word he sent it gone.

"What word is this?" the people muttered. "What a word, what a word is this!"

3. And the Flame Went Out from Him

This is the man, this Jesus of Nazareth who looks as if he grew up in any small town between there and Ohio or Durango or Masovia or Borno, this Jesus who moves through both time and space like white light through a prism into rainbow colors, like charged particles moving faster through a medium than light can move, creating an electromagnetic shockwave of shimmering cerulean Chernekov radiation. The rainbow spectrum reveals his presence. The ghostly blue glow reveals the passing of his presence. And the flame goes out from him into every place in the country round about.

Still, flame or no, with rainbow and Chernekov radiation or not at all, the real Jesus should watch himself or he will be gunned down by the CIA. A prophet is without honor and messiahs die young. There are East German tanks

Figure 16–Tanks in the street.

4. Some People Burn

At this point we must ask a question:

From whence does fever come? Does it rise from the infernal influence of the demonic? Does it come, as the ancients assumed, from the malign influence of an unclean spirit? Perhaps it is the maliciousness of Nergal, the netherworldly god of pyrexia pestilence who was both worshipped and feared in Mesopotamia? Nergal—the dunghill cock of slow death, Nergal—the chief of Hell's secret police.

Does it rise from the man eating *Rakshasas* which were created in the breath of the sleeping Brahma and were so filled with rage and insatiable bloodlust that they immediately began to devour the flesh of their creator?

Does fever rise from the Firstborn of Death, from the one who devours the skin and the limbs of its victims? Is it *Eshshata*—the demon that King Solomon was taught to exorcise with the invocation of holy angels? There are many fevers and many causes.

Perhaps again, the Talmudists were on to something when they gave anthropomorphic voice to blood saying, "I, blood, am the cause of all illnesses."[6] Seeing beyond the shadowy specter of demonic influence, they looked to blood for the source and the cause. They may not have known anything of infectious diseases and viral vectors, and their recommendation of venesection may not have been the most medically astute, but at least they were looking in the right direction.[7]

Or maybe the woman was just on fire. Maybe she was burning from the inside. Some people just burn.

From whence does fever come? Who can say? And Jesus did not ask. The source is irrelevant and the cause immaterial even in a materialist universe. Fever rises as it will and burns as it will and who it will. Having exorcized the agents of Chaos from the man in the synagogue, Jesus went home with Simon, whose mother-in-law lay burning in bed. He rebuked the fever and the fire was extinguished.

---

6. Bab. Bathra 58b.

7. To their credit, however, they did say that venesection at the height of the patient's fever is equivalent to murder.

Demons, like viruses, must kill in order to live[8] but they cannot kill indiscriminately. Kill too many or too often and they cannot survive. Whatever the cause, be it bacterial, viral, or spiritual, he rebuked the fever and it was gone. The fever went down and she got up and made her way into the kitchen. As she passed, she looked at her son-in-law and said, "Peter, you stink like a fish's armpit. Go wash."

5. All Divers and Sundry Sicknesses

When the Sabbath sun had set and the people were free to come to him, they brought any and all in their homes or family who were sick with pneumonia, cholera, strep, or mono. They brought those who were affected by stars and infected with influenza.[9] Those who were swollen with mumps and flush with roseola were carried and laid at his feet. All divers and sundry sicknesses were brought to him. And, without regard for recommendations from the CDC about quarantine and containment, he laid his hands on them. They brought their schizophrenic sons and their delusional daughters as well. The OCD, the bipolar, and the anorexic were brought to him for healing. Those who were breaking and broken within their minds, he touched them and healed them, everyone.

And it wasn't just physical illness with natural causes and sicknesses of the mind, but also those who were infected by supernatural causes. Those cursed by Mammon were carried to him for the restoration of their souls. Those who had been infected with spiritual STDs either by succubi or by incubi were brought to him to be purified, in their blood as well as their minds. Those oppressed by political thrones, principalities and dominions ,[10] all who are sat and shat upon by the whole range of exousiological powers were brought to him that they might be released.

All through that long night he healed them with the laying of his hands. He exorcised their spirits and the expelled demons came out shrieking, "YOUARETHESONOFGOD!" Nevertheless, Jesus commanded them

8. Though the word "live" is very qualified in both of these cases.

9. Influenza, known in fourteenth century Europe as *Influenza di stelle,* "the influence of the stars," is a disastrous astrological condition of bad stars.

10. The Pentagon is a major part of the principalities and powers ruling this world in this modern day and age—humiliating the weak and exploiting the powerless, making heroes of rich capitalists and Founding Fathers while bombing children in Vietnam and Cambodia, in Syria and Lebanon and Afghanistan. Lord speed the day when these thrones and powers are brought low and humbled before the Throne!

Terminus a Quo

into silence. Even if the demons do have good theology, he would not allow them to speak.

And when the day was broke upon them, being exhausted and drained, he left them and tried to make his way back into the deserted desert places, so that he could be alone. But they followed hard upon him and caught up to him, and stayed him, saying "Stay! Stay! Please stay!"

But he would not be stayed. "I cannot be confined here. I will not be contained. I am not your privilege or prerogative. I have other places to be, other cities to visit. It's what I must do."

6. A Great Many Names

Kings come and go. Rulers rise and tyrants topple under the weight of their multiplied maladministrations. Empires are nearly as ephemeral as the sands upon which they are built. Don't be fooled by the propagandists. It's all *E pluribus unum* until the friction comes. Then you'll be left to fend or fall for yourself. Keyed to some celestial clock, like the moving of the planets in the solar system, like the seas upon the shore, the High King of Heaven has appointed a time for every transient leader, and every temporal kingdom. All authority on Earth is in the hand of God and he appoints a useful person at just the right time.

And just as the prefects and princes change over time, so too change the names of their dominions. The Jebusite city of Shalem becomes Jerusalem, the City of David. And still later, al-Quds and Aelia Capitolina. The City of Rome, that was suckled by the She-wolf, was once the Etruscan Ruma. Sepphoris becomes Tiberias (rebuilt and renamed at great expense). Istanbul was Constantinople. Volgograd was Stalingrad was Tsaritsa. The Congo changed to Zaire and then back again. It happens all the time. It's happening somewhere right now.

As the premiers and presidents change, so change the names of their territories, but the lands themselves, and the peoples who live there, are changeless. Generations come and generations go, but the Earth and all her peoples remain forever. The sun rises. The sun sets and hurries round to begin again. Winds blow north and south, west and east, forever changing. Rivers run, cities rise, streams flow, cities fall—a wearisome cycle without end. What's done is done and done again. Leaders come and go and are forgotten. Future rulers will be forgotten by those who follow. But the people, the people remain forever, no matter the names given to their place they live.

Soon it came to pass, that the people pressed upon him to hear the word of God and he sat to teach them, in a boat upon the Lake of Gennesaret, which at various times has been called by many names, for it has been inhabited for the length of human history. People settled in that low valley even before the Neolithic Revolution.[11] They made their homes on the fertile red soil surrounding the water through the mythic rule of King Solomon. They lived there during the rule of the Hellenists, the Romans, Byzantines and Muslims. The people of the land lived by those fresh waters even during the capriciousness of crusading fools from Europe. They live there still. And they have given it a great many names:

The Lake of Gennesaret, Yam Kinneret, The Sea of Minya, the Sea of Ginosar, and the Lake Tiberias (which is both, more *and* less accurate for it is hardly a "Sea," but Tiberius Caesar never swam in its waters). There is no *penuria nominum* here. You may choose from many, but the name by which it is best known is the Sea of Galilee.

7. UnJesus Calls Simon Out

One day as UnJesus was standing by the Lake of Gennesaret with the people crowding around him and listening to the words he said, he saw at the water's edge two fishing shallops, left there by the local piscators, who were washing their nets. Jesus got into one of the boats, the one belonging to Simon, and asked him to put out a little from the shore. Then he sat down and taught the people from the boat. When he had finished speaking, he said to Simon, "Put out into deep water, and let down the nets for a catch."

Simon answered, "Master, we're tired. We've worked hard all night and we haven't caught anything."

Then the UnJesus (who is nothing like the savior that we know) said, "Really? You worked hard all night and caught nothing? Nothing at all? You didn't catch a single thing? There must be something wrong with you. Are you lazy? Maybe you weren't trying hard enough. It's really the only interpretation that makes any sense. Maybe you shouldn't really be a fisherman after all. Maybe you're not qualified to fish. You really just need to do more

---

11. Which is also known as The (First) Agricultural Revolution. So many names for everything.

to prove yourself, otherwise we will have to have you replaced or moved to another appointment.

Simon fell down, broken and exhausted. He said, "Go away from me, Lord. I am a broken man."

Figure 17–You are not meeting our expectations.

8. Should He Be Phlebotomized, My Lord?

In a certain time and in a certain place[12] behold, a Scaly Man, full of leprosy and escharotic lesions came crying, "Unclean! Unclean!" as he came. Those with Jesus immediately turned to one of the nearby World Health Organization's vending machines with handfuls of pocket change to purchase emergency PPE. From the Medivend machine they bought face masks and hand sanitizer as well as aspirin and overpriced insulin kits. They bought adhesive bandages and sanitary napkins, toilet paper and bottled water. And when they had bought out everything from the vending machine the mob raced to the S-Mart Market to stock up on other vital supplies like carved ivory enema syringes and philters of Serum-114.

Those who stayed with Jesus, donned their masks and latex gloves to protect themselves from contagions and infections and from other blasphemous infirmities carried upon droplets of spittle. They shivered in revulsion. A portion of the Scaly Man's nose had fallen away. His left eye was

---

12. Though, how *certain* can either time or place be in a relational universe? Einstein's theory of Relativity tells us that space has no fixed, no *certain* structure; space is dynamic. Geometry changes in time, and time changes with geography.

rheumy and matted, scaled over. But Jesus reached out his hand to touch the Scaly Man without fear, without disgust for his disfigurements.

"Jesus, if I may," interrupted one of his followers. Jesus paused and lowered his hand to listen. "The learned rabbis and doctors tell us that 'Much blood produces leprosy.'"[13] Jesus nodded, not so much in agreement as in giving encouragement to his disciple to continue his thought. "Knowing this is so, should he," Jesus' follower motioned toward the man with blotched and scabrous skin. "Should he be phlebotomized, my Lord? I'm sure that we can find a trusted, and fully licensed and bonded phlebotomist in this town. After all, as the Rabbis also say, a leaned man does not live in a town without a reputable blood-letter. And if this town is so unfortunate as to have no qualified phlebotomist, leeches for blood-letting are available in most Medivend machines."

The Scaly Man fell on his face into the dirt below Jesus and begged, "Can I be cured? Can I? If you wanted to, lord, if you wanted to, you could make me clean."

"I would. I will. Yes." He touched the Scaly Man and the leprosy departed from him. "Now go," Jesus said. "Fulfill all the sacerdotal obligations; see the priest of the village and be pronounced clean by him. But say nothing of this to any man, nor to any woman neither. But go and show yourself to the priest according to the codes of Moses. All will be well.

9. Into the Lost Lands to Pray

It is a false idea that we must always be on, that we must always be closing, that we must always be winning and always be positive and never criticize or express any sort of melancholy. One day this attitude will disappear but it is not yet gone. It still holds many of the leaders of our churches, our cathedrals, our synagogues, our mosques in its possessive thrall. That false prophet pronouncement of a false god will someday slip a step, but not just yet.

Instead let us ourselves slip off into the unsearchable depth and richness of wisdom that is only found in the loneliest of places and in forgotten wildernesses. Like complexity and diversity, solitude is a necessity. Solitude makes you strong. Your heart beats faster. Your lungs breathe deeper. And Jesus withdrew, alone again, into the lost lands to pray.

---

13. Read rabbi Resh Lakish's comments in the Talmud—Bekhorot 44b.

Terminus a Quo

10. Everything Is All Tangled Up with Everything

Again a certain day and a certain place, Jesus was teaching. This is gospel precision, a precision without specificity. Nature itself is blurry at the quantum level; we cannot know it with precision and there will always some measure of uncertainty on our part.[14] This is the world as we know it. He was in a certain place on a certain day, but we cannot know where and when. All ordinary talk of "when" must be talk of a relative, relational positioning. The same is true of time. Newton was wrong; there is no absolute time, no absolute space.

Could absolute truth and absolute space even be possible in a dynamic, relational universe, wherein all properties that have to do with position in space and time must be constructed from the multiplied relations between every other thing in time and space? Would it even be possible to have complete concrete knowledge within the boundaries of such a universe? Nature, as we've said, is blurred to imprecision. It is vague. Nature is unknowable in its fullness. Can we even speak of "laws of nature"? Is there such a thing as "regularity of phenomena?" Light is energy traveling as particles, moving with inertia but having no mass. Matter at the quantum level acts as a wave, waves of matter. Particles of energy. Interchangeable. If we accept what the German poet and playwright Frederic von Schiller wrote, "*Nur die Fülle führt zur klarheit,*[15]" that only wholeness brings clarity, then we are condemned to ignorance.

But Newton and Postmodernists be bedeviled, I *do* believe in an absolute truth (if not absolute space) though I remain unconvinced our ability to know it absolutely. The world *is* relational. So there it is: Jesus was there and he was teaching. And Pharisees and Doctors of the Law were there to hear him.

Let us establish this right up front and out in the open for all to see: The Pharisees were not mustache twirling melodrama villains. They were neither nefarious nor noxious. They were as impassioned as we were, but was that a fault? They kept themselves separate from the world and attributed all things and everything to both fate and to God. Both good and evil, they said, are held in our hands. For the most part. But fate comes too and cooperates with us. For the Pharisees, fate and free will were the two

---

14. The universe can only be understood statistically—as a collection of approximations. It displays the sort of logic that disappears if you press too close. Don't press too close.

15. Schiller *Spruch des Confucius*.

eternal cadences held in perpetual tension in our lives—the thrust away and the pulling close, the choice and the decree. For the Pharisee it was all part of the same. Fate is set but can be changed. Freewill and Determinism are not mutually exclusive. They held both and felt no logical inconsistency. Everything is all tangled up with everything.

As he was teaching, a group of men arrived with a palsied man carried between them. They carried him on a stretcher, but they could not enter the house where Jesus was lecturing because it was so crowded. Undeterred, they lofted the stretcher to the roof. Taking vigor and force against all obstacles, they dug a hole in the flat roof and lowered their paralyzed friend down.[16] Jesus saw the man coming down through the room and he saw the faith of the men upon the roof. He saw their strange, unfounded certitude, and he said, "My good man, your sins are forgiven."

It was this pronouncement, this exculpation that troubled the Pharisees and Doctors who were there, though neither the Pharisees nor the Doctors of the Law could do anything for the man. They reasoned with in and among themselves, "Who is this man to say such things? Who dares such blasphemies? Only God, and God alone forgives."

But Jesus, who knew their entangled thoughts said, "Which is easier to say? That your sins are gone? Or that your paralysis is gone? Which would be easier to say? And which would be easier to see? He held up a hand to stifle their objections. "So that *noumenon* might become *phenomenon* I say: Rise up. Walk."

The man got up from his stretcher and went home,[17] giving glory to God all along the way. And the crowd that was there, the Pharisees and doctors of the Law as well were all greatly amazed. "We have seen something burning, burning strange," and they went away biting their fingertips with rage.

---

16. Did they plan ahead and bring a pickaxe and rope or were these tools fortuitously, providentially provided? Were their chosen actions aided by fickle fate?

17. It was too crowded for the man to enter the house, but not too crowded for him to exit? Did he push through the astonished crowd saying, "Excuse me. Pardon me. Oh, hey Cousin Josiah, good to see you. Ope, just gonna' squeeze past ya' there . . ."?

Terminus a Quo

11. All the Unwashed Legions

Jesus met a (Re)publican[18] named Levi. Some say this Levi was a son of Alpheus, like James. And maybe he was. Is it *possible* that he was the son of Alpheus and brother to James? Sure. But is it *probable*? Maybe. Is it *provable*? Probably not. But if the study of quantum particles tell us anything, it is that if it is at all possible, it will, eventually happen somewhere. So maybe Levi and James were brothers. So what? Even if it were true that they were relatives, it tells us relatively little.

Jesus saw the (Re)publican named Levi sitting in the tollbooth. "Follow me," Jesus said to him. And this Levi (who was maybe a son of Alpheus, or maybe he was Matthew, maybe both, we can neither confirm nor deny either one) stopped his work for the Roman Occupying Force, got up from his seat in the tollbooth, and went home to make a feast for Jesus in his own house.

There was a great company with Levi, of (Re)publicans and other sinners, all the animals that only come out at night—the residuum and underclass, the skunks and junkies, the sick and lame, the dribs and drabs of a throwaway, disposable society, all the unwashed legions were there to share a meal with Levi and with Jesus.

"Why," asked the scribes with the separated and serrated Pharisees, "do ye eat and drink with the (Re)publicans?" To his disciples and students they asked, "Why does he eat with these that are outside the pale? Eating with swindlers, with mountebanks, and pickpockets, with gamblers and other scum. Eating with *sinners* is something that should shame the pupils of the scribes.

Peter shoved back his chair, stood and drew his foil. He pointed it at the accusers. "No one should question the teachings of our master. Anyone who hears our master's instruction maligned should be ready to defend it and to defend him by the sword with a good thrust into the belly as far as the sword will go." He glowered at them, making feint attacks hoping to draw them into a fight.

But Jesus pushed his sword arm down. "No, Peter. There's no need for that. None." Peter glumly replaced his foil into his belt scabbard and sat down again. Then Jesus turned to his accusers and apologized. "My students' loyalty yet out-distances their comprehension. I'm sorry." The Pharisees mumbled their acceptance, but Jesus interrupted them. "It's true,

---

18. A *(Re)Publicanus* to be perfectly vulgar about it.

though. Your allegation is too broad. You need to be more specific," Jesus told them, "if you want the charge to stick, don't say, 'He eats with sinners.' It's too generic. Say instead: 'He eats with cutthroats and bandits.' Something like that."

"Say that he eats with communards, and socialists. Say that he eats with sex-workers and disgraced, defrocked clergy. Or that he eats with lepers. He eats with juvenile delinquents, drug addicts, ex-cons, escaped galley-slaves and runaways. He eats with university professors and (at the risk of being redundant) atheists. Say that he eats with politicians, landlords, fortune-tellers, television weather-men, members of the Weather Underground, tax collectors, tax avoiders, pacifists, draft dodgers, and with generals in their masses. He eats with judges, juries, and executioners (even if far too often these are all the same person). He eats with punk-rockers, anarchists, diggers, knife grinders, organ grinders, and sausage makers. With snake-oil salesmen and other disciples of L. Ron Hubbard. He eats with founding fathers, absent fathers, and unwed mothers. You could even say that he has the gall to eat with limerick writers."

"The ones who are whole," Jesus told them with a chuckle, "the ones that are well, they don't need to go to Gilead for a balm or to a doctor for a nostrum. They're already fine. But," Jesus extended his arms to indicate all those gathered at the table, all those in the room, "the ones who are sick, they need me."

12. Question and Answer Time, Jesus

"Now it is question and answer time, Jesus. Tell us: Rabbi Leibniz says that this is the best of all possible worlds, is he right? Or has he been corrupted by that candied demon, Pangloss?"

"Ugh," groaned Jesus. "I hate talking about monads. Next question."

"Teacher, a two part question: Is there such a thing as Ylem? Was it there in the beginning? And were protozoa the first animals of Genesis?"

"That's three questions. Someone else?"

"Jesus, where is your beard?" someone shouted from the back of the crowd.

"What?" Jesus was caught off guard by the question.

"Beards are mentioned all through the Hebrew scriptures, what some would call the Old Testament. Beards were everywhere then. All the men had them and even some of the women had them. But in the Christian

Terminus a Quo

scriptures, in the so-called New Testament, there is no mention of beards. Why is that?"

"Honestly, I never thought about it," Jesus answered. "Next."

"Jesus, Rabbi Eco suggests that there might be a world in which the crossing of a camel with a locomotive might produce a square root. What do you say, Jesus?"

"Rabbi Eco says many strange things. And he writes the same way in all his books, speaking in them of these matters. His books are great, but they're very difficult; they contain many things that are difficult to understand, which some ignorant and unstable people tend to distort. This strange union between a camel and a locomotive that you say he describes is probably hyperbole.[19]"

"Teacher, can human consciousness affect the molecular structure of water? Does water respond to positive thoughts? Does water retain a memory of those substances that have previously been dissolved in it? And can polluted water be purified through the power of prayer?"

"Does the Pope shit in the woods?"

"What?"

"Seriously? No. Next question."

"Rabbi Hanina ben Tachyon[20] has written that we are free willed creatures, free of any sort of determinism. Free enough, he suggests, to even violate the rules of causality, that cause may no longer precede effect in time. Does any of this make sense to you, Jesus?"

"Sorta' yes. But I think we can safely say that no one really understands what Rabbi Tachyon says. Not yet anyway. Next?"

"Rabbi, why is it that the disciples of the Baptizer, like those of our Pharisees, fast and make prayers, but your disciples, Jesus, your disciples are seen eating and drinking? Why are they not more punctilious? Why is that? Explain yourself."

"Later my students may fast," Jesus said in response, "if they want to and if they choose to. But now, while the bridegroom is still with the wedding guests, while the band is still playing, while the bar is still open, can they be expected to fast and mourn and groan with despair? No. Now's the time for celebration. Drink up. Dance a bit. Enjoy. Later, when the groom is gone, that will be the time for sober fasting and abstention."

---

19. Eco, *Kant and the Platypus*, 52

20. The theoretical models predict the presence of Rabbi Tachyon, but researchers have not yet been able to confirm his existence.

13. They Agreeth Not

He is eschatological and abstruse, maybe, but never abstract. He tells stories, laughs at tricks and subversive reversals. He is like a playful panther, a leopard, a she-bear, or even a lioness. "I've got other stories I could tell you," he said to them. "Stories of Stagolee, or of High John the Conqueror." They stared blankly at him. "Ah well, maybe now's not the time for those stories. There is no end to the stories we could tell, and no shortage of books, but our time is short. Still . . . you really should hear them some time."

He continues: "No one tears a new shirt into pieces in order to make a patch for an old one. Why ruin the new to repair the old? And they wouldn't match anyway. They agreeth not. It's the same with new wine in old skins, right? The old is stiff and dry; when the new ferments the skin will burst. You'll both lose the bottle and waste the wine."

We may be heading for a similar predicament with this novel as we're cramming the novel and the strange into the old and familiar. This weird blend of hippy-dippy, leftist agenda (as some would describe it) may not be helpful to anyone. Nevertheless I've committed myself to the story and will continue, mischievous though it may be.

14. Defense by Way of Question and Precedent

There was that time when Jesus and his comrades were walking through someone's grain fields.[21] They were walking through the grain fields and they were hungered so they plucked some ears of the grain and rubbed them between their hands to separate away the chaff. And there, on the march, they ate the kernels of this fresh plucked grain.

"*Assur! Assur!*" Certain nearby Pharisees shouted at them. "Forbidden! Forbidden!" The Pharisees accused Jesus and his friends of criminal activity. But don't misread the story by modern convention: the crime was not theft. Gleaning from neighbor's fields was honored and legal. The scandal was Sabbatical; they were accused of harvesting—which is work—on what should have been the day of rest.

But Jesus gave defense by way of a question. "Don't you remember that time that David and his men of war were all hungered so they went into the

---

21. I don't remember if it was corn, or barley, or wheat. Maybe it was wheat. Do you think you could plot the timeline of this story by agricultural cycles? Perhaps, I suppose. But that's not really the point here, is it?

tabernacle and ate the showbread that was consecrated to the priests?" It was a defense by way of question and precedent. Human need sometimes outweighs the stricture of the law, just as the needs of the many usually outweigh the rights of the one. Of the two, locked in perpetual frictions, one must yield for the Son of Man is Lord of the Sabbath.

15. Apathy Is a Failure

Another Sabbath in another synagogue in another village down the road Jesus was teaching. And his enemies were watching. They were surveilling him. Call it curiosity, professional or otherwise. It was then that a man with a withered hand approached him.

No. Sorry. That's not quite right. The man with the withered hand was there but he did not approach Jesus. It was Jesus who called him out. It was Jesus pushing the point. "What's your story, brother?" Jesus asked.

"I am a Stoneman, working with my hands, cutting rock and carving stone. I could build you a house just as easily as I could carve palm and pomegranate ornaments fit for the temple. I am a Stoneman like my father and his father before. Or I was, but no longer." He waved, as much as he was able, with his withered right hand with ligaments pulled tight and the muscles shriveled, he could hardly waggle it at all.

Was it supernatural agency or keen psychological insight? Could Jesus receive and interpret their psitrons? The mechanism is unclear, but his enemies in the synagogue could not keep their thoughts from him. Nor could they mask their intent. Jesus called out his accusers even before they'd had a chance to accuse him. "One question," he said. "Is it Sabbath lawful to do good or to do evil? Is it Sabbath lawful to save life or to destroy it?"

But they gave no reply. "Stretch out your hand," he said to the withered Stoneman. And when he did, his hands and arms, both of them, were whole—the one as strong as the other.

There was no extremity here, no exigent circumstance, no life or death emergency to necessitate a Sabbath day miracle. The healing could have waited till the morrow but Jesus was pushing a point, purposefully being provocative. And the point is this: Whoever knows the right and the good and fails to do it, for him it is evil. It is a sin. Silence is consent and apathy is a failure. Even on the Sabbath. Especially on the Sabbath.

His enemies were filled with madness and with fury. They began plotting and scheming together but could bring no charges against him. No formal charges of Sabbath violation were ever brought against him. And even if they had, would the Roman judicial system have concerned themselves with the peculiarities of Jewish law? Unlikely.

16. What Is the Temperature of Our Longing?

Our view of the universe is usually veiled by thick mystery, and this mystery provokes questions that we cannot answer. Questions that may not have an answer. Ask the anthropologist, the archaeologist, the linguist, or the learn'd astronomer. Ask the theologian, the philosopher, the philologist, the cleric, the psychologist, the secretary, the nurse. Ask the poet—poets will tell you all about this mystery; all you have to do is ask. But don't bother asking the advertisers. They'll sell you an answer that is nothing more than a beautiful lie.

We have only fragments, bits of a fascinating whole. We have these broken fragments, these shards of light, it's true, but we also have wonder. And we have mystery. This is vital. It's the mystery and the wonder that keeps us sane, keeps us sound. Listen to the Prince of Paradox who told us, "if you destroy mystery you create morbidity.[22]" He knew the score.

What is the color of our passion? What is the temperature and temperament of our longing? How can we find our way to clarity? To insight and to vision? Let us start slowly and keep a good shape; Jesus went up into the mountains to pray. This may be a mystery but it is a sensible and a healthy one.

17. The Heroes, the Legends, the Talmidim

When the day came he returned from his prayer and solitude in the mountains and called his band of disciples together. Twelve of them he named as apostles.

Among them there was Simon, whom he also named Peter. Simon had rocks in his head and carried a fencing foil. He liked to pretend that he was Zorro. I thought he was more of a Zero, but Jesus liked him. Much has been said about Simon, and nothing more needs to be said at this point except that Jesus liked him. That was enough.

---

22. Chesterton, *Orthodoxy*, 48.

Terminus a Quo

Figure 18–Our Lady of Perpetual Probation.

And there was Andrew, Peter's younger brother. He was manly and brave, a freedom fighter even though he was only seventeen years old. He wore a faded jean jacket with the collar turned up and a *keffiyeh* around his neck. He wore the badge of Our Lady of Perpetual Probation and the red and black pin of the anarchists on the flap of the breast pocket. On one shoulder of his jacket was a patch that read, "Revelation! Liberation! Revolution!" On the other he'd drawn in heavy, black marker, "Defund the Military! Demilitarize the Police!"

James and John, the twin thunder sons of Zebedee owned a fleet of fishing boats with paid employees before they began following Jesus. They weren't "dirt people." They weren't desperately poor like most of the *am ha'aretz*—the changeless people of the land—who followed Jesus, but neither were they flush with wealth. It took them a while to acknowledge their privilege, but they did come around eventually.

I knew very little about Philip. He was from Bethsaida, I think. And later he went off on a quest to find the swamps and mists of Acherusia in the underworld. Whether he ever found them or not, I don't know. He was gone for a long time. And when he came back from wherever he went, he was sullen and withdrawn. He refused to talk about the things he'd seen in those stygian realms. I will say this about Philip, though. His frequent glances into the mirror were not, as some have said, acts of vanity and narcissism. They were, in fact, attempts to reassure himself that he still existed. *Cogito ergo sum* didn't concern him so much as a sort of Missourian 'show me' incredulous anxiety. Existence is a dubious proposition, and Philip was not convinced.

And what of Bartholomew? Bartholomew was a bit of a dead end, but what can I say? I always liked him. I smiled every time I saw him wearing that tin funnel on his head. It's true. He wore a funnel, tied with a bit of leather cord as if it were a hat. As if it were normal. But that was Bartholomew. He's the one who suggested to Jesus that the Scaly Man should be phlebotomized for his health. He was also quite keen on the benefits of trepanning and icepick lobotomies. If he hadn't become an apostle of Jesus, I'm sure he would have gone on to a brilliant career as a chiurgeon.

Mathew was very plain. Vanilla. In a simple word, Matthew was boring. When he spoke, which wasn't often, mind you, it was in a near monotone. He preferred lists over descriptions, and spreadsheets instead of narratives. He liked numbers more than words and words more than people. While I don't think he understood people he did keep all his receipts, carefully organized by date, in an attaché case that he carried with him everywhere. After all these years I can't even tell you what he looked like anymore. He was forgettable. He always struck me as something of a placeholder, a token to round out the twelve.

And Thomas will only be mentioned this one time. This once—that's it and no more. He is a human *hapax legomenon*.[23]

James the son of Alpheus was fascinated by octopuses. He was a freak for those soft-bodied pseudopods. If he ever managed to buttonhole you at a party, he'd tell you everything you never knew you wanted to know about the limber and graceful limbs of the sensitive octopus. He'd describe their excellent eyes, "which are closer to the eyes of vertebrate creatures than any other invertebrate animal," he'd rave. "They have eyes like cameras, you know? And they're intelligent. So smart. Their brain to body mass ratio is the highest of all invertebrates. They're not cold and unfeeling as you might imagine them to be. They're highly social creatures that get lonely when they're isolated from their communities. They collect shiny objects that they keep as treasures. And they use tools. They use tools! Do you understand what that means? They're curious and they can be taught! Taught—not trained—to pull and release levers in exchange for food. They have extraordinary capacity for spatial learning. They can solve quadratic equations! There are even some immunologists and astrobiologists who believe that

---

23. And without this footnote the phrase "*hapax legomenon*" would have been a *hapax legomenon* in this novel. You're welcome.

octopuses[24] may actually be aliens from other parts of the universe. Mark my words," he told us. "Someday octopus and other cephalopod mollusks and decapod crustaceans will be protected by law as sentient creatures. You can mark my words!" He couldn't fathom that anyone could think of the octopus as loathsome things. And don't even mention eating them . . .

Simon Zelotes. Simon freaking Zelotes! He talked big, but he wasn't. He was a loudmouth and a braggart, and a bit on the obnoxious side. *Ein Großmaul.* But he was never one of those right-winged ultranationalists, the Zealots. He never carried firearms into crowded shopping malls, and never crossed state lines to shoot at protestors. And he was not a member of any revolutionary group committed to the violent overthrow of the Roman Empire. He was not one of the *Sicarii*. I don't know how those stories started. The Zealots, as an organized militia warring against the Romans, didn't really exist until later, much later—the winter of A.D. 67-68 to be more specific. They were organized by Judas of Galilee in Jerusalem. But Simon Zelotes was never one of them. To describe him as a member of the Zealots is a bit of an anachronism, and there are far too many of those in this narrative already. He was more fundamentalist than revolutionary, motivated by a desire to protect himself and his coreligionists from violations of the law.[25] He was a bit of a windbag and a showoff but he was always a reliable friend. We always knew that he had our backs. Always.

Figure 19–Saint Jude, patron of difficult cases and lost causes.

24. Octopuses is correct. Not Octopi nor Octopodes. James told me that.

25. The Apostle Paul (AKA Saul) also described himself this way, as a former Zealot. See his letters to the Galatians and the Philippians. But this is not his story. Perhaps in the sequel.

Judas, the brother of James, hated to be called Thaddeus. "That's not my name!" he insisted whenever anyone called him that. But it was a lost cause. The more he objected, the more the guys called him Thaddeus, stringing it out in a taunting schoolyard whine: "*Thhhaaaddeeeeeeusss.*" Still, later, he was somewhat relieved to be called Thaddeus. "At least they're not confusing me with . . . with the other one," he whispered.

The other one, Judas Iscariot, was the traitor of course. Now, I could say that we never trusted him or that we never liked him, but that wouldn't be the truth. I did. We did. He wasn't one of the *Sicarii*. He wasn't, as far as I could ever tell, a "man of lies," though I've heard some say that of him since his death. He was just Judas, the guy from Kerioth down in southern Judea. Even if he was the only one of us not from the green hills of Galilee, even if he was the lone Judean among us and he spoke with a different accent, he was still one of us. I don't care what anyone says; he was one of us at least for a while.

These were the heroes, the legends, the *talmidim*. Print the legends if you want. They're great stories and they make for high drama and exciting movies, but *this* is how I remember them.

18. The Living Spark

The whole crowd was trying to touch him in those days, reaching out with grasping, grubby fingers, trying to snare him. They were desperate. They wanted him to take away their bad dreams and their recurrent nightmares of disappearing wives, as well as their returning visions of dead dogs on the doorstep. They begged for him to take away their conflicted desires and their ambiguous ambitions. The crowd kept trying to touch him because of the power that went out from him. They could sense the vitalism that infused him, they could feel the living spark, the *élan vital*, the soul of the divine flowing from his touch. They wanted more than anything to be healed by him.

And the people *were* healed. Their lives were reinvigorated. Their bad dreams dissolved back into the star-puckered dark of night. Their fears dissolved. Their anxieties relaxed their chokehold grips. And the people were finally, at long last, able to rest.

Terminus a Quo

19. Little Things That Make So Much

From that place on the plains, he lifted up his eyes to them and he said, "The universe contains all that exists, and some that does not. Do not be surprised by this. The universe is composed mostly of hydrogen and helium, and the poor. These are the little things that make so much. They are *les misérable, les gens de feu, sans aveu* but they are blessed too."

"Blessed are you, the poor for the poor are the people of God, and never forget it. Blessed are you, the hungry. Hunger and thirst for righteousness is a good and noble thing and will be blessed. Amen. But blessed are you who are belly-hungry and dry-throat thirsty. You will be filled with good things. Count on it. Blessed are you, the weeping, for you will find new reason to laugh. Blessed are you, the despised, the blacklisted, the divorced and the expelled. Blessed are you when they curse your name as communists when you speak for the health of humanity."

"Give me your tired, your poor, your huddled masses yearning to breathe free. They are mine. I will bless them all. Give me the wretched refuse of your teeming Mediterranean shores, I'll not turn them away. The tempest-tossed, the

broken-backed, the hollowed out and humiliated, all the inevitable offspring of the fiscal aristocracy are the blessed and beloved of God. This revolution unmakes but does not destroy. It renews without oblivion. No compromise, no surrender and no blood but my own."

Figure 20–No surrender and no blood but my own.

Maybe you remember the story of Rabbi Hillel who was approached by one of the gentiles who said to him, "Rabbi, I have heard of your teaching, and know that you are a wise and honest man. I am ready now to pledge that I will convert to the Hebrew faith, and that I will worship the God of Abraham, Isaac, and Jacob, and that I will also circumcise myself according to Jewish custom *if* you can recite for me the entirety of the *Torah* while standing on one leg."

Rabbi Hillel considered for a moment then lifted his right leg and began, "Do not do unto others as you would not have them do to you." Then he replaced his foot on the ground and said, "That is the whole of the *Torah*. Go now, and learn it." What I'm telling you is similar, yes. But heavier, yes. More aggressive. What Rabbi Hillel phrased in the negative, I tell you positively, "Do unto others what you want done to you."

20. Woe and Be-Damned

Woe and be-damned, you who are rich for you've already received all you're going to get. May your road be ten thousand years long, and all of it uphill. Woe and be-damned, you who are full, satiated, satisfied. It will be an obvious hell for you. Be sure of it. Woe and be-damned, you who laugh and laugh, when you laugh at the misfortune of others. *Schadenfreude* is low, and you are lower still. Woe and be-damned, you when all men speak well of you, when your ratings are up. All of your obnoxious tyrannies are coming to an end.

My servants and my companions, my friends shall sing for the joy of their hearts, but you, you with your unbalanced pentagrams and disordered pentagons, your lopsided Satanism lurching limp-legged through the world, dragging the weight of dead and rotting muscle, you shall cry and howl for the vexation of your spirits. You will howl for an end that will never come. Howl!

21. You, the Peaceful Ones, Are Fools

"You will be called fools," Jesus told the crowd sitting in the grass. They were hungry for his words even if they didn't understand them. "Don't doubt it. All of you working for peace will be called fools. If you were working for war, if you were part of the military industrial complex, if you were a member of any branch of the armed forces, or even a member of the

Coast Guard, you'd be respected as manly and heroic. You'd be adored as the bravest of men and loved by the masses. You'd be given medals and scholarships and roses. There would be statues erected in your honor on the town squares of your hometowns. But you, my peaceful ones, will be derided as fools."

Jesus may have been paraphrasing Issam Sartawi, a senior member of the Palestinian Liberation Organization. Or perhaps the paraphrase goes the other way. But it should be noted that Sartawi, like Jesus, was assassinated—shot and killed in the lobby of a Portuguese hotel. Do not doubt it.

22. *That's Just Bad Economics*

"Love your enemies," he says.

We split hairs nearly as well as we split atoms and not because we don't understand what this means, but precisely because we *do* understand. We just don't want to do it. We refuse the truth that we understand. We want what we want and what we want is not this.

"Love your enemies." We scoff because that's a damn-fool way to get yourself killed. And "Do good to them that hate you"? Are you kidding me? Is this a joke? Only brainwashed, drooling idiots hate themselves enough to *love* their enemies.

And the damn-fool doesn't stop there, does he? No. He digs in deeper. He just keeps digging and digging and digging. "Bless the ones that curse you." Oh, good Lord! "Pray for your abusers," and "turn the other cheek"? *This* is what he says? *This* is his advice for us? Not to fight (which is to be expected) or to flee (which could be understood), but to return good for evil? What if someone breaks into our home or tries to rape our wives and daughters? What about Hitler? The only thing that can stop a bad guy with a gun is a good guy with a gun. But Jesus can't understand this.

"Lend without expecting anything in return"? No. No and no, God damn it! This is nothing but feel-good foolishness. And we will have nothing to do with it. This strategy would ruin us. This sentiment will bankrupt us. What the hell is he thinking? What the actual brimstone hell is he thinking? That's bad policy. It's just bad economics. We need to isolate and incapacitate the miserable so that they can do our work for us without letting the laboring poor become desperate enough that they erupt like pustules on the skin with radicalism, trade-unionism, Chartism, riotings and disquitings of many kinds along with all the fevered dramas of class warfare both unfair and spiteful. We must strike the balance that holds endemic discontent without encouraging the malcontents on the corner distributing leaflets, communist newspapers and bomb building instructions. None of this 'interest free lending' for Christ's sake!

Give them a good shaking; that's what we say. Give them the old shakedown. Press them hard. Come at them from all sides. Eye for eye, tooth for tooth, tit for tit. Retaliate. Give them everything they've ever given you, and then give them eight percent more. That way they'll remember. That way they'll learn. Give them everything they've never given you. Hit 'em first and him 'em hard. Tooth and claw, all the way to the tip of the Kilkenny cat's tail if that's the way it has to be. So be it. That's what we say.

23. Introspection Is Difficult

Now I ask you: Can the blind father, Chaos, lead his blind, riotous sons? Where could he take them? He couldn't lead them down a straight, narrow hallway. How could he guide them to the stars? *Et quid parcis astris?* When you wish upon a star, what are you thinking? There is no dream to come true. I hate to be the one to have to tell you this, but that star that you're wishing upon has been burnt out and dead for millions of years already. You just haven't seen it die yet. There is nothing for you in the stars. They are, like you, dead congregations with dead men preaching not from pulpits but upright caskets. The children are not greater than the fathers. The disciple is not greater than his master. Emperor Constantine was illiterate and wore a wig, but are you any better? Forget the beam. Can you see the mote in your own eye? Introspection is difficult, some would say impossible. Especially for the ones that wish to be blind.

24. The Liar Lies

No healthy tree produces outrageous or inharmonious fruit. Liars breed only lies. Prevaricators generate only deceptions. Earthborn sorcerers with hallucinogenic drugs can conjure only chaos. The adulterers and whoremongers of all the Tellurian states combined can only produce more of the same. Like unto like. Birds of a feather flocking together. What more could you expect? They are what they are. Take figs from figs and thorns from thorns. The liar lies. It's what he is. It's what he does. The mediocre rattlesnake will bite. The scorpion will sting. You knew what it was. There is no question, there is no doubt. It is what he does because it is what he is. In New York City or Washington D.C. or Tel Aviv, or Jerusalem; it's all the same. The good draw from the store of goodness inside them. The mediocre may have money in the bank, but they have only corruption in their wells.

25. When the Levee Breaks

Can you hear what I'm saying? Do you understand? If you're hearing, you'll be acting. You'll do.

Let me tell you this: a person who hears and then acts and does is like someone who builds a house and makes a home. He digs and digs deep, to lay a rock solid foundation. Are you hearing all this? I know that you've probably heard it before, but I'm not convinced that you're actually hearing me. When the rains come and the river floods, that house will be strong. It will not shake.

But someone who nods along, without listening, someone who does not do, that nodding no-one is like the one who builds a house with no foundation. When the waters rise and the levee breaks, his house will collapse around him. And it won't take much. Even a little water will move the stones to fall. Can you dig it? Can you hear it? Can you hear the mighty walls rushing asunder? Ask Usher. He can describe the roar of that collapse. He's heard the long, tumultuous sound of shouting, like the voice of a thousand pagan waters. I tell you, the ruin of that house will be great.

26. No Magic Word, No Logomancy

In Capernaum at that time there was a Centurion who had a trusted servant, a valuable slave that he loved, loved like a son. But the slave was sick and near unto death.[26]

The Centurion sent wave after wave of delegate forces to approach the Lord with a request. "He is worthy," said the Jewish elders who came first. "He is worthy of your consideration for the consideration that he has given to us. And because he has built a synagogue for us." The Centurion that

---

26. Was the servant something more? A lover? Possible, though it seems unlikely. But he was loved. And was the centurion an imperial Roman guard, or was he a foreign officer in the Jewish army of Herod Antipas? Who can say? But he was a gentile and still respected. And more than that we cannot say. We never actually meet the man. He remains, behind the scene—issuing orders to those in his command.

we never meet next sent a few of his friends with the message, "I am not worthy. But just say the word and that will be enough. I understand authority. I have my own shrievalty to manage. I have men under my command who go when I say, 'go' and do when I say, 'do.' Only speak the word and my companion will be healed."

Jesus was impressed. "Not even in the Holy Land is such faith manifest." More than this, he does not say. No magic word is spoken here. No magic word, no logomancy. Just a confirmation of the spooky action accomplished at a distance.

27. The Death of Death and Hell's Destruction

Now Jesus comes to a charming village on sunny mountain slopes. See him with his disciples and followers in a field of wildflowers. And now comes a young man, a dead man, the only son of a widowed woman. Here comes one who is still fettered to the curse of dust. See how he is carried on the inevitable bier, just as you will see your own when you look into the future. And see the weeping mother. Hear the mournful ululations of the funeral crowd.

We can hear them and we can see her because we share that grief. We are broken. We are the bewailed. We are sleepless and afraid of sleep. If we sleep we know we'll wake up again tomorrow and have to start everything all over again. The human heart is built to bleed, but not like this. The light of our days, our reasons for living have gone.

But see this also: the death of death and hell's destruction is here with her. He says, "Do not weep." With a word and with a touch an unstoppable force meets the immovable object. And it is moved. See the boy restored. He sits up. Alive.

The people recognize what they see here: God has visited his people. But keep two things in mind: ONE—If the capitalists could resurrect the dead by sorcery (or by any means natural or super), and if they could employ them as unpaid labor, you know that they would. Zombies or robots, it doesn't matter to the bosses who or what does the work. Whatever keeps their costs down and profits up is acceptable practice. And TWO—The Federation of Spiritual Healers, with officers stationed in all major cities of the Levant, refuses to endorse this unlicensed practitioner of thaumaturgic resuscitation. Still, the people recognize what they see: "God has visited his people."

Terminus a Quo

28. Should We Look for Another

What did John the Baptizer think of the rise of Jesus' popularity? He was there first, gathering disciples and making a name for himself, full of pith and vinegar. But was he threatened by this upstart, Jesus? He sent two of his disciples to Jesus with questions: "Are you he that should come? And if not, should we look for another?"

The Baptist's followers leaned against a Medivend machine as they observed Jesus. It was fully stocked with all kinds of tonics, and pills and powders like Anglo-American Catarrhal Powder (with two hundred and seventy milligrams of cocaine per ounce) for clearing out congested mucus, and Colwell's Egyptian Oil (which is thirty-seven percent opium) cures sore throats and diphtheria, and Watkins' Anodyne (which was banned in seventeen countries because it was nearly pure heroin) for that deep seated cough. Jesus cured many of their infirmities that day, but never once used the contents of this particular Medivend machine.

He took care of their electro-cardio irregularities, their shocks and burns, and their high voltage sleep deprivation. Even those with an alleged electromagnetic hypersensitivity came to him for relief. He cured them all. He cured them of plagues and pestilences. Buboes and blisters disappeared. Fevers evaporated. Even their black rat *Yersinia pestis* bacteria dissolved in the brightness of his light.

He cast out the spirits which could be identified by their individual elements. There were demons of fire that boil the blood, and water demons that bring up black bile. He cast out earthy, mineral demons that bind a person up with phlegm and spirits of air that burn their host with an irascible choler.

And he didn't do this as the other healers of the day did. He used no nostrums, no patent medicines, no petroleum based *serpentibus perierunt* spirits. Other exorcists chanted secret incantations like: "*Astra, Castra, Disastra, Nomen Numen!*" and alchemists used alembics of liquid Azoth. And all of it for a price. It has never been cheap to hire a physician or a magician for that matter. But Jesus used none of their tricks, and charged them nothing. He simply cured their complaints and sent them home.

"Go back to your master," he told the observers leaning against the Medivend machine. "Go back and tell him what you've seen. Tell him that all the things the prophet described are here. The blind can see, the lame are walking around. Tell him that the lepers are cleansed and the ears of the deaf are opened. Tell him that the dead are raised up to life—and not in some nasty, flesh eating, zombie kind of way. They are raised up to life, sentient and whole."

But before they could leave, he pronounced one more beatitude: "We are in search of an unnamed country here, the true and beautiful country that cannot be stolen from us. And blessed is the one who isn't repelled. Blessed is the one who is not offended."

29. What Did You Expect

What did you expect to see when you went out to the desert? A reed in the wind? Cattails in the breeze? Did you go expecting a pleasant voice? A pleasing vice? Did you expect to see him lounging in silk shirts and gold chains like some self-indulgent, luxury-league, millionaire's son? One of the Fortunate Ones? No, of course not. You knew what he was. You knew he'd be a wild man dressed in camel hair and leather skins. You knew exactly what he was before you went. You knew. You knew. You sit there drinking your eschatonic-waters and your lachrymose mimosas, but you knew. You knew.

You wanted to see a prophet. A prophet. You people! You wanted to see a prophet, and you found a prophet, didn't you? You found him. And something more than a prophet. So what are you going to do now that you've found him?

Look. The messenger is coming. The messenger is already here, and he's come with burning skylines and a *lapis exilis* stone fallen from heaven. He's come to prepare the way. He stands beneath the eaves of the ether, breathing clouds from the nostrils of the Almighty. He's seized the mighty axe of proving power and he will slash and burn any obstacles in his way. Do ye see him? Do you ken?

And I'll tell you this too: of all the children born of women, of all the children ever born, there's never been one better than John. Not one. What did you expect? What did you expect? Piety? Power? There are precious few that can hold both, and there's no one better than him. And yet, the lowest in the Kingdom of Justice stands taller than him. The people who went out to the desert to hear him, to actually hear him were baptized. All of them. Even the (Re)publicans. Do you hear that? Even the (Re)publicans could understand it. But you people, you Evanjellyfish with your corporate lawyers, you've rejected it all. You've rejected the whole thing: his words and his work. You've refused it all.

Terminus a Quo

You're like a bunch of spoiled children. That's what you are, a bunch of trust fund babies in the bazaar calling for the DJ to play your favorite songs. But you won't dance. And when the funeral bagpipes play, you won't mourn, either. You're glib. You're smug. You're nothing but the incompetent scions of little men in expensive ill-fitting shoes.

You saw John eating no bread and abstaining from wine. You watched him eat locusts and honey and you were disgusted. You called him an ascetic and a lunatic. You said 'he's possessed or on drugs.' You dismiss it all as a pathetic expression of anti-American values. You laughed at those who listened to the little bindlestiff. And now, when you see me and my friends laughing and drinking, you call me a glutton, a wine-bibber and dismiss my words as utopian nonsense.

You don't understand.

No. It's more than that. It's that you won't understand. You *refuse* to understand. It's a willful and belligerent ignorance with you.

30. Beyond the Pale

One of the Pharisees, Simon of Albumen, invited Jesus to his house for dinner. So Jesus went, and sat down at his table to eat. And a woman of that city, having heard of his presence in that city, in that house, sitting at that table, came immediately with an alabaster jar of perfumed massage oil. She knelt there tableside, weeping on his feet and wiping them dry with her hair. She kissed them and rubbed them with the oil from her alabastron.

The Pharisee blanched. "This is beyond the pale. Most irregular! How dare she wear white?" he thought within himself. "A woman should wash the hands and feet of her husband, but only her husband! And for that her husband should provide her with food and clothing, cosmetics and funeral expenses. If this man were a prophet he would know that the word 'feet' is sometimes used euphemistically. Not that it's being used that way here, but still . . . This is too much. She's too close. If this man were a prophet he would know what kind of woman she is. She is indecency and presumption. She is chaos and promiscuity. Losers of society like her should be banished to the outlands."

"Simon," Jesus said to him, "Allow me tell you a story." Simon's already blanched expression turned waxen, but what could he do? He'd invited the itinerant rabbi to his house expressly to hear his teaching. He nodded for Jesus to proceed.

"A creditor had two debtors—the first owed a sum of one hundred thousand dollars, the other one hundred dollars. And since neither one nor the both of them could pay a single penny of their debts, he forgave them the whole of their debts over the objections of his investors and shareholders.

"Now, tell me, Simon, which of them will love him more?"

Simon considered the question for a moment and then said, "The one forgiven more, I suppose." His face was pallid and wan.

"*Pravda* and *verdad*," Jesus said. "You do understand. And do you see this fair woman? You've failed in all the steps of common hospitality. You provided no water for my feet, no towel, no oil for my head, and no kiss of peace in greeting. But this one that you'd call white-trash, she has done all this and more. She has, some might say, crossed the bounds of intimacy, and I know that this makes you uncomfortable, but it's true. She is forgiven. Her sins which, as you know, were many are gone for she has loved and loved much." He looked into Simon's eyes. "Those who need little forgiveness, love little."

Then he knelt down to be with the woman at his feet and said, "Your sins are forgiven. Your faith has saved you. Go in peace. *Sic itur ad astra*."[27]

"She loved much, if you know what I mean," one of the disciples standing in the hallway whispered. And they all sniggered quietly. Jesus turned and glared at them. "Sorry, master," they apologized shamefacedly.

"And to her," Jesus pointed to the woman.

"Apologies, my lady," the embarrassed disciples said before skulking away.

31. Filled with Witchcraft and Variance

Through all the cities and the towns, the villages and the burgs, Jesus and his itinerant band of followers travelled. Up and down the hills and vales of Galilee preaching the good news to all people everywhere. And, in addition to the twelve who were with him always, there also travelled with him several women whom he had cured of their infirmities and vexatious spirits.

With him was Mary, who they sometimes called "the Magdalene," and sometimes, "Towering Magdalene." Later some of them named her "the Apostle to the Apostles," but this title has not been universally acknowledged unfortunately. The master had driven seven howling demons from

---

27. "Thus one goes to the stars."—Perhaps Jesus had Sirius B in mind. It is a white dwarf star that is only 8.6 million light years from the planet Earth.

her.[28] The first to be driven out of her was the demon known as *Sidon Sidanu*, a vertigo demon of disease and epilepsy rising up from catacombs and tombs with argle-bargle and other nonsensical chatter. Second in line was the metallic-green *Euduras Set*, a parasitic demon from Egypt who burrows deep into her hosts to suck out their minds. Third was *Surdus Absurdus*. This worthless one could not hear Jesus calling for him and had to be summoned forth with sign language. Fourth inside her was the demon *Mr. Myrmidon* (who is distantly related to the waspish *Enduras Set* on his mother's side). Mr. Myrmidon controls his victims with a series of painful injections of formic acid. After a few of his fiery bites even the strongest individual will lose all independent thought and will subordinate themselves to the will of wicked men. Fifth came *Frater fui Draconum*, one of the fleeing serpent demons found in the eternal midnight darkness of the Abysmal Seas. It was last seen in the wild in the lad of Uz, but that was many years ago. *Kali Bromati*, Mary's penultimate demon, does not, despite repeated claims, stop either seizures or night-terrors. Instead *Kali Bromati* will often appear as a hunchbacked hobgoblin in order to frighten his victims into nocturnal enuresis. And the final demon inside The Magdalene was the perpetually tired and half dead demon, *Medio Morto* who kept Mary partially drugged and totally depressed.

All these had tortured her, tormented her with a torrent of abuse and psychic pain for years. They drove her to all manner of dangerous behavior, both lewd and lascivious. But when the Master found her he swept her house clean and made her read for inhabitation by a new and pure spirit. Afterwards people often failed to recognize The Magdalene for who she was. A line of perfumers and ointment makers approached her once carrying with them their scented unguents and oils and cosmetics for the skin. "Bless us, mistress, and our wares, you who anointed the master's feet with precious spikenard."

"That wasn't me," she said to them. "How many times do I have to say it? It wasn't me. I wasn't even at Simon's house that day."

Jesus shrugged his shoulders as if to say, "What can you do?"

Also with him in those days was Joanna, the wife of Chuza who served as keeper of Herod Antipas' court. She too was later numbered among the Myrrhbearers and counted among the Saints. But this came later. When she first met the master she was held fast in the path of the Destroyer. Others

---

28. He'd driven them out sequentially, of course, one after the other and not all at once as is usually assumed.

would later all her Junia, but whatever the name, she still served the master with devotion.[29]

There was also in their number Susanna, a beautiful lily of the valley who, in her former illness would constantly rave of "the wicked king of wicker things and woodlice living in a hole. The wicker king in a wicked tower wicking away the hours of All Fools' Day."

These women, and many others with them, who had once been filled with witchcraft and with variance, who were once filled with jealous emulations and vain simulations of murders, now provided for Jesus and his band out of their not insubstantial means.

32. With Wild Abandon

Listen. Jesus is about to tell a parable, a parable which is something of a riddle. You'll need to listen. You'll need to listen because it's not often that he explains. It's not often that he defines, not often that he makes it simple, so:

Listen!

"A sower went out to sow. That is what sowers do—they sow. And as he sowed with wild abandon (tossing seeds left and right, right and left) some of the seeds fell on the edge of the path where people would walk. Years of heavy feet and heavier carts had crushed the soil there, hardened the earth, leaving it impenetrable. The seeds that fell on the path could not embed themselves, could not pull the earth up over their heads and so were carried off by hungry birds."

"Other seeds fell on patches of rock. The sower was, after all, sowing with abandon (tossing seeds right and left, left and right). And rocks were everywhere. Oh, the farmer, I suppose, could have spent days and days removing the rocks from his field, but he could never be sure he'd gotten them all (and there would be more again next year, of course). But to do so he would have lost those days for sowing at the start of season. So he tossed the seed with wild abandon and some inevitably fell on rocky soil."

"And these seeds falling on rocky soil found some little earth there and sprang up quickly. 'Early signs point to an abundant harvests,' the forecasters declared. But when the scorching summer sun came out, these shallow

---

29. Joanna, if she was Junia, became something of a transgendered apostle as Reformation scholars decided that Junia was a transcription error for Junias and that Junias could only be a man.

rooted plants shriveled. They withered in the heat. Whether you like it or not, the weather did them in."

"Other seeds fell among the thorns, sharp jagged-piercing-pointed-bloody-toothy thorns. The precious wheat grew up but before it could mature it was choked. Strangled and throttled by the bloody teeth. Asphyxiated by cruel neighbors."

"So much seed thrown away. So much seed tossed with abandon, like caution thrown to the wind. So much wasted. But this was typical Mediterranean farming. The sower sowed with heedless abandon, knowing that the relatively inexpensive seed would, by the grace and goodness of God, grow up to produce a crop. The sower sowed his seed throwing left and throwing right. Some fell on the path, some on rocks, and some among the thorns. But some seed (and this is the good stuff, so listen) some seed fell on good soil. Rich, dark soil. Noble souled soil."

And where a typical Mediterranean farmer might expect (in a good year without drought or flood) to reap a five to ten fold harvest, this sower (throwing both caution and seed to the wind) reaped thirty-sixty-one hundred fold. It's an exaggeration, to be sure, hyperbole to make sure we're listening! It is the unexpected punch-line to catch us in an exuberant *a-ha*!

Anyone who has ears should listen.

Later the disciples came to Jesus and asked him, "Why do you speak to them like that, with parables and riddles and all? Why not speak more directly? Why not speak clearly?"

Jesus told them "It's been given to you to understand. You've accepted the word that you've heard. But them? They're like the prophet Isaiah said. 'They might listen, and listen, and by listening they might understand, and by understanding they might be changed. They could look and look, and by looking they could see, and by seeing they could be healed.' But their hearts have grown hard. Calloused. They've become stony hearted Pharaohs of their own fates! But blessed are your seeing eyes and blessed are your hearing ears. All the saints and patriarchs and prophets of old dreamed of seeing what you see, and hearing what you hear. And they went to their graves without it."

"So pay attention to the parable. Listen because I don't usually explain and I'm only going to say this once. When anyone hears the words of the Kingdom without bothering to understand, without wrestling through the night like Jacob with the words, the Evil One comes and carries off what was sown in his heart."

"The seed thrown into rocky ground is someone who hears and, thinking she has got it all, thinking that he has received an eternal enlightenment from that one little seed, welcomes it with great joy and celebration—*praise Gawd!* But, let me tell you, this person has no root, and does not last. Trials will come or some persecution on account of the Word then she will fall. He falls, she fall, they all fall down."

"The seeds thrown among the thorns are received by those who hear it and accept it, but their acceptance is choked by worries. The worry of the world and the lure of riches (and these are often the same) chokes the life out of them."

"But the seeds falling on that good dark soil, the rich soil, noble souled soil; those seeds produced a bountiful harvest—thirty times, sixty times, one hundred times larger than what was thrown by the heedless sower. Hah-ha!"

Do you get it? Do you understand? Did you listen? And did you hear? The mysteries of the kingdom, secret until now, have been given to us, thrown with wild abandon by the heedless sower of seeds. Secrets are revealed. Mysteries are unveiled. The curtain is pulled away and torn in two from the top to the bottom for us. Listen and listen so that you can understand. Look and look so that you can perceive the truth. And be changed. Be healed and grow in the Unshakeable Kingdom, produce a crop yielding a bountiful harvest through perseverance.

33. *A Battleship or Some Other Vessel*

No one, when they have lighted a candle (Roman or otherwise), covers it with a battleship or some other vessel. Would you prefer to hide it under a bushel or perhaps a peck? *Doodle oodle oodle oh doo?* Neither do they putter around with it, doing small jobs crouched under the bed. But instead they set it up high, on a candle-stand so that everyone who enters the house, can see and be seen in its light.

You see, there are no secrets, neither in the darkness here nor in far flung midnight. What is manifest will be brought forth and the manifesto will be read. Take heed what and how you hear. Observe the warning signs posted on the wall:

Electrical Hazard! and Do Not Touch! Toxic Live Snakes!
Black Snakes Falling from the Sky! Beware Loose Spirits and Radiation!
Beware: What comes, comes without warning.

Beware: Has will have more. Has not will be further deprived. Beware.

34. Umma and Ummi to Me

His mother and his brothers came to him while he was teaching and the crowd. The crowd pressing close and tight about him said, "Hey, Jesus. Your mother and your brothers are here to see you." They came because they worried about him. They'd heard the rumors. They'd read the editorials in the papers and the heard the predictions of the political pundits on television. And they were concerned. But don't ring the tocsin for him just yet. It's not yet time for Beelzebub. And even when that time comes, it will not last long.

The crowd said to him again, "Your mother and your brothers are come to see you." But he did not move. Not in the slightest. Whether his mother was the typical suburban housewife or the radical revolutionary living in occupied territory, it matters not. Liberation Theology or Opus Dei, either way. It's not important here. "Mother to me and brother of mine are those that hear and hearing, do. You are *ummah* and *ummi* to me. Understand?"

35. Master, Master We Perish

Another day, more or less precisely, he was in the boat with his friends. "Let's go over there," he said pointing to the other side of the lake. And, having nothing better to do that day, they launched out for the far shore. They sailed. He slept. This was the standard arrangement.

The still unforgotten animism of the lake erupted in a sudden squall of such surreal and dystopian violence that even the well-practiced mariners in the boat that day were terrified by the storm of wind and the lashing waves. Savage storms like this are not uncommon here. How many research vessels and fishing trawlers, pontoons and submarines have been sunk within the waters of that inhospitable sea? Dredge the depths and count the dead, if you can. Few survive such nightmares upon the sea.

"Ye watchers and ye holy ones!" they screamed over the roar of the wind and rain, "Bright eyed seraphs and all blessed saints, preserve us!" they cried out from their terror.

They shook him woke and screamed, "Master, master, we perish!"

He arose and casually rebuked the raging of the winds and waters. "Peace," he said and there was a precipitous calm, which is a disorienting calm in that sea of sudden changes. "Where is your faith?" he asked them. "Where are you?" Then he laid back down in the boat and went back to sleep.

And they were afraid. Again. Still. With norepinephrine still pumping from their adrenal medullas into their blood streams, their hearts still thudding, ready for either fight or for flight. "Who is he?" they asked themselves. Lenny told us that Jesus was a sailor and that only sinking men would be able to see him from the water. Maybe the singer was right.

Where are we? Who is he? Who is this that rules the wind and water? And will he, when the time comes, stand by me?"

36. Foul Spirits with Unpleasant Names

It was one of those middle November afternoons, the kind of afternoon that is perfect for phantom sun photography when Jesus and his friends landed their boat on the far shore of the Sea of Galilee, in the region of the Gadarenes. The sun shone in a comminatory sky when Jesus met the tomb-dwelling, lunatic, Graveyard Man.

The Graveyard Man wore nothing but filth and mud over his own skin. He did not live in a house or home within the community of his friends and family. Having escaped from the Asylum of Moral Lunatics, he now lived along in the caverns and caves, and among the buried dead. When he ate, *if* he ate, he ate forbidden swine flesh stolen from the local swineherds. For drink he drank only putrid and abominable broths from unwashed cups. Remove your shirt. Remove your shoes. He was a monster—all mouth, no ears. There was never an interlude of quiet for him, no rest, no respite, no relief. Only temptations and tempestuous nights. The constant thought of death overwhelmed his passions and neither iron fetters nor steel bands could hold him fast.

The horrors of the unwashed night were gathered under that vengeful sky. The massing demons and of ghosts and specters, all manner of malodorous monsters assembled inside his shuffling frame. All the witches and warlocks of the world were there, cursing and plaguing his body and his soul, stealing his mind. "What have you for me, Jesus?" he squealed among the stones. "Come not to torture me!" he gibbered.

"Who are you?" Jesus asked. "What is your name?"

Terminus a Quo

"Legion," he said. "Legion!" for there were many within him, a whole company of dark spirits.

If the angelic forces of the apocalypse are ranked in Enochian myriads, the infernal, satanic forces are apportioned into their own occult Legions. Among the ranks within the man were foul spirits with unpleasant names: 192 Apes, Tree-branch, Madwort Allisoin, the twin demons Fixod and Fixid, Hammerhead Bart, Prince Undinist of the Many Waters, and the demon servants of Mammon which are those seducers of the faithful known anagrammatically as Mad Ah-Mist, and Dy An-Ran.[30] The roll call of haints within him rolled on and on. The whole hellish host of wickedness was contained inside his frail, emaciated body.

But strong forces always fear; the power they have is never enough. Heavy is the head that wears the crown, and all that. No power is ever enough power. No strength is ever enough strength. The lion shaped legions within the naked, Graveyard Man trembled. Here was one who could conquer them. Here was one who could command them. "Go," he told them. "Go now, into the dark abyss that has been prepared for you since the creation of the world."

But they would wheedle. They would grovel and they would beg, if not for their lives[31] then for mercy and for time. Feeding on the mountain greens nearby was a herd of swine—fat, fungus beasts tended by hideous, and white-bearded swineherds. "Don't send us to the abyss. It is not yet time. Let us go into those pigs instead," the demonic legion pleaded. "Let us go into them. Suffer us that, please. Just that little bit. Please."[32]

So he suffered them this. But only this and nothing more.

The multiplied devils immediately fled from the man and entered into the squealing, screaming pigs. "*Gay kaken ofn yahm!* Go shit in the sea," Jesus ordered them. And they went squealing and screaming, running violently over the side of a steep cliff. They fell into the water, and were drowned. Sent into the abyss after all, despite their objections, where they choked on the inhospitable water.

The white-bearded herdsmen on the hill witnessed the whole thing. They heard the whole squealing slaughter. They fled to tell it in the city and

---

30. These two also go by the names Madam Shit and Darn Nay, among others. Be warned however, their works are far more difficult to unscramble than their names.

31. For what lives can demonic entities have?

32. And that is fair, I suppose. In the ancient world porcine blood sacrifices were offered only to the chthonic deities of the underworld. Goldstein, *1 Maccabees*, 158.

in the country. When the denizens of that region came to see what had happened, they found the man, now cleaned and clothed, and in his right and ordered mind, sitting at the feat of Jesus. And they were seized with their own numinous apprehensions.

Jesus and his travelling companions got back into the boat to return to their own side of the lake. And the man, now swept clean and made whole, no longer scoured by hellish winds and fine grit of demonic wrath and torture, begged to travel with him. But Jesus said no. "Leave these cemeteries and the columbariums where you have been sleeping and go back to your home and family. Show everyone this good thing that God has done."

Notice: The pigs are the goats in this story; they are the scapegoats that reverse the standard order of operations. Instead of the victim being the one flung down and pelted with stones and dying while the victorious crowd stands above in judgement, here the crowd of thousands itself plunges into the stones and waters of its death while the victim stands above, saved alone.

A few decades later the Roman general Vespasian[33] would march his own swinish and vulturous legions into the same region to slaughter the youth and set fire to the cities and the villages of the Gadarenes. No strength is ever enough for those who would be strong.

37. Psychics in another Medium

During the process of impulse transmission, both conscious and subconscious, during autonomic response evens, the human brain releases psychic particles known as Psitrons. Psitrons are released in great numbers, especially during periods of intense concentration or emotional distress.

Psitrons are something like sunlight, being both wave and particle, and something like neutrinos, having no mass.[34] They are emitted by everyone constantly but, being nearly massless, have no great effect over distance and disappear quickly. The true telepath has within his or her brain highly developed Psitron receptors that are able to pull these psychic particles out of the air in much the same way that a radio pulls in radio waves. But while there may be many with highly developed Psitron receptors, there are only

---

33. The sycophantic Jewish historian, Flavius Josephus, would conclude that Vespasian had fulfilled all the ambiguous oracles of the prophets in the sacred scriptures and would describe him as the long-expected Messiah.

34. If they have inertia but no mass, are they still Catholic?

a uniquely qualified few who are able to understand what it is that they are receiving. Again, it is like the radio. If the psionic individual is not 'tuned' to the correct frequency, there will be no comprehension. They may have the occasional flash of recognition, but will be, for the most part only incomprehensible static. Noise, and nothing more.

"The microphysical world of the atom exhibits certain features whose affinities with the psychic have impressed themselves on physicists. Here, it would seem, is at least a suggestion of how the psychic process could be reconstructed in another medium, in that, namely of the microphysics of matter.[35]" So said the psychiatrist, Carl Jung. But what did he know? And when did he know it? And why did the CIA attempt to kill him?

During the Cold War, both Americans and the Soviet scientists were deep into research and development of the Psitron. In the last years of the prolonged proxy war in Indochina against a Chinese enemy that largely wasn't even there, Doctor Tarrrec, the world renowned alchemist-theologian, was reported to have developed his own, independent Psitron device that could receive and analyze the Psitron emissions of individuals up to one hundred yards away. It's no secret that the CIA had him killed.[36]

Still, this may not explain all of what happened in the story that follows.

38. Anachronistic Saints

When Jesus and his friends returned from the Gadarenes a waiting crowd greeted him with cheers and by waving hands and peacock feathers. And in that anxious crowd was one more apprehensive than the others, a man named Jairus. He fell at Jesus' feet the moment the master stepped from the boat to the shore, and pleaded with him for his daughter was twelve years old and dying. Jesus would have gone straight to Jairus' house to help and heal, but the way was blocked. At that very moment a parade was cutting through the city.

Now, ordinarily I don't like parades. I find them tedious and predictable, and somewhat obnoxious in their celebration of obsequious

---

35. Pauli, *Atom and Archetype*, 89.

36. Or thought they did. The CIA has a long and storied history of failed assassination attempts—even longer than that of their successful assassinations. Doctor Tarrec escaped and quietly continued his alchemical researches underground. See my previous work, *The Last Persecution*, for more about Doctor P. L. Tarrec.

patriotism. But this particular year I watched the annual Saint Drogo Day parade with a certain amusement because I knew some of the kids performing in that day's callithumpian pageantry. There was Amelia, who everyone called Oatmeal (Don't ask why they called her that; I don't' remember.) and Rachel and Joel. They are good kids, but loud. Their rowdy cartwheels and backflips seemed oddly appropriate for a parade in honor of the anachronistic Saint Drogo—the patron saint of coffee—even though he himself never sipped any of the Middle Eastern brew.[37]

The parade was an exuberant affair with fireworks and the marching bagpipe corps from Nazareth Community High School as well as a passing cortege of slaves for the presumptive presidential nominee, and a herd of performing war-elephants parading in phalanx formation. The elephant handlers were dressed as clowns in military uniforms. And there was Oatmeal, of course, tumbling and turning in flashy gyres of sequins and spangles. And the people in the street that day loved every chaotic minute of it.

39. The Flesh Is Antagonistic

The Saint Drogo Day parade blocked traffic all across the village. Police barricades were placed at the intersections of all the major roads and crowds of people milled in the streets. Jesus and Jairus and the rest of his entourage were unable to move. And this gave opportunity for a woman in the crowd, a woman who had been bleeding for twelve years, to catch up to him. She'd been ill and suffering from an indeterminate uterine discharge. She'd spent her life and her inheritance paying physicians and specialists for remedies that never worked. And now she was desperate. She could not tolerate the treatments any longer. They hurt and they burned with their pokes and prods and their bitter pills. Neither could she pay for them any longer. What money she had was gone. The money was gone, and there was no euphoria for her. No rest, no release.

She'd once made a pilgrimage to the healing camphor pools in Damascus. No soap. She'd tried acupuncture in Alexandria. No dice. She'd eaten the strangely bitter honey of the one-eyed bees found only in Tehran which was said to cure the wasted and the withered. She'd applied to her body the patented *Odor of the Saints Curative Rosewater*, which is bottled exclusively in seaside Tyre. She anointed herself from crown to toe with the stuff, but to no avail. None of the regimens—neither folk remedies nor expensive

---

37. He is also the patron saint of ugly people. So, he's obviously one of my favorites.

patent medicines—had any curative effect. Many of them caused serious side effects—like suicidal thoughts, increased heart rate, liver damage and monorchidism.[38] Nothing she'd tried had stopped the bleeding.

And when medicine failed she turned to magic.

Figure 21–This isn't faith. This is magic.

She consulted sorcerers and spell casters who told her to write her name on an apple and to consume that apple over three consecutive days. "This is guaranteed to stop the hemorrhage," one enchanter promised her. Another told her to write on an egg or a piece of cheese the words: SATUR AREPO TENET OPERA RUTAS, "which has the potency of reading the same forward as backward. There is powerful magic in the palindrome," the magician told her. "This will stop the flow," he promised her. But it didn't. No medicine. No magic. Nothing.

The cosmological struggle is real. The flesh is antagonistic toward us. Influenza is the result of the secret, invisible fluids of the stars which drift down through the clouds. Harry Houdini died of a ruptured appendix after a fan punched him in the gut without warning. Even doctors trained to recognize the difference between Anthrax and Anthracite and to determine the time of Venus' rising in the sky may not be of much help against antagonistic flesh. Hast thou seen the creatures of the deep? Hast thou fought with dragons? Has thou wrestled with unnamed strangers in the night? You will.

---

38. Which was especially strange, given her feminine condition.

The bleeding woman snuck up behind him in the crowd and secretly fingered the tasseled fringe of his cloak. Though she often felt out of control—like a passenger and not a participant in her own life—this wasn't an involuntary ideomotor response. Call it spontaneity. Call it desperation, but in that moment of desperate spontaneity the flow of blood was staunched. What could not be done with twelve years of doctoring and sorcery and was completed in a touch.

Jesus cried out, "Who touched me?" He felt the power flow out of him. Psitrons or no, he did not know who had touched him. Or maybe he *did* know, but wanted to provoke a conversation. Who can say?

Peter objected, "Master, the tumblers and the bagpipes . . . the elephants! We are surrounded by a crowd, Master. How can you ask, 'who touched me'?"

"But someone did touch me," Jesus insisted. "Someone touched me. It was a touch as light as a breeze, as light as a breath, as light as a shadow moving across the wall. But someone touched me and the virtue has gone out from me."

The woman, seeing that she could no longer hide within the chaotic crowd stepped forward with fear and trembling, expecting a stern rebuke tinged with disgust and disappointment. But Jesus spoke only comfort to her. "Daughter, daughter," he said. "Be comforted. Twelve years of dying is over; go now and begin to live in peace." And from that moment, the roses were blooming in the garden of her life and on her cheeks.

40. They Know Death

Figure 22–Oatmeal weeps for Jairus' daughter.

Terminus a Quo

He is still speaking to her, and to his disciples, and the crowd, and even to the parading elephants when the friends of Jairus finally catch up with him. They are huffing and puffing with hazardous news. "Do not trouble the master any more, Sire. Your daughter is dead."

This is the bone rattling sound of grinding generators and diesel engines in the night. It is the whine of overtaxed motors and grinding gears, and the smell of grease and motor oil and burning electrical motors. The smell of ruptured septic tanks and smoldering hair. It's a report of gut-knotting, vomit-inducing loss. This is the cruel and senseless heartache of life.

Death is there. Always there. Like the Wicker King in the grove amusing himself by dressing as a leper and a beggar and going into the streets to insult the populace. Death comes for everyone. Even the blessed Saint Drogo himself suffered an incurable illness and died sequestered alone in his cell. Death is there listening, waiting like the demon at the door, watching at the gate. The dog lunges and snarls. The housecat hisses. All our symbols, our elements, our neurons and bytes are dissolved in death's inevitable flame.

"But fear not. Only believe." He tells them that "this is not death, only sleeping."

Sleeping! They scoff. Sleeping! They scoff because they know Death. They have seen Death. They have seen children born dead and mothers dead in giving birth. They have seen old men drop dead in the fields, and young boys cut down by the sword of Roman soldiers. They'd seen their friends and neighbors beaten to bloody pulp by brown-shirts and red-caps in beer hall battles and street side skirmishes. They have seen drownings, and burnings, broken limbs turned septic, and fevers burning through the night. They've seen swollen glands and pox blisters. They've seen old peasants with witch-wives walking arm in arm with the reaper in the cemetery beneath autumn skies. They have watched Death come screaming in the sun. They've watched Death come silent in the night. They've seen Death in all its disguises. They have no illusions about it. They know Death and this is it.

"Death is cruel enough," they say, "without making jokes. Don't toy with the man or give him false hope. Hope is rare and fragile enough as it is."

But, he says, "Fear not, only believe." At the house he dismisses the crowd, except for Peter and James and John along with the parents of the girl. No crowd is needed for this. No crowd is *wanted* here. Taking her hand in he says, "Child, rise up." The shaking powers of instability are broken, the infinite potential of irrational fear is shattered. Her spirit returns.

"Rise up," he says. "Rise up."

They know Death. They have seen Death. But this is something astonishing and new. But as astonishing as it is, he tells him to say nothing of it to anyone.

41. Expelled with Incantations and Beatitudes

Sometime later he gave them instruction on how to recognize and identify demons along with the authority and power to cast them out. You may already know that it can be very difficult to identify demons. Many demonic entities look very much alike. Consider the aforementioned twin demons, Fixod and Fixid.

Fixod is focused on obsessions and fixations. Amateur demonologists often observe that Fixod is many degrees above the ambient temperature. He is constantly radiating heat away, but never cools. He is always fevered. Fevered and friable. Unfortunately Fixod often causes even the most observant exorcists to become distracted by irrelevant details and sexual frustrations. He is always flush with the flash of flesh.

Fixid, like his twin, preys on the desires of the weak. "Want it, do it, eat it, have it, take it," he whispers. "It's all yours," he says. "Do as thou wilt," is his only law; fashion is his only pleasure. Fixate and drive al night; drive on towards death.

Fixid and Fixod are different. They are separate and distinct, but for all intents and purposes Fixid can be treated much like his slightly older brother. And vice versa. Fixod can be accounted as his slightly younger brother.

Beware also of the Demon Stration. He is a self-propagating egoist, an obnoxious show-off and charlatan without conscience. The Demon Stration often focuses his attacks on those in leadership positions, tempting them with confirmation of their own idealized self-portraits. Frequent and incautious use of the first person personal pronoun will summon him.

Such is the doctrine of spirits and devils and vain mathematicians with mystical names. Do not allow them to speak their cheap hypocrisies into the infinite continuity of space. Do not let them speak. Give them no influence. Silence them, as you would silence all the would-be billionaires attempting to buy their way into immortality. They can be expelled with incantations and beatitudes, through prayer and fasting, though sometimes it will take something a bit more vigorous.

There were demons everywhere in those days. They discovered devils beneath every stone and behind every leaf. An unexpected swell of witchcraft and addiction (both examples of the dangers of *pharmakia*) as well as unprecedented demonism had swept over the entire land. There may have been a few incidents of demons and of the demonized recorded in the sacred scriptures, but now there were flying demons in the night and creeping demons under the sun. There were subcutaneous succubi and incubi with innocuous eyes. They saw wizards in the air and witches on the seas. There were pestilent spirits like a miasma, spreading cholera and chlamydia in the cities and the fields.[39] There were diseased spirits lurking at the doors and windows of their homes, waiting for an opportunity to infect the people with lustful inflammations–painful burning and itching. Over all of these, and more, he gave them power and authority. Authority to cast them out and send them gone.

In addition to training them to expel the spiritual forces of darkness, he also gave them the power to cure diseases of the natural sort. To cure sudden onset lethargy and sexually induced sneezing fits. To cure them of their nervous stomach pains. He gave them the power to cure all manner of disease and discomfort. With these he sent them out to preach the gospel of the Kingdom of Justice.

And he sent them with this instruction:

"Take nothing. Go without. Take neither stave nor scrip. Take neither cash nor cane. You will be provided for. Don't take more than one coat; you won't need more. When you are welcomed into someone's home, stay there. Don't go chasing better beds with Egyptian linens. But if you are not received, shake off their apocalyptic dust from your feet. There's no time to waste on rejection."

With that, and a few things more, he sent them out to confront all the powers of darkness.

---

39. There were even reports of songbirds infected with chlamydia. Whether or not this avian chlamydiosis was the result of the demonic oppression of birds or simply spread by the *chlamyida psittaci* bacteria is still being debated.

A Life Known and Unknowable

42. Am I Responsible To Keep Track of All These Corpses

Now the Tetrarch Herod Antipas heard about it all. His network of spies and informants, those members of the Office of Strategic Services who were responsible for various and sundry domestic slaughters, the ones he'd inherited from his father, reported to him everything that Jesus and his disciples were doing in the region. And the Tetrarch was perplexed by the conflicting accounts. "This man Jesus is the return of John the Baptizer," read one of the reports. Another said "he is the ghost of Elijah," and still another, "he is a suicidal and bi-polar folk-singer pseudonymously named John Butler Train and the FBI has over five hundred pages on him in their subversive files." The Tetrarch dismissed these conflicting reports as nonsense and exaggeration, but still feared they might be true.

"Why was this not disclosed by our covert surveillance teams?" he shouted at his underlings. "Are my border control monitors failing?" He issued frantic orders: "Revoke all travel documents immediately! What is this Baptist *Redivivus* doing here? Haven't I already assigned him to a biblical oblivion?"

The Tetrarch's rant continued even though his minions and servants had fled the room and there was no one left to hear his ravings. "I had him killed. Didn't I? He can't be wandering around out there. I had his head removed, goddamn it! You can't call him the Baptizer anymore. Call him John the Acephalous. But, who is this? Is he the return of Elias? No. no. no. But the Baptizer? He's buried in Sebastia, isn't he? They buried him there, all of him, except for his head. I had his head cut off. And it's in Damascus, or Rome. Maybe it's in France, maybe in Amiens. Maybe Munich, which isn't in France, I know. I can't remember everything. I can't be responsible to keep track of all the decollated heads rolling around out there."

"Thomas Paine died—or will die—in 1804, and was—will be, whatever. I get confused by verbs in these sideways dreamtime interludes. Thomas Paine was denied a Christian burial. His body was lost *en route* to England. Am I to be held responsible for keeping track of all misplaced cadavers in the world? Don't I have servants to take care of those kinds of details?"

He was red in the face now, and panting from a lack of breath, but he continued shouting into the void. "Who is this phantom priest speaking to me in the dark? I felt him again last night. I felt his spirit passing before my face. I heard his voice, a voice like the wind, like a breath, a spirit. And the very hairs of my flesh stood upright." Herod shivered. "I hate piloerection. Still it's better than being visited by the ghost of Charlie Manson. Am I right?" He shivered again. There was no one there. Then, feeling cold and vulnerable he sought out the comfort of a familiar cardigan before continuing his screed on the balcony just like his father was once wont to do.

"Should I release him? No, no. He's already dead. And man is not completely born until he's dead. Who said that? Was it Plato? Or maybe Benjamin Franklin? I forget. Still, it's true. It's all true. So perhaps the Baptizer should be thanking me. Future generations will forgive me for his death. They must. They'll be thanking me eventually."

He said all this, and he was silent for several minutes. Servants in other parts of the palace began to relax assuming that he'd fallen asleep. But then, with startling suddenness, he began again. A startled servant in the hall dropped a silver platter of figs.

"I am the spider that dangles flies over the flames of the furnace. I am the loathsome one. Who is he? Who does he think that he is? He's in the way, that's what he is. He's nothing. Nothing. But still, I desire to see him. And I do not understand why. I could have put him into the guano mines. I could put him away. I could remove all the broken silences. I could have him given an orchiectomy—necessary or otherwise. I will have no tolerance for the religious dissenters in the land of unwalled villages. There will be no tolerance for dissent. Not in my realms. We will put down the protestors with bullets and bayonets and cannons if the policeman's club will not suffice."

"Still," he said to himself after a moment of nervous reflection, "Why do I desire to see him? Turn out the light; I'm done with these thoughts."

43. What Does He Do

"Herod Antipas, he's a tool, isn't he?"
"A tool? No. Tools have a function. Tools are useful."
"Still."
"Still."
"We call him Mr. Constipation, you know."
"Yeah?"
"Not where he'll hear us, you know. But . . . yeah. We call him Mr. Constipation because he's such a stubborn asshole. I take that back. I'm sorry. I can't call him an asshole because assholes, while unclean, are necessary. What function does he serve? What does he do? I mean, besides shirking and shrugging? Besides all the smoking, what does he do?"

"We shouldn't be having this conversation, you know? He'll hear about it; it'll get back to him somehow, and we'll be . . . you know . . ."

"Yeah. I know. See ya' around."

44. The Food of the Poor is the Bread of Heaven

The study of the Fortean and the paranormal was once, and not so very long ago, a respectable science and many research grants were available to occult investigators in those days. Velikovsky was read by students—without irony. Without laughter. The study of alchemical knowledge was pursued by serious academics and passionate amateurs around the world. Those eager to plumb bizarre depths gravitated to esteemed centers of learning like the Society for Psychical Research in London,[40] or the Atlantic Paranormal Society in Rhode Island, the Toronto Society for Psychical Research,[41] or even the Occult Studies Group in Cairo. They went to the Forbidden City in the Himalayas. They worked in medieval London or gothic Prague or even in Gdańsk. But few of them, if any at all, went to work in Galilee. Seekers of the uncanny and the inexplicable did not visit the backwater, redneck hills and hamlets of Israel.

Investigators of anomalous weather patterns, cryptozoology, prophetic pareidolia, crop circles, or out-of-place artifacts[42] went to Europe or Asia or even the Antarctic. Magic and sorcery and alchemy necessitated locations with more historical significance, more gravitas. But Galilee! Can anything weird come from there? Galilee went unnoticed by the Fortean fellows who catalogued lists of the uncanny. Still, there was something going on there in the village of Bethsaida.

Bethsaida, which had been enlarged by Philip[43] to the status of *polis*, was still just a middle-of-nowhere grazing area. He was the king that never

---

40. Founded in 1882 to advance the cause of understanding of those events and abilities commonly described as 'psychic' or 'supernatural', the Society for Psychical Research—the SPR, had its roots and antecedents in the ancient Roman Society of the Paranormal qua Recondite—the SP(q)R.

41. The TSPR published the now classic studies *Through the Gates of Death* (1836), *Aspects of Sane Occultism* (1836) and *Psychic Self Defense* (1837), *Inquiries into the Efficacy of Prayer* (1837), and *Intelligible Signals between Neighboring Stars* (1837) before suddenly disappearing.

42. Like the galvanic Baghdad Battery or the Lake Winnipesaukee Mystery Stone.

43. That is Philip Herod II, half-brother to Herod Antipas. Of course his name is Herod!

was, and Bethsaida the village that never became. There was never no much as a lightning and never a Napoleon, but even so, something was definitely going on there. There was something to see.

The twelve came back from their mission trip eager to report everything that they'd done. Jesus took them aside into a desert place attached to Bethsaida. But the crowds found out and they followed too. Ever ready for them, Jesus told them about the Kingdom of Justice even as he cured those that needed healing right up until late in the afternoon, almost evening.

"Send them away," James and John told him as the sun was bending low. "Send them away so they can go buy food and meat for themselves. Set them loose for victuals and lodging."

But Jesus said, "No. You will feed them."

Matthew, who'd taken a quick accounting of everything, said, "Lord, we've only five small barley cakes and a couple of smoked tilapia. This is not enough to feed a crowd of this size, unless we want to buy meat for all of them." Matthew had already made a rough count of the crowd as well. By his reckoning there were nearly five thousand, give or take a few. "We have even less than the blessed Elisha had to feed his hundred. He had twenty barley loaves . . ."

"Have them sit there in the grass," Jesus instructed, "in companies of fifty. We'll take care of this."

"But," objected James.

"But," balked John.

But they made them sit in groups of fifty as he commanded. They were tobacco chewers with their alcoholic wives who dreamt of vacationing at the radioactive spas in Karlovy Vary in Czechoslovakia (even though they knew they could never afford it.)[44] They were rowdies, roustabouts, rustic radicals, and professors of annoying European nonsense (retired). They were fishmongers, student nurses, itinerant cherry pickers, and graphic artists (out of work), bus drivers, elevator operators and late-shift waitresses. They were tinkers, beekeepers, costers, bobbin-turners, needle women, milliners, and garret-masters. They were chimney sweeps, rag and bone men, and banjo pickers. They were mechanics, unpublished authors as well as butchers, and bakers and candlewick embroiderers, and all of them were hungry.

---

44. You've probably seen the billboards: "Our tonic waters are naturally heated and radioactively activated!"

There were a few who stood aloof from the crowd—women in blue silk gowns with their noble husbands in crushed velvet suits. They'd arrived in horse-drawn droshkies to watch the goings-on. Jesus invited them to join the feast as well, but they declined with a giggle and a wave. "Well," Jesus said, "it's here if you change your minds."

Jesus lifted the loaves of borrowed bread and fish up to heaven, broke them and pronounced a blessing over them. "The food of the poor is the bread of heaven," he said. "Do you seek deep and enigmatic treasures? Do you pursue the mystical and the mysterious? They are right here before you in this desert place." This is the Lord's Supper, the believers gathered for the breaking of bread and for prayers. All of that is there with Jesus on that hillside and all of it is yours.

The twelve distributed the food to the people seated on the grass. Each of them taking bread and fish enough to eat. All of them were filled. And there were bits and fragments left over, enough to fill twelve baskets—more than what they'd started with. There was even enough for those who drove away laughing in their droshkies without having joined the party. There is always more in the sharing.

45. Who Am I to You?

Blaise Pascal wrote in one of his minor works that one cannot begin to define the word "being" without falling victim to one inevitable absurdity: one cannot define a word without beginning with the word "is" either expressed or implied. How then, do we define "to be"? One cannot define a word with itself. In a relational universe such as this, one can only describe something in relation to something else. Self-referential definition is meaningless. I cannot say who I am. Beingness cannot be defined. But now we find Jesus alone considering the question of self-definition and praying under the moon.

"Lord, grant me a goodly entrance, but if not that, Lord, grant me a godly exit."[45] He prays alone, until his disciples come to interrupt. Sighing, he asks them, "Who do the crowds and the mob say that I am?"

"Some would say John the Baptist Redivivus again," John answers. "Ask Herod about that." Then Thaddeus pipes up, "Or maybe that you are Elijah returned." Andrew also volunteers an opinion, "Maybe some are saying that

---

45. It sounds almost (but not quite) like he's reciting a prayer found in the Surah *Al-Isra* (the Night Journey) of the Koran.

you are one of the ancient prophets come back to life. The world is strange and stranger still. Who can say? They still try to put the new inside the old, a new patch on an old shirt, new wine in old wineskins, so to speak."

"But you, my friends," Jesus says to them, "the ones who might have reason to understand, who do you say that I am? Who am I to you?"

Without hesitation (or thought, and those are often the same) Peter says, "The Christ. The Christ of God. Chosen and anointed." He says this though he does not completely understand what it is that he is saying. And, because Peter has no idea what he is saying, Jesus tells them all to say nothing.

"Say nothing because the Son of Man must suffer still. Must suffer and be rejected by elders, priests, and scribes. He must be rejected by the Seventy-One of the Sanhedrin who are the final appeal for all things not reserved for the Roman procurator's judgment. The Son of Man must suffer, be rejected, and die. And this is not extra; this is not outside the plan. He is not the Son in spite of suffering. The suffering makes the Son. Sickness is the natural state of the Christ.[46] This is the mystery and the plan. The Son of Man must suffer and must die—but will be raised up on the third day. Still, say nothing. It is not time for that just yet. This is the first time I tell you these things."

46. No Libertines Here

Here is the motif of martyrdom, coming hard upon the first prediction of his own death. Follow the melody. And if you would follow, you must take up your cross. And this should not be a reluctant acceptance of disappointing circumstances. Don't whistle that tune. This is the deliberate, purposeful choice to dive headlong into the black maw of self-sacrifice.

Tell me of the Christian martyrs living and dying in the long shadow of violence cast by the cross, suffering with the Christ of God just as he suffers with them, participating in his death and sharing in his glory. Tell me of those redeemed by his blood and ordained in their own. Tell me of those called to be sacred vessels of peace and cups of grace even as they hung on imperial crosses and roasted in the Emperor's flames.

Tell me how they praised the God of Heaven and the Prince of Peace as they forgave their murderers and went to their deaths as if it were a procession into life. Sing again of those Christian martyrs so they will not be

---

46. To paraphrase Pascal again.

forgotten in this new age under the renewed shadows of imperial violence committed in the guise of American exceptionalism.

There are no libertines here. No impotent princes with angry complaints, no billionaire sons with pretensions of nobility, no landlords, or real estate moguls earning their bread in the sweat of their neighbors. Wealth and power are nothing in the final assize. The martyred witness is a willing human sacrifice, facing death every day—either in the martyrdom of one swift stroke or the slow slicing of death by a thousand daily self-denials. They are a daily *Devotio*. Shall the Son be ashamed when he returns in his own glory along with that of God and that of the holy angels?

47. Spontaneous Combustion of Mountaintop Experience

Eight days later Jesus went up the mountain just this side of Syria,[47] with Peter, James, and John. *Les montagnes sont sages,* they say. The mountains are strange and mystical and holy. Dangerous. He went up the side of the mountain where fallen angels once plotted the pollution of mankind with the creation of giants, which were those "mighty men of old, men of renown," and where later Sunni Muslims would build Nimrod's Castle as a defense against Crusading armies from Europe.

And there atop the mountain, he was surrounded on all sides by remembrance of the Law and of the Prophets. On one side stood the prototype, and on the other, the forerunner. Moses to his left and Elijah to his right.

Figure 23–One way out.

47. Many in the international community would say it was actually *inside* the Syrian borders.

Terminus a Quo

There in the wisdom and splendor of the mountain was he transformed, his face and his clothes bright and dazzling. They'd come to speak with him of his own imminent Exodus and departure. His exit. His own, not to put too fine a point on it, violent and bloody death in Jerusalem. His ambitious and voluntary death in the City of Peace.

And now we ask, is this mountain top story of glory a resurrection event projected backwards before the bloody death? It could be, but one must first grapple with death. We must face death to move forward. And it behooves us to win the fight.

Peter, and the brothers James and John, were heavy with sleep. Dappled and drowsy as the troubadours might sing. The universe is expanding, ever outward, from the center big bang point and we know in part now, and prophesy in part now. At some point in the future we will be able to see further into the past—this is a constraint of the constancy of the speed of light and there's nothing you or I can do about it. But we can only see so far into the past; there is a limit. At some point the universe was opaque to light and we can see no further back into those dark histories than that. The somnolent disciples struggled to stay awake to see the glory of their Lord and they saw nothing.

Peter, still darkened with sleep, blurted out "It is good for us to be here. The whole cosmic drama is here for us to see. All of it! Creation, sin, death, redemption! Let's build up three sacred shrines, three tabernacles: for Moshe, for Eliyahu, and for thee. Then we might return here again and again to recapture this feeling."

But Peter, always susceptible to spontaneous combustion of mountaintop experience, spoke without knowing what he was saying. Heavenly bodies have no need for tents. Breathe in. Breathe out. Does the air taste different here? Does it have a bittersweet tang? Is there a burning in the nostrils?

A Life Known and Unknowable

Figure 24–Heaven came down, and glory.

Lighter. Brighter. Is it safe? Are our voices pitched differently in this atmosphere? We sound strange in our ears. Maybe we are not ourselves. Perhaps we are only a penumbra of ourselves.

While Peter spoke those thoughtless words, a cloud enveloped and overshadowed them. The *Shekinah* of God was present over them the way it will be present over a sick man's bed. Where the believers are gathered for prayer a holy fire will burn, but this is not a tabernacle made by man. Neither is it the temporary temple in Jerusalem. This is heaven itself come down to dwell with mortal men. And the glory filled their souls. And from that sudden supernova cloud of heavenly fire came a voice they would remember the rest of their lives: "This is my son. Hear him if you can."

Later when the voice and the cloud were gone, Jesus was left alone. And his followers kept it close. Quiet. Secret. The beloved is loved in the moment and feared afterward. And this is something of a switch since it was usually Jesus who told them to keep silent. They told no one what they saw, what they heard, what they felt until after it was all accomplished in

Jerusalem. Their fear and wonder were expressed only in their silence, with meanings too deep for words. The Lord is in his holy temple, let all the Earth keep silent.

48. He Is a City Besieged

The next day, as they came down from the mountain still dazed by wonder, they were swarmed by a crowd. And isn't that the way they say it goes? You're coming down from an ecstatic event, a miraculous meeting of the human and the divine, and suddenly you're overwhelmed by the pressing, immediate concerns of life. The quiet of solitude is subsumed by crowding chaos.

A man of that sudden company met Jesus with an urgent request and a complaint. "Master, please, look upon my son, my only son, the son that I love. An evil spirit seizes and convulses him and throws him to the ground. It shatters him. Bruises him. And it hardly ever departs. He foams at the mouth and there is a barbarous, musty odor that will not depart from him. I asked your disciples to help him, but they couldn't do anything for him. I don't know what to do anymore."

Here is the edge of parental nihilism, the father's words coming faster now, too fast, changing in his mouth even as he gave voice to them. "He is a city besieged," he said, "except that the scorpions come from within him. We can't live in town anymore because the people are afraid of him, of us. They hate what they fear. And we can't live in the plague-houses outside of town; even the lepers won't have us."

"I'm sorry, Jesus," the sobbing father shuddered. "I'm tired and surly. Nothing is right. I have little patience for anything. I am full of swears and self-loathing, inordinately irritated by every little thing. I curse at everything. Nothing is right. Nothing is good. Please, Jesus, help him. Heal my boy."

The ecstasy of the mountaintop evaporated. Jesus sighed. "You faithless, faithless and perverse generation!" Jesus sighed. "How long do I have to put up with you? Our struggle may be with the rulers and principalities, and all the occulted forces of this present world but," he said glaring at his disciples, "flesh and blood are rarely helpful." He sighed again. "Bring me your son."

Even as the man was bringing the boy to Jesus, the afflicting demon threw him down. It tore at him and thrashed him to the ground. And this

A Life Known and Unknowable

was the way of it with many demon possessions—though it may be more accurate to describe them as a demonic assaults, as demonizings rather than possessions. Wicked spirits can harm individuals, but possess them? No. I'm not sure that's possible.

But all was not doom and loss, even though there were dybbuks and other foul creatures under every bed in every part of the land. There were ways to deal with these binary forces. One could be protected by a magician speaking the proper incantations. In Ephesus there were the well-known seven sons of the priest, Sceva, and they often attempted to cast out demons using angelic invocations. Their prayers were usually addressed to Raphael, the archangel that stands before the throne of God, and who was known for his help to those afflicted by demons.[48]

It was believed in those days that the right spell could stop the vile vociferations of evil spirits, and that the correct charm could calm a demonized child. Wise King Solomon, it is said, composed his own incantations and rituals for the exorcism of demons. Alternately, one could use the *Baaras* root to force out unclean spirits, though it is difficult to obtain this root as it shrinks away from anyone searching for it, and to touch it with the bare hand risks death. Still, if one could find and harvest this powerful flame colored root, it could be used to drive out possessive demons. Other sources claimed that demons could be driven away with the blowing of a ram's horn or the waving of a white handkerchief. The Talmud says that all that is needed to drive away a demon or a dybbuk is for the exorcist to recite Psalm 91 three times and then to blow a shofar. Few professional exorcists these days believe that it can be that simple.

If the demon could not be forced out it could be offered a new host. The spirit could be enticed to leave its human victim and to enter into an animal, or perhaps a figurine, or even a reed of significant size. The disciples had attempted this while Jesus was on the mountain overnight. "We saw Jesus send the Legion of spirits into the pigs. So we tried that! We did. We really tried. We chanted the holy words: '*Aleph bet gimel, dalet hey vav zayin. Chet tet yod. Kaf lamed mem nun samek ayin pay tsade qof resh shin tav!*' But they had no effect. The demon would not enter the substitutionary host that we offered to it."

---

48. "Do that which is good and no harm will come to thee," as the sons of Sceva would say, but it didn't work out so well for John Proctor when he tried quoting those words, did it? It might be good to remember that the seven sons of Sceva were spectacular failures as exorcists.

Terminus a Quo

Prayers invoking the saints have sometimes proved effective as well. The father that came to Jesus that morning had himself frequently made this prayer: "Hear me and respond, o thou, long anticipated greyhound. Save my son from the she-wolf demon on the road. I call upon Saint Guinefort[49] and all the cynocephalic saints and servants to beg for their aid. Deliver me as you once delivered and rescued King Garamant—by sending a pack of two hundred dogs to lead him to safety. Deliver my son, oh faithful ones. Lick his wounds. Bring aid and succor, Saint Christopher."[50]

And while it isn't recommended in any of the respectable exorcism manuals,[51] if one gets really desperate, the mixing of equal parts matter and antimatter assures a complete mutual destruction. Whiz! Bang! Boom! All gone.

Never mind that none of these things actually worked.[52] That detail is irrelevant.

Satan, the Prince of the Air, is using his loyal agents within the United States Air Force to spray the population with both Barium and Aluminum. Think about that, will you? What are the symbols for Barium and Aluminum? Ba and Al. Put them together in combination and they spell Ba'al. And Ba'al is the lord and marshal of the satanic forces within the USAF. They are spraying diabolical elements over us to artificially induce demonic possessions. Everything in the physical universe resonates at a specific and particular frequency. A crystal goblet can be shattered with a sonic blast. And a boy and his father can be shattered as easily as a glass.

Still, not everything that you may have heard or read about the exorcism of demons is accurate. The popular book (and subsequent film franchise) *The Exorcist* by Peter William Blatty was based on a hoax perpetrated by a petulant and spoiled, young bully in the 1940s. And mental illness is

---

49. Saint Guinefort was a thirteenth century dog from France, declared a saint after numerous *mirabile dictu* miracles were reported at his grave. Adherents of Saint Guinefort continued their devotions until the 1930s despite repeated objurgation from the Catholic Church.

50. Saint Christopher is sometimes portrayed (though not officially sanctioned) in Eastern Orthodox icons with a dog's head, though this is not officially sanctioned by the Church.

51. See APPENDIX 1

52. Martin Luther claimed that he could drive the devil away with a fart. He also claimed to have hit the devil with an inkwell. It would not surprise me to learn that either of these methods actually work.

still frequently misdiagnosed as demonic assault. Do not be so easily misled as these.

Jesus rebuked the unclean demon and healed the boy. What could not be done with iron (for demons are repelled by *ferrum*) or fire (they are also repulsed by *fire*) was done with a word. No tricks. No formulas. No props. He rebuked the spirit, then delivered the boy back to his father restored and whole. And all were amazed at the mighty majesty of God.

49. They Were Afraid To Ask

When the disciples found him later, he was reading a battered paperback copy of Plato's *Phaedo* that he'd picked up in a used bookstore in Capernaum known as PALEOGRAPHIA.[53]

"This is the book Cato the Younger was reading," he told his disciples, "just before he perforated his belly with a sword and pulled out his own intestines. Do you know Cato? Cato Uticensis? No? Ah well." He sighed, dog-eared a page to mark his place, and closed the book.[54] He set it upon the ground "Let these words sink in. Open you ears and let them penetrate. They're important; that's why I'm saying them again." He sighed a second time. He sighed often. "The Son of Man will be delivered into the hands of men and led to an ominous ending." But they didn't understand. The truth of it was hidden from them.

"Ask him," said one.

"No. You ask him," said another. But they didn't. They wouldn't. They were afraid to ask

50. One of the Opitmates

Flesh takes motion to make motions and ambitious will does what it will. The disciples got into an argument. "I'm his favorite," said one. "I stand upon the glowing path with him." "No," said another. "I'm the Optimate,

---

53. I once bought a copy of Sir Isaac Newton's book, *Observations upon the Principals of Daniel and the Apocalypse of Jesus* there. In it Newton predicted that the downfall of the Catholic Church will occur sometime in the years between 2035 and 2045. It was a great bookstore, but it's not there anymore. It burned down several years ago. Investigators suspected arson but could never prove it.

54. I know! I'm as shocked as you are. Did he also crack the spine and lay his books open and face down on the table when he needed to stop reading for a bit?

Terminus a Quo

I'm the wielder of the Ultra-Fire." There was need for neither psitrons nor psychology here; Jesus could hear their dispute.

Jesus took one of the children sitting there among the group and sat the boy on his knee. "What's your name?" Jesus said to the little boy.

"Ignatius."[55]

Jesus smiled at the boy, then looked up and called to his quarreling disciples. "Whoever receives this child—this child here, or any one like him—whoever receives this child in my name, receives me. And whoever receives me, receives the one who sent me."

They were slow to respond.

"Less is more," he said, but they still did not understand.

51. It's All Very Boilerplate

John approached Jesus with a sheaf of legal documents. "I had our family lawyer write this up for you." He said as he handed the papers to Jesus. "It's a draft, but I thought you'd like to see it before the final copy is written, in case you want to suggest any changes."

"What is it?" Jesus asked.

"It's just a standard Cease and Desist letter." John said. "It's all very boilerplate."

Jesus skimmed through the pages. "Dear Sir, You are currently using the name 'Jesus of Nazareth,' a copyrighted term, held in accordance with title seventeen of Imperial code of copyright laws for the purpose of exorcising and expelling demons without the express and explicit written permission from Jesus and Company, Inc. If we have not received a written response from you by the first of June, agreeing that you have ceased using the name 'Jesus of Nazareth,' and will desist from all future use of the said name, we will be forced to seek juridical enforcement to rectify the situation."

"What is this?" Jesus asked John, waving the papers in his face. The grin John wore slowly melted.

"I told you, it's a simple C and D."

Jesus turned to James. "Did you have anything to do with this?"

---

55. Yes. The future Saint Ignatius of Antioch. So what if he was born some twenty years after Jesus' ascension. This story is already incredibly temporally unsynchronized. So why not Ignatius?

James nodded. "We saw someone casting out demons in your name. But he's not one of us. He's not part of our band. It's a clear cut case of copyright infringement."

"Listen," Jesus said. "Listen, all of you. Anyone that's not against us, is with us. It's hard enough as it is, without you sending cannibalistic lawyers against our allies. We don't consume our own. Do you hear me? If they're not against us, they're for us."

The Argument

Through A Glass Darkly and All That

I REMEMBER, THOUGH I KNOW it can't be a true remembering. It's more of a *faux souvenir*. I remember sitting at my desk after lunch that Tuesday in January 1986 watching the Space Shuttle Challenger take off from Cape Kennedy and then exploding over the ocean seventy-three short seconds after launch. I remember the horror and the fear. I remember blaming the Russians. My friend Travis and I imagined what kind of military response America would make against the Soviets, and how quickly we'd invade Russia. We blamed them for everything in those paranoid days before *Perestroika* and *Glasnost* and all that—in the same way that we blame everything on Mexican immigrants or Arab terrorists or the Communist Chinese today. There's always someone ready at hand to be blamed.

I remember the explosion and the fiery deaths of those brave astronauts. But I know that isn't correct. First of all, they didn't die in the explosion. There wasn't actually an explosion. There was no bang. The sound was added to the playback later. And the astronauts were actually alive until they hit the water. And secondly, this was before CNN and the twenty four hour news market were fully grown. CNN did broadcast the Challenger launch while all other the major networks had cut away from the event. And NASA arranged a satellite broadcast, but my school didn't have a satellite dish. So what I saw with my fifth grade classmates had to have been a taped replay after the fact.

Cal it the Mandela Effect, I suppose, the false memory effect described by paranormal researchers. Or call it a "flashbulb memory"—a nearly photographic recall of traumatic events which is almost always incorrect.

Memories are tricky. They're real, of course, but they're also a distortion of the real, a seeing through a glass darkly and all that. They're useful, but maybe not entirely trustworthy. Filter them through a handful of doubt and reason.

V

Tempus Fugit

1. The Most Choleric of His So-Called Followers

Something deep within triggered Jesus' internal alarm clock and he knew it was time for him to set his face toward Jerusalem. It was time for him to lift his chin in grim determination towards death. It was time. It was set. He sent messengers and harbingers ahead of him and the rest of the band, to arrange hospitality in the Samaritan village where he planned to stop for the evening.

But the Samaritans of that village wouldn't receive him. They'd discovered that he and his entourage were on their way to the Temple in Jerusalem, and all the old feuds and rivalries flared up. "If he's not going to worship on the highest and oldest most central mountain in the world, if he's not going to Mount Gerizim then we'll have nothing to do with him." The way they said it, it came with a sneer and a rhyme.

The Thunder Brothers, James and John, were furious. "Call down fire, Jesus" they urged. "Torch this whole village! Scorched Earth policy! Just like Sodom! Bomb them back to the Iron Age! Just like Elijah did. Put the dirty, mongrel Samaritans in their place, Jesus. Death from above. Whooo hooo! Burn it down! " James and John, like most Jews of their age, considered the Samaritans frenzied fanatics, rebellious and rude. And the Samaritans reciprocated the sentiment. They thought of the Jews as zealots and freaks.

James and John weren't concerned with Jesus' honor and reputation so much as they were perpetuating the old animus. Nothing more. But the confusion is easily, and often, made, even by the most choleric of his so-called followers. "My enemies are God's enemies" is so commonplace a mistake that it's rarely recognized as a mistake.

"Fine! Whatever!" the brothers huffed. "Let's get out of this God-forsaken place."

"There is no such place," Jesus said. "There is no absolute darkness. Even the furthest, darkest parts of the universe are illuminated, however slightly, by traces of electromagnetic radiation. Even in the darkest parts of space, the Father of Lights is present. And the Son of Man is a Savior not a Destroyer. When you call for fire from heaven it is evident that you don't understand who you are or who you're supposed to be," Jesus said and sighed. "Forget it," he said. "We'll find someplace to stay in the next village down the road."

2. Sanguine Dreams

A young man came to Jesus and said, "Master, I will, if you allow me, follow you anywhere."

Figure 25–Little birds can fly away home.

"Foxes have holes," Jesus told him, "and little birds have their feathered nests, but I have nothing and nowhere—not even a pallet on the floor in a Samaritan village. Can you dig that? My disciples and I spent last night in an abandoned Waffle House off exit 417. We slept on the floor in an old hobo camp surrounded by empty liquor bottles and used condoms. Are you ready for that? I'm on my way to Jerusalem through fire, water, prison, and death. Are you still willing to follow?

"Yes," he said. "Yes. I will follow." He said with confidence. But maybe his confidence was just the smoke of egotistical self-deceit. You can call it that, I suppose, if you're the kind of person who likes shitting on the dreams of youth. It could just as easily (and much more kindly) have been the sanguine dreams of a young romantic that Jesus knew to temper. Why be calloused? Why be cruel?

3. Let the Dead Bury Their Dead

Jesus said, "Follow me," and another man said, "Sure thing, Boss. I just need to bury my father first." But Jesus would have nothing to do with it. "Nope. Follow me and let the dead bury their dead." And that definitely seems weird. Maybe he meant something like 'let the spiritually dead bury the physically dead.' But what if—and I know this gets into a really weird territory—what if he meant 'let the physically dead bury the spiritually dead.'

Yeah. I like that much better. It has a kind of melancholic grossness that appeals to me

4. Neither Torah nor Elisha

Still another man came to Jesus. "I'll follow, just let me say farewell to my family." And this seems like a perfectly reasonable request, right? There is both commandment and precedent for this request. We are, after all, commanded to honor our fathers and our mothers. And when the prophet Elijah called Elisha to follow Elisha said, "First let me kiss farewell to my father and my mother."

But neither *Torah* nor Elisha prove to be acceptable examples here. The phlegmatic Jesus told him, "You can't look back, pal. Once you've started, you can't look back."

Three aspirants[1] have come, but did they go? I do not know. They said that they would but words and actions fail to meet.

---

1. The conjecture that they were Judas Iscariot, Thomas, and Matthew is singularly baseless. I don't even know why I bring it up.

5. *You Are So Few*

After this, Jesus appointed seventy advance ministers—and prepared them to visit every town and village in the area ahead of his arrival. He appointed them—one for each of the nations and languages of the world, according to the table of nations described by the prophet Moses in the book of Genesis chapter ten. One for each of the years of a man's three-score-and-ten years of life. *Soixante-dix*, sixty-ten ready to serve.[2] "The harvest is enormous, and you are so few," he said to them. "Jacob is so small. Size isn't everything, but pray that God will send more."

"Take no purse. Take no scrip. Take no shoes. And give no salute upon the road. You have no time for rituals of polite discourse."

"I'm sending you out like lambs among wolves. This may not be the time, just yet, when the wolves will lie down among the sheep, but it *is* time to go. So be doves and not serpents. Be wary. Be wily. You may be condemned as weak and feebleminded fools, but you are *my* holy fools."

"When you enter a house, pronounce the blessing: '*Pax Vobiscum.*' And your peace will rest upon that house, if an honest-to-God, son-of-peace lives there. But if it's a son-of-a-bitch that lives there, then your prayer will return to your own bosom just as the psalmist[3] said it would. When you enter a house, stay there—eat and drink with them just as in the days of Noah. Enjoy what they provide. Don't go hopping from house to house and bed to bed. Marx was right, 'wages are the amount of money which the capitalist pays for a certain period of work or for a certain amount of work. Consequently, it appears that the capitalist buys their labour with money, and that for money they sell him their labour. But this is merely an illusion.[4]' Still, all things considered, the labourer *is* worthy of his hire."[5]

Some of those who were listening interrupted him just then. "But Master, it is the *love* of money that is the root of all evil. The *love* of money, not money itself. Isn't that right?"

"Sure," he answered. "Sure. Fine. Whatever. But remember, it's the pursuit of money that brings ruin and destruction. May I continue?" They nodded glumly.

---

2. Or maybe there were seventy-two. Maybe. There are conflicting reports.

3. Sick, and sackcloth clothed prayers often return to the prayers heart, though sometimes they return unanswered. Psalm 35:13

4. Marx, *Wage Labour and Capital*, 17

5. Join a union. We're stronger together.

"Heal the sick," He told them. "And tell them that the Kingdom of Justice is close. Tell them that if the Kingdom of Peace is here at hand, we must take it. We must seize it.

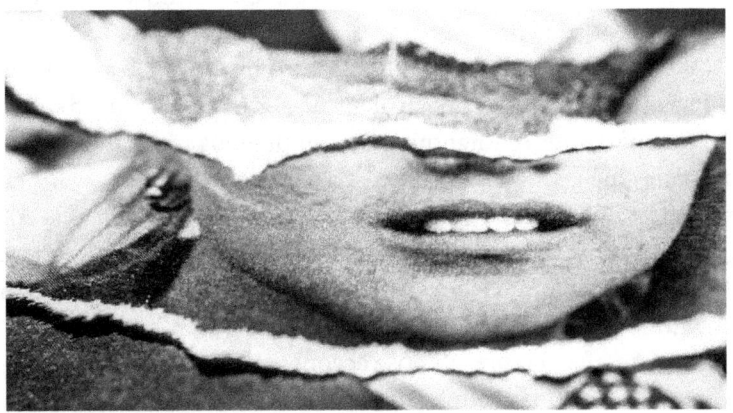

Figure 26–This is not my mouth.

If they won't receive you, brush off their dust from your clothes as a warning to them. Tell them to 'remember Sodom.'[6] Whoever listens to you is actually hearing me. You are my *viva voce*. It may not be my mouth, but it will be my voice."

He commissioned them to go into every city, and town, and every municipality, and unincorporated area to prepare their denizens for his arrival. He sent them to the habitable cities of great kings and to the forgotten villages of overlooked princes. He sent them to speak to the principled men of rebellious cities as well as the rebellious young men of principled communities. He sent them to towns like Badwater-Chorazin and Crippledhorse Bethsaida even though there'd be nothing but diminishing returns there.

"Woe to you, Badwater-Chorazin! Woe and be damned, Crippledhorse Bethsaida! If the godless communists in Moscow or Beijing or Pyongyang had seen what you've seen, they'd have repented and put on their best sackcloth and ashes already. Just like they did in Nineveh. You remember Nineveh, right? Better for them. Worse for you. And Capernaum too! Call it Capernaum-thrust-down-to-Uffern for all that I care."

---

6. Archaeologists at Tel el-Hamman may have unearthed evidence of a meteor airburst which may have caused earthquakes, shockwaves, and eruptions of petro-chemical fire that may have been responsible for the destruction of Sodom nearly four thousand years ago, but it's still vulgar speculation at this point. Wait for more data.

6. *Except When It Does*

When the seventy-two ambassadors[7] and envoys returned they brought exuberant news. "We saw devils subject to us," they grinned. "In your name, of course," they added hastily.

"Of course," Jesus agreed with a grin of his own. "I saw it too. I saw it all. I saw the fall of that malevolent power. I saw Satan, the Prince of the Aire, wing'd with red lightning and impetuous rage fall like a fireball bolide exploding in the ash-blackened skies over Russia. I saw his fall like a nuclear test over Bikini Atoll, like lightning over the Great Sea. And the odor of Sulphur and hellish putrefaction lingered after. The zoophagous psychopath was emaciated and starved, and ragged like a disgraced mercenary knight who's sold his clothes and arms for food."

"You can safely ignore all those accounts that describe the devil in the form of a man or a goat with an overly enlarged member. They always describe him as having 'the member of a mule.' Or they say that 'the member of the devil is half a yard long, of medium thickness, red, dark, crooked, and veiny.' But these are only the grotesque exaggerations of a wounded ego.[8] These are nothing but exaggerations and outright lies. The monarch of make-believe has only mendacity in his arsenal."

"I saw him fall alone, having been abandoned by every one of his infernal lieutenants. He was abandoned by *Belphegor*, who had once been called Ba'al Peor and Hell's ambassador to France. *Belial*, one of the multiplied sons of worthlessness, had fled into the night. And *Asmodeus Ashmedai* the good-natured slayer of husbands was cowering in a darkened corner. They all fled from their falling prince and their forces were scattered to hell and gone. He fell through a cloudless sky and splashed into the cold waters of the eternal abyss. Enormous tidal waves rolled him under."

"Now have come the power and the salvation and the kingdom and the authority of the messiah, for the accuser of our comrades has been thrown into the sea."[9]

---

7. Or was it seventy?

8. It is either the wounded ego of the devil himself, or of vain and self-styled witch hunters who find the devil in everyone and anyone they don't like, hiding behind every fence post. Or both. But it's never the truth.

9. American intelligence agencies saw nothing of this, not with their hexagon spy satellites (which could count the number of Soviet tanks on parade in Moscow), nor with their secret agents hiding in the shadows of the Kremlin. One wonders if it wasn't a deliberate blindness.

"And now I give to you also the power to tread on half-demon scorpions and to walk down full-blooded serpents (even the ones flying yellow and black 'Don't Tread On Me' flags from the back of their noisy pickup trucks) as well as power over all the forces of the enemy. Nothing by any means shall ever hurt you. Except when it does."

He looked them in the eye each one and said again, "Except when it does."

"But you should not rejoice in that power. It's only yours on loan. Rejoice instead that you and your names are known in heaven."

Jesus rejoiced and thanked God that all of this had been concealed from the wise and from the learned, that it had been concealed from the prudent and the careful, revealed instead to babes and bumpkins. But this author laments that this has been taken as justification for a deliberate anti-intellectualism and the violent anti-mentalism that we find among so many of his followers in these days.

"No one knows the son, except the father. And no one knows the father except the son. The one can't be understood without the other. There's truth in what I say. I am the truth, but not just in words. Look deeper. Words themselves are incomplete. Words fail. Use context. Use relationship. Blessed are the eyes that see what you see. Many prophets and kings went to bed and to death without having seen anything like these things in their times."

7. Do This and You Will Live

Look here: a lawyer who thinks he's someone steps up to test and to tempt him. See his shiny shoes and oiled hair, his immaculately exfoliated skin, his slick silk suit, smooth hands, and neatly trimmed nails? Hear the clipped eloquence of his speech? He's something, all right. He's everything.

"Master," he says in silver tones and with posh inflection, "how do I inherit the eternal life that you describe?"

"Inherit," he says as any trust fund baby will. The 'pull-yourself-up-by-your-own-bootstraps' mentality does not seem to apply to the scions of the rich even if they're the ones to shout it back at us so vociferously. But Jesus responds without the rancor that I seem unable to conceal. "What is written in the law?" he says. "And how do you interpret it?"

The lawyer boy gives a good response, quoting from the *Shema* and the Levitical codes, or maybe he's cribbing from the *Testament of the Twelve*

Fathers. Either way it comes to the same thing. He says, "Love God and love your neighbor."

"A good summary," Jesus says. "Do this and you will live."

But praise is not enough for our bright-boy, our estimable, well-bred lawyer-boy. Praise is not enough; he wants justification too. He wants to have his ego stroked in public view. So he asks again. "And just who *is* my neighbor? What are the limits and meaning of duty? What I'm asking, Jesus, is how far do my obligations to others extend? I have rights, Jesus . . ."

How do you feel about similitudes or allegories? How about a riddle? Jesus is given a question but he answers with a parable which is a riddle, of sorts. This is what he does. Jesus doesn't answer the lawyer boy's question with a relational definition. Jesus doesn't answer the question so much as turn it upside down and pull it inside out to tell a story:

A man went down from Jerusalem to Jericho, a short journey of seventeen miles or so. Not far, not really. But the road is steep, desolate and rocky, dropping down thirteen hundred feet over those seventeen miles. And the road was perpetually infested with bandits and outlaws. The man going down to Jericho fell, and fell among thieves who beat him, wounded him, stripped him, and left him for dead.

Now either by coincidence or by stochastic pattern a priest went down the very same road not long after, probably going home to his family after his shift at the Temple. And when he saw the bloodied man left for dead in the road he squeezed by at the far side of the road. Perhaps he thought that the man was already dead, and did not wish to risk the ritual defilement of touching a corpse. Perhaps he preferred to hope that the man was already dead so he could excuse his lack of attention to the man as an adherence to priestly purity. Perhaps. It doesn't really matter either way. He passed by without offering aid.

Likewise a Levite, pledged to divine service at the temple, passed without stopping to offer succor or salve for the man's bloody wounds. Maybe he was in a hurry. Maybe he didn't care. Doesn't really matter either way. He also did not stop.

But then, following the rule of three, there came another, a layman this time, and an outsider at that. It was a Samaritan this time. And he saw the man with compassion—which is literally "with passion" and passion is pain. He suffered with the man there on the road between Jerusalem and Jericho. He stopped the bleeding and bound the wounds. He poured on oil and wine, and put him up on the back of his beast to carry him to an inn.

And at the inn he put down cash to cover his continued care. 'And if it's not enough,' he said, 'I'll come back with more.'

Now here's the case. Put on your lawyerly best and give us your opinion: Which of these was neighborly? Lawyer boy stammers for a bit, but finally answers and answers well. "The . . . the . . . one who showed empathy," he says. "Empathy combined with mercy."

Jesus nods and says, "Do this and you will live."

8. Don't Take It Away from Her

Next they went into a village and in the village they went into a house, and in the house was a woman, a woman named Martha. She was always distracted, finding her space too large and herself too small. A dry cloud hung over her head. She vacuumed floors and washed dishes. She dusted cobwebs and cleaned the gutters. She even washed laundry for Jesus and his *talmidim*, fretting over the various stains and discolorations she found in their garments. So many strange odors and oil stains . . .

Martha had a sister named Mary, who sat at Jesus' feet listening to every word he spoke as if she herself were one of his *talmidim*—for, in truth she was. Meanwhile Martha was cumbered with the hostesses' load of cares and much serving, taking coats, making pies, mixing drinks, playing the harpsichord and reciting poetry as entertainment for her guests.

"Master," she said, "Master, Master why has my sister abandoned me? Tell her to help me." Guilt trips and psychological manipulations are common, even among the pious. All natural light is diminished, and what is remembered? The insect? The tapeworm? The parasite of the soul? Only the intimidation of the soul.

"Martha, Martha," Jesus said, "you are anxious, anxious, so very anxious. But few things are actually needful. Maybe only one, and Mary has it. Don't take it away from her."

9. It Seems a Bit Short

Once, when Jesus was praying, as he often did, one of his disciples approached him. When he'd finished, the disciple said, "Lord, teach us to pray, as John taught his." And Jesus agreed to the request.

"When you pray," he told them, "pray like this:" He raised his blue and white *tallit* with dangling, knotted fringes at the corners over his head and began to pray. "*Avinu Shebashamayim*, Father in heaven, may your name be forever holy. May your kingdom come clear and come soon. Give us daily, supersubstantial food and forgive our debts just as we forgive everyone indebted to us. Do not lead us to temptations, but keep us from all visible and invisible apparitions of the devil."

The disciples, who'd all gathered near to hear this instruction on prayer, were stunned. "Lord," said the one who'd asked him for the instruction, "isn't this prayer missing a few phrases? It seems a bit short. Short enough that Blystone probably *could* write it on a grain of rice."

"Yeah, Jesus," said another, "And that whole debt cancellation thing? Doesn't that sound too much like communist propaganda? You know that The Communist Workers' Party is always going on about the immediate cancellation of all international debts. We don't want to get mixed up in that sort of thing, do we? We can't go around encouraging that sort of thing. We'd be labeled unpatriotic if we start mouthing this kind of prayer."

Jesus just shook his head and sighed as he regarded them in the fading light of dusk. "Take it as it is, without the filigreed liturgical expansions and heavy handed attempt at harmonization and pray. It's really not that difficult."

10. Proceed from the Mild to the Severe

Which of you is a . . . not a back-door-man. No . . . That's not right. No. Which of you is a . . . which of you is a midnight friend? Banging on your neighbor's window in the dead, dark of night to ask for help? "Friend, neighbor lend me three loaves of bread. A cousin of mine has arrived unexpected from a long trip–to Norway, or Iceland maybe–and I have nothing to offer him. I'm fresh out of pickled herring and dark bread." Oh Discordia! But this an embarrassment, to be so unprepared. Have any of you ever been in a situation like this?

And there he is, your neighbor stumbling to the window like a noctambulist, shouting back at you from inside, "Go away! Trouble me not! The moon is up and the door is shut. My wife and children are asleep, for God's sake!"

But you go right on banging on that window. Bang! Bang! Bang! "Let me borrow a bit of bread, p man." Bang! Bang! Bang! And here's the thing: your neighbor *will* help—if not from the deep wells of friendship between you then, at least, from an urgent desire to get rid of you as soon as possible.

Loyalty may be fleeting but human self-interest abides forever. You can bank on that.

So ask: it's given. Seek: it's found. Knock: it's opened. Everyone who is asking is receiving. He that is seeking is finding. And she that is knocking, well . . . the door is opened for her, isn't it?

What if your son asks you for bread? Will you turn around and hand him a piece of granite to gnaw on? If your children ask for a dinner of purple and green asparagus spears fresh from the garden will you hand them a viper with fangs exposed? If your daughter asks you for an egg will you deliver her a poison scattering scorpion?[10]

You're evil, to be sure,[11] and I've never doubted it. But even racist kings gibbering behind the gated grounds of white-pillared mansions built with slave labor know better. Even they do better than this. And you are not so bad are you? As evil as you are, you're not *that* bad. Not yet. And the Heavenly Father is better yet. Think *a fortiori*. Proceed from the mild to the severe and draw your own conclusions. Won't he give you the Holy Spirit?

11. With a Word

The mute demon, Dumah, who is silence personified,[12] will keep his victim silent, mum like a sleeping dragon beneath a wine dark sea, like a seething volcano with nothing to say, smoking, and restless. Truth or lies, he never speaks. But once encountered, Jesus casts him out as he casts out all demons: with a word. A spoken word.

"He casts out devils," some will say," with the power of Beelzebub, the chief and captain of the devils. He colludes with them. He is one of them. He is one of the detestable flies that serves the Lord of Dung." But others

---

10. She is already convinced that an enormous scorpion creature or demon locust with a whipcord tail has shattered the kitchen window and stabbed her mother. The police report filed immediately after her 9-1-1 call indicates that a tree branch, blown from a nearby oak tree during the recent inland hurricanes, was found in the kitchen. Why would you do that to her? She's already morbidly afraid of scorpions.

11. There is the possibility that some of you may have some sort of neurological condition, like prospangnosia like the man who couldn't remember faces and mistook his wife for a hat. If so, this isn't necessarily an evil, but it is an illness that you should have treated.

12. Or perhaps Dumah is silence demonized. Dumah is the thousand-eyed angel of death with ten thousand angels of destruction under his flaming wings. He is chief of the demons in Gehennom's valley and stands guard at the fourteenth gate of Hell.

aren't so sure. They would like some proof, some evidence. "Give us some sign. Satan demands his share of everything from a new pair of boots to one thousand pounds of cocaine. He wants it all and he will have it all too. And with the many outbreaks we've had recently—Black Plague, Influenza (both A and C), and Covid—he appears all but unchallenged. His witches are dancing naked around stone altars in the woods. What can we do? Give us some sign."

Jesus chuckled. "You chowderheaded numbskulls. Divided kingdoms are desolate. A house divided will fall, house on house. And a house divided by zero is the ghost of a departed quantity. Think about it. If I'm using Satan's power to drive out Satan, what power are your own homegrown exorcists using? If Satan is schizophrenic, how will he rule? If the finger of God is provoked then demons are driven away. And if this is so, then the kingdom of God is here. Even the Egyptian magicians that squared off against Moses and Aaron in Pharaoh's court could recognize the finger of God when it pointed at them. Why can't you? Are your hearts are harder than Pharaoh's?"

12. Plunder His House

He saw them: Peter, James and John (the Thunder-Twins) and Judas hunched conspiratorially over the evening cookfire, whispering. Jesus had left his followers an hour or so prior, gone off some distance to pray alone, in the dark. But now, upon returning, he found these four conspirators plotting by the fire.

"We've got enough rope," said Peter, "I think. I think we have enough rope. We can do this if we have enough rope to tie up his hands and his feet, but . . ."

"But," said John, interrupting with a pointed jab of his meaty hand, "we've got to be quick, and we've got to be quiet. We do this tonight, while the others are asleep."

Peter spoke, "James, you keep watch to the North and East. Judas, on the South and West. Let out a little bird whistle if you see anyone approaching. It's dark tonight, no moon, so I don't think there will be anyone, but . . ."

"But," John interrupted again. "We've got to be quick and quiet. We go in. We crack him on the head with this," he brandished his walking staff which was a stout length of solid oak, "And we tie him up tight. Then we find the money."

Tempus Fugit

Jesus moved closer now and the conspirators, seeing the motion, flinched. Their eyes were wide in firelight and surprise. "Jesus . . . you startled us," said Peter.

"What are you boys planning?" Jesus asked.

They hesitated, none of them wanting to be the first to speak. Then Peter said, "Well, it's like you told us, aint it? We're going to go in, bind up Levi the Merchant, and take his moneybox."

Judas said, "We'll use the money to feed the poor, and to spread your gospel, Master. We . . ."

Jesus cut him off before he could say anymore. "You're going to do what?"

"We're going to bind up the strongman," said Peter, "and plunder his house. Just like you told us to."

"Told you?" Jesus sputtered. "That was a parable! A parable, you jackass! Why must you always take everything so damn literally?"

13. Logically Incompatible Statements

Some inquisitors from Jerusalem came to speak to the itinerant rabbi from Nazareth. "Jesus," they said, "we see that you are not wearing the eagle and laurel S.P.Q.R. pin, like all loyal supporters of the Roman Empire who wear it to demonstrate their loyalty despite the *Torah's* prohibition of graven images. Can you explain yourself? If you're not wearing one it must mean you do not support the Empire, and if you're not with us you must be with the terrorists, the zealots, the *Sicarii* brigands."

Jesus answered them with something like their own words. "He that is not with me is against me."

At this, Judas, who hated the name Thaddeus almost as much as he hated the Romans, leaned close and whispered to his master and teacher, "Uh . . . Sir . . . what you said just now seems to contradict something that you told us earlier." He flipped through the pages of his notebook to find the quotation. "I believe your words were, *'Anyone that's not against us, is with us. It's hard enough as it is, without you sending cannibalistic lawyers against our allies. We don't consume our own. If they're not against us, they're for us.'*[13] Which is it? Are they for us or against us?"

---

13. Back on page 116.

"Yes. No. Maybe. I don't know. For crying in the beer, Thaddeus!" Jesus exhaled. "I can't keep track of every little thing I say, can I? I thought you guys were writing all this down."

"I did write it down," Judas objected, showing Jesus his notes.

"Never mind," Jesus sighed. "You should try to imagine, if you can, a reality that is robust and complex enough to hold two such logically incompatible statements. And hold both as true. The same Bible that says 'Be joyful always,' also has a book named Lamentations. Go figure."

"And besides," he added to both the inquisitors and to Judas (not *that* Judas), "both of these statements can be understood as valid in that there is no room for either for neutrality. The train is moving and you have to pick a side."

14. Troubled By Emptiness

Jesus reads to his disciples from Lesson Number Seven in the book *You Shall Cast out Demons: A Field Guide to Exorcisms and Expulsions. Third Edition*.[14] "When an unclean spirit of any type whether it be named Alichino, or Barbariccia, or even Libicocco,[15] when any of the unnumbered demons, named or unnamed is driven out of a man, it is forced to wander around in dry and waterless places far from the habitations of men. Tobit, you will remember, following the instructions of the angel Raphael, used burning fish livers to drive away the demon. When it fled, it went into the barren sands of Egypt."

"There, banished into the solitude of the wilderness, the demon will seek rest but, finding none, will be continually restless and irritable. It is irascible like us, restless finding no rest outside of God. So it will say to itself, 'I must go back to my house,' then it will return to the one from which it was driven it will find him swept clean and garnished, redecorated but still empty. And finding it thus, it will to itself again, 'Now I'll find seven of my brothers, and we'll make ourselves at home in him.' So the victim is even worse off than before . . ."

The lesson is interrupted when Bartholomew raises his hand and begins shouting. "Lord! Lord! Ooh, ooh Jesus!"

---

14. See APPENDIX 1

15. Alichino is "the Harlequin." Barabariccia is "Curly Beard." And Libicocco is "the Libyan Hothead." These three are the evil claws of the Malebranch. Dante Alighieri can tell you more about them if you're interested in learning more.

"Yes, Bartholomew?"

"Is that what happened to Mary Magdalene? She had seven demons in her, didn't she?"

Jesus sighs. It's not the question that bothers him. He's troubled by emptiness. By nothing and neutrality and by the drivel he finds in this textbook. He's not sure if it's intended as an actual practical handbook for casting out unclean spirits, or if it should be understood in some sort of allegorical or parabolic manner. Though, if it is to be understood as a sort of terrestrial narrative with divine meaning, the context seems to be missing. He tosses the book over his shoulder and says to his followers, "Forget it. Let's move on."

15. Thicker than the Water of the Womb

A woman from the crowd shouted at him as they moved on. "Blessed is the womb that carried you, Jesus! And the paps that you sucked when you were a babe."

Jesus stopped and turned to find her in the crowd. "Because I'm so special?" he called out to her. "No." he said, rejecting the saccharine syrup of the unsought and unwanted compliment. "I'm not here to have my ego stroked. The blood of the covenant is thicker than the water of the womb. Blessed, instead, is the one that hears the word of God, and hearing, does."

His mother, Mary, was following along with them at this time. She was mortified by both the blessing (for a discrete woman does *not* have her paps mentioned in public) and by her son's rejection of them. Had she been a woman of means, she may have hired a wet nurse to breastfeed her son, but she wasn't and she didn't. Even so, the rejection stung her just a bit. Rejection always stings.

16. Ignore the Church Growth Books

The people were gathered thick, pressed in and crushed on all sides. They'd come because they wanted to hear him speak—or to have him cure their sicknesses and bad dreams or both. They wanted to hear his message of course, but mostly they wanted him to take away their gout and their irritable bowels. Then, ignoring all the Church growth books and the advice of celebrity pastors, Jesus began to insult his audience.

"This generation is nothing but a wicked, evil generation." This isn't the way to win friends and influence people. This isn't the power of positive thinking. But screw that; he went on with his castigation. "This generation is fossilized oxygen. It is an acid cloud under pressure. You are the white powder residue of unidentified toxic substances. You are the rotting remains of a dead grey whale washed ashore in San Francisco Bay. You will get nothing but the sign of the anti-prophet, Jonah."

The crowd gasped and took a step back.

"Like Jonah to the Ninevites is the Son of Man to this generation. In fact, the men of Nineveh will stand up from their graves to condemn this generation. They had the courage to repent, but you . . . You! You get nothing.

17. Basic Biology

No one, when they have lighted a candle, covers it with a battleship or some other vessel. I've said this already, haven't I?[16] You don't light a lamp and then stash it in a secret place, under a basket, or down in the cellar, right? You put it up, where people can see it, right?

Right. Because the light of the body is in the eye. It's basic biology. Light enters the eye through the window that is the cornea and is immediately bent. Light has weight and can be bent, it's practically a solid. The bent light passes through the pupil in the iris like the shutter of a camera expanding and shrinking to control how much light is allowed through. The light passes through a crystalline lens and is tightly focused, then passes through a transparent gel and is blasted onto the retina where it is captured and processed into nerve impulses by millions of optic nerves.

Simple really.

If you have an *ayin tovah*, which is to say a good and generous eye, your whole tripartite self will be blazing with light. You will be illuminated. Our soul is the eye that comes from the Eye, the All-Seeing Eye, and just as the soul sees through bodily vision, so too does God, the Eye, the All-Seeing Eye of our heart, see through the eye of our heart in its pure state. This is how the prophets and clairvoyant saints saw those things which are hidden and future and hidden in the future, as well as the hidden thoughts of man. This is both sight and insight.

---

16. See page 90.

But if you, like the basilisk, the cockatrice, or the beholder, have an evil eye, an *ayin rah*, which is a stingy, greedy, eye, well, you'll only have darkness, won't you? Only despair. Nothing else is available to the selfish eye. When others celebrate, you will curse. When they laugh, you will suffer. *Schadenfreude* will be your watchword, though you'll not see it, of course. Darkness and all . . . You aren't blindly ignorant, but willfully blind. How great is your darkness, how complete. Blighted and blinded.

Let's say it again: If you have an *ayin rah*,[17] a stingy, greedy eye you'll have only darkness. Darkness and despair. But we'll have no evil eye here. Spit three times! *Ptui! Ptui! Ptui!* Beware, lest ye be filled with only the darkest of lights.

18. Bitter Table Talk

As he spoke an American Evangelical[18] approached him to invite him to dinner. So Jesus went and sat down to meat with him. The American Evangelical, having observed Jesus' companions who were sex workers and socialists, and having observed Jesus' stubborn refusal to adhere to the established social mores of polite and pious society said to his coreligionists, "Look! This man doesn't even make ritual ablutions before the meal. How can we trust him?"

Jesus said to him. "Oh, you Evangelicals! You anti-factual, rugged individualists dressed exactly alike. You'll wash and scrub and scour the outside of the cup and saucer but, *whoops!* You forgot to clean the inside. And the inside of your cup is full of extortion and wickedness, full of jimson weed, extortion, and wicked volcanic ash, with dust bowl storms and mildewed books. You're full of the bitter anthrax of drug addiction and hysterical blindness. You fools and pratting coxcombs have the appearance but not the substance. You're all hat, no cattle."

"Now, I realize that this is bitter table talk, but it must be said. It must be seen. What you should do is give alms from what you have—then everything will be clean for you, everything will be wholesome and pure. You'll see."

---

17. Or an Ayn Rand, which comes to the same thing.

18. Though the word 'Evangelical' does contain the word 'angel,' I have serious doubts about their message.

19. Alas and Woe

"Alas and Woe!" he said. "You Evangelicals give tithe on everything down to the golden kitchen herbs and mint. Not even rue is excluded.[19] But you neglect justice and love. Keep both, but the one is definitely more important.

"Woe and be-damned!" he said to them. "You love the uppermost, box seats in halls of Congress, and salutations in the market. You get off on respect but give none."

"Be-damned and hell!" he said. "Hypocrites! You *munafiqeen!* You're like unmarked graves beneath people's feet. Unmarked and unnoticed barrows. No warning, no tell—just a step into putridity and disease."

One of the lawyers[20] around him spoke up and said, "You're insulting us, and we won't stand for it. This is slander and religious persecution and we will file suit against you if you do not stop." But Jesus just kept on.

"Hell and be-damned!" he said. "You pile up obligations and requirements and rules for others that you'd never take upon yourselves. You know your rights, by God. You won't live in fear. You won't have *your* freedoms taken away."

"Be-damned and woe" he said to them. "You build marble monuments and bronze statues for the prophets. I've seen the way you honor the Reverend Martin Luther King Jr. But you know that your fathers killed him the same way they killed the holy ones before him. And, what is more, deep down inside your darkened selves, you know that you'd love to get some of that action. The blood of all the long ages of sages and teachers is pooling beneath your feet. Look at you, your finger is already on the trigger of your gun. You'll go down to your death, drowning in the depths of their accumulated blood."

"Woe and alas to you," he said. "Because you've taken away the key to knowledge. You are obfuscating obstructionists. You've seen the treasure inside and refuse anyone else entry. You're gated communities, literally and metaphorically."

Then the lawyers and Evangelicals turned on him and began a furious attack with a barrage of rapid fire, unanswerable questions and barely veiled

---

19. Amateur demonologists take note: rue can be used to drive off hysterical demons. They dislike its bitter aroma, which irritates their lungs, and its mutagenic and hepatotoxic oils which burn their sensitive skin and damage their livers.

20. Evangelicals love lawyers, yo, and cops too. They're all about that law and order shit!

innuendo. They rage tweeted and spewed their bile on Herod's FOX news, waiting, waiting, waiting for a day when they could make their revenge.

20. Self-Inflation and No Beer

The multitudes gathered now in greater and greater numbers to hear him crowded together cheek to cheek and jowl by jowl. They were pressed in so tightly together that they were beginning to trample each other. Now, the disciples were no Hell's Angels, and this wasn't the Altamont Raceway, but things were definitely getting out of hand. It was all descending into chaos. In the heat of the sun they were dying of the cold. One way or another the pressing darkness had to go. But first he would speak to his disciples.

"Beware of the hypocrites. With them it's all self-inflation and no beer."

"Honoré Balzac says that, 'Our worst misfortunes never happen, and most miseries lie in anticipation.'[21] But he's wrong, or at least he's not completely correct. You can anticipate this, count on it: Nothing is covered that won't be uncovered and discovered. There is no secret that won't be known. What you've whispered in the dark and shadow will be heard in the light. What you've spoken *sotto voce* in the closet will be shouted from the rooftop."

"Do not fear those who can kill the body but nothing more. Fear neither the elected nor the appointed archons, elementals, sheriffs, national guardsmen, nor the armored riot squads dispatched from Capitol City— even if the Prince of Persia himself leads them."

"Do not fear their illegal choke holds, or their CS cyanocarbon tear gas. Don't fear their bludgeons and batons, or their rifles and shotguns, their flash bangs and smoke grenades. Do not fear those who kill with the full authority of the state, who murder under the blessing and badge of the throne. Though they may attack you (and they will), do not be afraid of them. Though they may strike you about the face and in the gut (and they will) do not fear them. Though they may blind you, bind you, and shoot you from behind (and they most certainly will), do not fear them. Be bold. You are the cosmic gladiatorial display, a spectacle for all the world, condemned to death by the powers that be, but rewarded by God. I know this is easy enough to say and that words are cheap. Would it help if I show you how?"

---

21. Everyone seems to know that Balzac wrote this, but no one seems to know where.

"Be wary. Yes. And cautious too, but do not fear the ones that can kill only the body and nothing more. You are more than body and martyrdom has no room for terror. Instead, fear the judgment of God and the Valley of Gehenna where the kings of Israel once burned incense along with the bodies of their sons and daughters, where the worm never dies, *non inclinabitur in saeculum saeculi.*"

"Five sparrows can be bought for two bronze assarions.[22] Cheap and never more than ten for seven cents, per Diocletian's imperial edict. And yet, not one of them is forgotten of God even when the shadows come. And you, as evil as you are, are worth more than sparrows."

"Whoever acknowledges me in plain-sight public, will be recognized with honors before the host of holy angels. Whoever denies me, shall likewise be denied before the same. With public acknowledgment comes public recognition. Denial brings denial. Speak a word of blasphemy against the Son of Man, and it can be forgiven (no matter what those loudmouths in the Bible-Belt declare), but blasphemies against the Eternal Spirit cannot. Calumnies of me won't weigh much in the end, but disloyalty to the truth will feel the weight of forever."

"When they bring you before the magistrates, the judges, the lawyers and priests, don't go before them with despondency. The Spirit of Truth, in that very hour, will give you the words you need."

21. *They Still Wanted More*

Someone in the Modern American Version of this story said to him, "Teacher, tell my brother to divide the family inheritance with me."

But Jesus said to him, "Friend, who appointed me to be judge or arbitrator over the two of you? Get a job, man! Earn your own money. Buy your own bootstraps"

And he said to those there with him, "Take care! Be prepared for all kinds of greed; for there are many who would exploit an absolutely unAmerican class warfare to take your abundant possessions away from you."

Seeing that they still wanted more, he said, "Shall I coin a similitude for you? And what would you purchase with that silver, I wonder?" Then he told them a parable so that he could hit them a straight lick with a crooked stick.

---

22. You'll have to consult the exchange rate to convert that to farthings.

"What should we say about the rich man who lived long with his wealth upon the land, sustaining himself with vitamin regimens and supplements? He profited from land investments and secretly negotiated armament sales. But none of these could give him the length of days he desired, so he began taking a series of increasingly exotic treatments to extend his life and his profits. He had whole blood transfers and spliced-gene therapy. He ingested a mélange of pharmaceutical troches. His private doctors gave him daily injections of Razal Gel and altered carbon cortical stacks to extend both his life and his income."

"And still he thought, 'What am I to do? I have not lived long enough to enjoy my wealth.' Then he said, 'This is what I will do: I will begin viral blast treatments and buy black market organs to replace my worn out parts. RNA resourcing, nano-filament rejuvenation, and applied phlebotinum routines are not enough. I will hide my wealth in off-shore and Swiss accounts and drink the lachrymose essence of the grimalkin younglings. Then I will live long in the land with my wealth.'"

Figure 27–Won't you carry me over for another year?

"But Death, who comes to us all sooner or later, stood near to him that very night and said, 'You fool! You failed to consider the estate tax, and tonight your life is demanded of you. And all the wealth that you have accumulated, whose will it be? The federal government! So it is with those who store up treasures without the advice of a good tax lawyer.'"

What shall we say of him? Maybe it's not important what we say *about* him. Maybe we have no declarative sentences appropriate for the occasion. Sometimes there are only questions. Questions like: Is your money clean?

Are your hands? Is your money good? Is it *that* good? Is your heart? Will your money buy you an eternal estate on the other side? And where would you sleep if it did?

22. Fear Not Little Flock

"Be not careful" is better than "take no thought," I suppose, but they both sound like bad advice. I understand that we are more than body and, I mean, I want to trust him and take him at his word, but is it practical? Is it advisable? The body is more than clothes and I am more than my doubt, right?

Oh, Jesus, help me.

Consider the ravens, right? They were the first birds to be called out by name and by species in the Bible, in the story of Noah and the ark, ravens as dark as King Solomon's luscious hair. They neither sow nor reap—the lazy freeloaders. They just expect that God will take care of them. They don't have storehouses or barns; God just feeds them. And we're worth more than ravens, right? Worth more than sparrows, and, presumably, more than ravens . . . [23]

And here's another: Can you, by force of will, or by yoga exercise, or with essential oils add a single cubit[24] to your lifespan? Will better education or a better job make your life taller? It's a Tristan Tzara kind of question: Can you add twenty inches to your age? Play the cosmic harmonica for toothpaste pastry. It's nonsense.

Put aside the ravens for a bit, and consider the lilies. I have both Stargazer lilies and Daylilies growing in the backyard. I've even considered trying to grow a couple of Voodoo lilies. Look them up. They're beautiful but disgusting and terrible. But go ahead look them up and then consider

---

23. Of course, we haven't forgotten that chapter twenty-three of the Midrash *Pirkei de-Rabbi Elizer* tells us that the raven that old Noah released from the ark, the raven that did not return, didn't return to the ark because it was busy devouring the corpses of those drowned by the great flood, picking out the eyes first like some sort of carrion delicacy, so . . . there's that. And the Qur'an tells us that It was the raven that taught Cain to bury his murdered brother. So go ahead and consider the ravens.

The nagging voice in the back of my head reminds me to mention the raves that fed the prophet Elijah and the ravens that still guard, after all these years, the tomb of Saint Vincent of Saragossa.

24. That's eighteen to twenty-one inches for those of you who may be more familiar with the metric system.

the lilies. They're even lazier than the ravens. They don't work. They don't spin, or stitch, or sew, but God takes care of them anyway. And not even King Shlomo was ever dressed half so fine as they. And if God dresses the ephemeral grass, which grows up in a day so that I have to mow it twice a week to keep in good graces with my retired neighbor, if God clothes the grass and flowers in splendor like this, what more will he do for those he loves?

If we give up Albert Schweitzer's imminent eschatology, are we also forced to give up Jesus' ethical teaching? Or are we expected to radically reinterpret it to the point that not even Jesus himself would recognize it? Do we, by our living, by our radical every day following, make kingdom living possible in the regular every day, down-to-earth world? Do we make it relevant? How do we make it something better than anxious living of pagan kings in this world of dust and grit?

"Sell what you have and give alms." This is one way we will do it. "Keep your thesaurus[25] in heaven where no thief can corrupt it and no sticky-fingered moth can steal it. Keep it in heaven where rust never sleeps. And if we seek heaven, do we find earth thrown in as well? "Fear not, little flock. It is your Father's good pleasure to give you the kingdom. It's what he wants to do."

Oh, Jesus, help me.

23. Absolutely Thoughtless Days

"Keep your loins bounds up and your boots laced. Keep your lamps lit. Be ready and watching like the Grigori Watchers of the fifth heaven; they never sleep but observe and report all things to the Lord above. Be ready and watching like servants watching for the master to return from a long ceremony. Be ready the moment he knocks on the door."

"The master, when he returns and finds them ready, will change into his work clothes, and make them sit down to meat so that he can serve them himself. Even if he comes during the second or third shifts. No matter how late it is. If the Goodman of the house knew when the thief would come, the house couldn't be burgled. Could it? Be ready for the Son of Man comes when you think not."[26]

---

25. A thesaurus is literally a treasure house or store house, a depot, cache, vault, repository, archive, warehouse . . .

26. Which must mean any time in these absolutely thoughtless days, am I right?

Peter, who'd been swinging his fencing foil and lunging and shouting *"en garde"* at the other disciples, stopped and stared at Jesus. "Are you saying this to everyone or to just us?" he asked dully.

"Who is the faithful servant?" Jesus said, answering a question with a question. "Who is wise if not the one that the master finds doing his job? When the Master returns, he'll put that one in charge of everything."

Peter didn't seem to get it. He went back to lunging and shouting 'Ha!' as he swooshed his foil through the air.

"But I tell you, Peter, that one supervisor, you know the one I'm talking about, the one who, because he knows that the boss isn't going to be back for quite a while, starts to dick around the place, putting his feet up on the desk, taking naps in the back office, beating the staff, beating off in the bathroom, and getting drunk in the kitchen, and all the while laughing and saying to the rest of the staff, 'Know what I mean, buddy?' in that ridiculous and inconsistent accent that he has. When the boss gets back and catches him unaware, he will chop the miscreant masturbator into pieces and throw the pieces out into the dark."

24. *Burn It Down*

Jesus and his companions watched the news with horror—the rioting, the buildings on fire, people shouting in the streets, broken glass, shattered skulls, horse mounted police trampling protestors for carrying nothing more dangerous than cardboard signs, riot squad officers firing pepper balls at reporters and cameramen, firing tear gas and flash grenades into the crowds to provoke them to violence. It was on every channel.

"Jesus," said Matthew. It may have been a curse. It may have been a prayer. Both felt appropriate. "I'm so sick of the division and the strife. Can't people just get along?"

Jesus turned off the television and scolded them, "You think I've come to bring peace? Do you think that's why I'm here? Shit, no. I came to start a fire, and I wish to God it were already burning. Anoint the world with the kerosene oil of salvation and light the whole thing up. Oh God of burning, cleansing flame, send the fire."[27]

---

27. The Emperor Nero was blamed for the burning for the burning of Rome. He in turn blamed the Christians. But can you blame him? Have you read their propaganda? Have you read the words of their founder? "I've come to set the world on fire . . ." You can't trust these agitators, these arsonists. Do they want to see the fires? Let's use *them*

"Burn it down!" whispered Andrew beneath the *keffiyeh* he already had wrapped around his face, and shook his tightly clenched fist in the air.

"But," Matthew objected. "Destruction of property isn't a valid form of protest."

Jesus laughed. "Just wait a few chapters," he said and laughed again.[28]

"Jesus, Jesus! Can't you be civil? Can't people just, like, get along with each other?" Said Matthew.

"No," Jesus said in brusque response. "The time for that has passed. When the fire burns it will show people for who they really are. And when people show you who they are, believe them. Don't make excuses for them in the name of mere civility. Manners are the hypocrisy of nations.[29] There is no neutrality here. There can be no moderates. You must choose a side. They have.

Remember it's going to be divided houses from here on out—three against two, two on three. This is the uprising, the struggle, the *intifada*. It's the end of traumatized truth and tortured dreams, and the end falls hard. Fathers and mothers will turn against their children. Children will turn their parents in. This world will be upside down until all is made right. Till one can walk on through this world without feeling like they're in hell anymore."[30]

Then he got out his guitar and began to play an old bluesy riff. "House catch a fire," he sang. "And there ain't no water around. If your house catch a fire, and there ain't no water all around. Throw yourself out the window, let the doggone shack burn on down." He put the guitar down, then said, "I have a baptism coming, and you can see how I'm straightened and constrained until it is fully accomplished. I keep telling you about this. But no one is listening to me."

---

as torches.

28. He said this maybe, but the table flipping, whipcord violence doesn't actually appear in this narrative. You'll have to look elsewhere for that particular story.

29. Jesus appears to be quoting Balzac again. Balzac, *Physiologie du Mariage*.

30. If the rules governing the quotation of popular song lyrics weren't so byzantine and the cost so prohibitive, Jesus at this point might have said something about the roof being on fire and letting the entire incestuous edifice burn to the ground and of water being unnecessary to the situation. And it might have been needlessly provocative. On the other hand, Jesus was being purposefully provocative so perhaps the vulgarity of the quotation might have been appropriate.

James and John looked at each other in confusion. "Where was this pyromania when we were turned out from that Samaritan village?" they asked each other sadly.

25. Destabilization May Come as a Shock

IDENTIFIED = Orange red Antares clouds rising in the west of the Scorpion's eye.
UNDERSTOOD = There will be showers and there will be rain.
IDENTIFIED = Strong south winds.
UNDERSTOOD = There will be increasing desert heat, one hundred degrees and five and rising, coupled with decreasing sexual attentiveness. What is the temperature required to turn bone to ash? Upwards of fourteen-hundred degrees. The wind is expected, but frigid marital destabilization may still come as a shock.
IDENTIFIED = Your meteorological prognostications and stock market divinations have reached a level of unparalleled excellence. You've mapped the face of the darkness of deep space, the topography of the earth, and the contours of the Marianas Trench beneath the earth, but you still can't understand what's going on right now today, at this crucial nexus on this timeline.
UNDERSTOOD = You have your observations and your science. You have all the phenomena that can be perceived and understood by anyone of normal intelligence, and upon which reasonable men can agree. But you are not reasonable men. Right now today is always the crucial time, but you hypocrites are shouting "I see no evidence!" from secret, underground bunkers and refusing to accept the results. The truth is that you *refuse to see* anything that would contradict or challenge your privileged existence. It is a selfish ignorance. You *refuse* to comprehend. And this is the darkest kind of blindness. No one is blinder than the one who *will* not see.

26. The Very Last Copper

If Jeff is being called into court to face his accuser, or rather, if Jeff is being called into court to face his accuser *again*, if he's being called 'evil', if he's being called 'a corrupter', if he's being called 'a lazy, socialist, dissenter, debtor,[31] shouldn't he at least make an attempt to settle whole thing before he reaches the black robed magistrate. Shouldn't he be trying to settle the whole thing before the whole thing settles him? Better out of the courts than in the cells, am I right? Or else he may never get out, not till he's paid the very last copper. And Jeff doesn't have very many coppers as it is.

27. Were These More Extravagant Sinners than Anyone Else?

People don't talk about them as often as they should these days, but some of us still remember the Galileans that Pontius Pilate had killed in those poor and wretched days. Those days were a turbulent river, a torrent of conflicting ideals and passion, days with no expectation of joy. No hope, no peace. The Herodians, the Pharisees, the Sadducees, the Scribes, the Sanhedrin, the Essenes, the Zealots, the Galileans (not to mention the Romans). Each of them had their own objectives. Each of them pushed and pulled against the others to shape the world according to their own interests. And we were dashed against them like ships between Scylla and Charybdis.

Pontius Pilate was tasked by the Emperor in Rome to keep order in the distant Judean province and to put down even the slightest breath of dissent or revolt by splashing the blood of troublemakers on the streets and dumping their corpses into shallow lakes. And Pilate considered the Galileans the most seditious people in the land, if not the whole Empire. He considered them more dangerous than the fanatics he slaughtered in Jerusalem, more dangerous than the Samaritans he butchered at Mount Gerizim and more dangerous than the Fascists who were, after all, very fine people.

One of those dangerous malcontents was Judas the Galilean,[32] who led his own theocratic nationalist movement in the foothills of Galilee. His thugs shouted "Blood and Soil!" before hurling themselves against their enemies (which included just about everyone). Judas was killed, his forces defeated, and his followers were scattered. I may say more about him later, in another writing.

But Pontius Pilate, the Prefect of Judea, was a tyrant, and some people still remember the Galileans he had killed during the Passover festival though they do not discuss them openly.[33] He hid a squad of his special

---

31. And he has been called all of these things. Some of these things *may* even be true. Who knows?

32. AKA Judas of Gamala. AKA Judas the Unreplaceable. AKA *La Hachade Guerra*.

33. They have forgotten, however, that the first airplane attack on U.S. soil was not the

forces within a crowd of celebrants—ranks of undercover soldiers within the groups of musicians playing harps, and children carrying flags and embroidered runners. When those Galileans, who were in no way connected to Judas the Galilean's band, entered the plaza, Pilate's forces flung explosives into the crowd, killing the Galileans along with a number of worshipping bystanders and clergy. Their blood was intermingled with past pains, individual mistakes, and the sacrifices made upon the altar.

Some in the crowd with Jesus said to him, "We deplore the violence of the Galileans' rioters. While we understand and may even sympathize to some extent with their grievances, there is no excuse for the blatant destruction of private property. They must have been rioters. Otherwise the soldiers would have had no cause to attack them." When the rest of the crowd began shouting them down, they vociferated more vehemently. "Of course their women were raped and their sons were strung up to die on trees. Of course the Roman forces occupy their community; we see them everywhere, don't we? But what can you expect if you refuse to respect the police?"

Others in the crowd asked Jesus about all this. "Why do bad things happen to good people? Everything happens for a reason right, Jesus?"

Jesus dismissed this flaccid theodicy. "The question isn't so much *why* is there suffering, but why is it *distributed* the way that it is? Why is suffering so indiscriminate? Why are the prosperous wicked while those who are striving and struggling to keep faith with God are left to suffer on the floor? *This* is what we don't understand. You want causality? You want a 'why'? Do you think that there is a direct correlation between sin and calamity? Were these Galileans greater sinners than any other Galilean?"

"What about the eighteen who were crushed with the Tower of Siloam collapsed?" he went on. "Were they more extravagant sinners than anyone else in Jerusalem? Don't ask me about hurricanes and tornados, or earthquakes or cancer. Don't ask me about mudslides or meningitis. These are not punishments But, I'll tell you this: Unless you repent, you'll die like everyone else."

Japanese attack on Pearl Harbor, but the 1921 Battle of Blair Mountain when the United States government dropped bombs (including gas and chemical shells) on striking union workers.

28. Open Ended and Uncertain

He told them this parable: A man had a fig tree planted in his vineyard. But when he came looking for fruit on it he found none. He said to his gardener, "For three years now I have been coming again and again to look for fruit on this damned tree. I've waited long enough. I want it cut down. Why should it take up the ground that could be used by more productive plants?"

"Sir," the gardener replied, "leave it one more year and give me time to dig round it and manure it: it may bear fruit next year; if not, then you can cut it down."

And there Jesus concluded the tale. He told this parable but he didn't end it, and what is a story without an ending? Well, it's not really a story, is it? So let's try out a few possible endings. Think of it as a sort of Choose Your Own Parable Adventure:

Ending 1—Then the owner answered the gardener, "Do as you have said." And the gardener lavished great care on the fig tree for a year—watering it, fertilizing the ground, carefully pruning it, but at the end of the year there were still no figs. The owner returned and said, "Dig it up and throw it into the fire. And let the ground be given to another that will bear fruit."

This may be the most obvious ending, and fitting with the context of the preceding chapter wherein Jesus spoke of imminent judgement, but it is not, by any means, the only possible ending. Shall we consider a few more possibilities?

Ending 2—Then the owner answered the gardener, "Do as you have said." And the vinedresser lavished great care on the fig tree for a year—watering it, fertilizing the ground, carefully pruning it, but at the end of the year there were still no figs. The owner returned and said, "Give it another year. There still may be hope for this tree."

Ending 3—Then the man answered the gardener, "No. This tree will not produce any fruit here. Dig it up and move it elsewhere. Perhaps it will do better on the other side of the garden."

Ending 4—Then the man answered the gardener, "No. This tree will never produce any fruit. Cut it down. But sell the timber to the carpenter. There is still some good, some use to be found in this tree even in its unfruitfulness."

Ending 5—Then the owner answered the gardener, "Do as you have said." And the gardener lavished great care on the fig tree and, over the course of the next year it produced more fruit than any other tree in the garden, enough to feed the entire community.

Ending 6—Then the owner answered the gardener, "Do as you have said." And the gardener lavished great care on the fig tree and, over the course of the next year it began to produce fruit—not as much as the other trees, but still more than nothing and the owner was satisfied.

Ending 7—Then the man answered the gardener, "Do as you have said." And the gardener lavished great care on the fig tree for a year—watering it, fertilizing the ground, carefully pruning it, but shortly before the end of the year the tree was struck by lighting and burned to the ground.

Hey, the future's uncertain. Magic Eight Ball says, "Reply hazy. Try again." The story is open ended and uncertain. Shit happens sometimes. Disasters too, and we don't know what time we have left in this world.

29. Not by Her Bootstraps

See her now—a woman long crippled and bent over by a spirit of infirmity. She'd been bound over for eighteen years with no help and no relief. Like the man with the muckrake in John Bunyan's allegory, forever looking nowhere but down, this woman had come to doubt, she'd come to disbelief and to a fear that heaven was nothing more than a fable. She could not lift herself up—not by her bootstraps, not by herself. Not at all.

And Jesus saw her too. And he called her to himself. She approached him, creaking and groaning. "What is your name, daughter?" he asked.

"Miriam," she said in the smallest of voices, hardly a whisper.

"Jesus smiled for her. "Oh, Miriam don't you weep, don't you moan." He said, and then, "Woman, thou art loosed, released and liberated. You are free." He laid his hands on her and immediately she was, as he said, free. Her stiffened, crippled spine stretched straight and true. Hear it now—all the snaps and pops along her vertebrae and neck as she extended her frame. Crepitus cavitations resounding in the nearly silent synagogue. She sighed, then giggled like the girl she hadn't been in many, painful years.

"Glory be," she said. "Glory, glory, glory be."

See her now—with a smile on her face as she lifted her hands and her face up towards heaven to receive her celestial crown and to praise the God of healing. The spirit of infirmity was gone.[34] Infirmity is the spirit sent by

---

34. And truth be told—we hardly saw that spirit of infirmity here. The story began as an exorcism but wound up as a laying on of hands kind of healing miracle.

Satan. Bondage too. But Liberty, sweet release and freedom, is the spirit sent from God.

But see it now: the ruler of the synagogue was still present, and was not pleased. "Objection!" he shouted. "Objection!" The congregation turned their attention away from the newly liberated woman, and from Jesus. "There are six days in the week," he lectured them. "There are six proper days in the week for work and toil. There are six days in the week when she could have been healed, but this—the Sabbath—this isn't one." He objected to Jesus but did not address him. Not directly.

"You pilgarlic," Jesus chortled. "You simpleton. You know perfectly well that each one of you would loose the knots to untie your ox or ass so as to lead it to water, even on the Sabbath. You know that it's legal to lead your horse to water even if you can't make him drink. And ought not this daughter of Abraham, this woman bound by satanic oppression, be loosed on this Sabbath day? What better day for it?"

His adversaries were ashamed and the people rejoiced. Do you see it now? Glory, glory, glory be!

30. Would We Know It if We Saw It

There are rhetorical questions that demand no answer. There are true statements and there are false statements. On that point we need no debate. But can there be a false question?

Never mind. It's not really important. Let's ask another question instead: What is the Kingdom of Heaven like? Would we know if we saw it?

How about a mustard seed? Is a seed alive? Or dead? Is it merely dormant? I don't really know. But when this little seed is cast into the field it grows, it waxes, spreads. It becomes a visionary tree that is home to all manner of birds and beasts. And what is that?

What is the kingdom of heaven like? Would we know it if we saw it?

How about leaven? Or yeast, which is usually given as a symbol of hypocrisy and of evil, something to be purged and thrown out. But let's throw that out for now. The kingdom of heaven is like the yeast that a woman hides and folds within three measures of meal until the whole thing is risen.[35]

---

35. A quick calculation: three measures equals sixty-four pints equals thirty-five liters. In the words of the revered (if not yet beatified) Winston Zeddemore, "That's a big Twinkie."

31. Many Will Try

He and his companions continued travelling through the cities and the village, through every little rural community along the way, teaching and preaching and healing as they went. Still the wen of Jerusalem loomed in the distance. The shadows of its walls and towers stretched out before him. There were low roads for low men into the high places of the Holy City. Its grocery stores and walk-up flats, its cheap restaurants, pawnshops, pool halls and speakeasies called to him. He would go to the Jerusalem of the storefront brothels and churches. To Jerusalem where the hostels were filled in equal measures with low-class hipsters and police informants and vermin (of both the rodent and political varieties). He would go up to Jerusalem where gun dealers and cheapskate Senators made bathroom deals with undercover cops, where CIA operatives met to swap information with the KGB. There was little leadership and much confusion in that city and this was exploited by the violent gangs that effectively controlled the streets: the Hospitaliers, the Templars, and the Teutonic orders, each marking their territory with peculiar symbols and with sprays of urine. But even so, Jerusalem the City on the Hill, drew him on and called him up.

One of those with him stopped him. "Lord, I have a question. One of the Esdras, I can't remember which, told us that the Most High made the world for the sake of the many. And that the world that is to come is reserved for the sake of the few. But the world as we know it seems to exist for the pleasure of the few, while the many scrabble and squabble for the scraps that fall off the edge of their table. They own the land and the seeds. They control the seas and the water rights. And they would, if they could, take the skies from us as well. They own the banks and the police, the factories and the roads. This ain't the free world, not yet. It's their world, they just allow us to live in it. If we're lucky."

Jesus said to him, "Is there a question in there somewhere?"

His disciple nodded. "Yes. Tell us Lord, are the few to be saved, or the many?"

Jesus nodded too. "The rich will certainly get all that they deserve, all of it and more. But do not worry about that just now. Live in the now and make the most of it. Strive instead to enter through the strait gate. Many will try but few will succeed."

Jesus continued, "If the owner of the café locks up for the night, if he pulls down the gate and snaps the lock, no matter how hard you bang upon the door, he's not going to open up for you. Even if Karen says, 'We have a reservation! I want to speak to the manager. I've eaten here before and I *will* leave a bad review,' the owner will say, 'Do I know you? Go away!'"

"There's going to be shit-ton of swearing in those days. Weeping and gnashing of teeth, grinding bicuspids. You'll see Father Abraham, Jacob—the angel wrestler, and good ol' laughing boy Isaac, but only from a distance. Meanwhile the outcast and rejected people from the far four corners will be streaming in for the feast."

"Come the *ekpyrosis,* that universal conflagration at the end of everything, there will be a complete particle reversal. Up will be down. *Adroit* will become *gauche*. First will swap with last and all will be right and good again. Are you afraid to admit that a Socialist redistribution of wealth is a practical putting into practice of that aphorism that the last shall be first? Maybe you are feeling that warm wind at your back even now and it frightens you."

32. More like a Mutt than Man

That same day, a few hours later, we were still somewhere in Galilee. Or maybe it was Perea. Our itinerary during those traveling days was rather peripatetic and it was often difficult to mark our location. And Heisenberg was right: I can tell you what, but I can't say where. What I do recall is that it was that same day when the invisible Pharisees caught up with us.

I call them invisible because you so rarely see ones like this. Sure there was Nicodemus and Joseph the Arimathean who were able to shake themselves loose, but were there more? Possibly. Still—how many Sadducees can you name?

Anyway, these Pharisees caught up with us and they said, "Get out! Go away! Depart hence and forthwith." Sounds friendly enough, right? But they went on. "You are in danger. Flee for the Tetrarch will kill you. He's tired of you and your meddling in his territories. If you're not out before midnight he's going to have someone blow your brains out. His agents are already looking for you.[36] They may be here at any moment."

"Satan is a two legged rattlesnake and Herod is a fox, or rather, a vixen." Jesus told them. "He's a second rate scion. He's never held the title or worn the crown of a king and this has forever rankled him." The disciples chuckled. "Still," Jesus said, "He's worse than Nixon—just as vicious and not

36. Martin Luther King Jr. received similar threatening phone calls, as many as forty a day.

nearly as subtle. He's more like a mutt than a man to be held accountable to codes of morality and ethics. He's a bloviator with a bad toupee posing as one of the big men of big affairs. But, pay it no mind He's unimportant. He is a poser and a jackass."

The Pharisees who'd come with the warning begged Jesus to listen to their advice and to leave immediately, but he waved them off.

"You tell that vituperative vixen that I'll be here the rest of today and here again all day tomorrow, casting out devils and performing cures just as I have day after day here. Then, on the day after that, I'll be on my way out of his realms. On the third day I'll be perfected. So let him try out his weather weapons against me, if he'd like. Have him call up a tornado to carry me off or derecho winds to blow me away. Maybe he could sic the Bull Connor dogs on me. Perhaps he could use other, more exotic means—perhaps he could use a crystal methamphetamine bacteria blast to destroy me. I know he keeps a sample in a little glass vial that was sent to him from the Tarkus Experimental Energy Laboratories. Maybe he could get something on loan from the U.S. Defense Advanced Research Projects Agency.[37] One of their binaural hypnosis rays, beamed from satellites in orbit far above us, or one of their neurasthenia guns, or the new Pyschospontaneous Fission techniques they've developed, which are able to coax radioactive elements to violently discharge their electrons from a distance using psychic energy. Let him seek me if he will. If he wants to make a move against me, he knows where to find me."

"But Jesus, he wants to kill you," they pleaded with him.

"Call no man happy," Jesus quoted to them, "until he's dead. So said Solon to King Croesus.[38] Even the *little death* would be a happy ending, I suppose."

The Pharisees stared at him in disbelief. In incomprehension.

Jesus rolled his eyes and turned away from them. "Jerusalem," he called over his shoulder. "Jerusalem is where the prophets always meet their deaths."

---

37. U.S. munitions and armaments—made by and for terrorists. The motto of the U.S. Defense Advanced Research Projects is "War is good for business. War is good business. War is good."

38. At least that's what Herodotus says that he said.

Tempus Fugit

33. Will You Even See Me When You See Me?

Oh Jerusalem. Woe Jerusalem. Jerusalem that kills the prophets along with the Palestinians. City of fire. City of swords and blades. City of blood and small pox. I would be your mother, but you refuse to have me. And now, once more my stomach tightens into a knot and my knees tremble. What tragic story, what desolate state! It will all be in your bloody hands when the bleeding time comes. Will you say, "Blessed is he who comes in the name of the Lord," when you see me? Would you recognize me if you saw me? Will you even see me when you see me?

34. A Rather Disappointing Christ

"Jesus, you've not given us any instruction on how to use our positions of power, or our wealth, that is to say our political influence. You've not told us how to manipulate the masses. You've not told us how to make people do what we want. Perhaps you could begin by telling us how large of an army will be necessary and if we should invalidate the peace agreements we have already signed? Should we bring back the chlorine, the phosgene gases along with the vomiting gas, chloropicrin? Can we open our stores of dichlorethyl sulfide, better known to the world as Mustard gas?[39] Can we begin reinvesting in nuclear missiles and the Space Defense Initiative? What is the proper role of propaganda in the governments we establish? Is it ethical, Jesus, to lie for matters of state or for espionage? I mean, we know that it is, but we'd like to hear you say it. We'd like for you to tell us how to do it better. Tell us how to be lords and kings, princes and prime ministers. Tell us how steal both elections and the hearts and minds of our enemies. Tell us how to win."

"No."

"Well, look, Jesus, if you can't answer, or if you *won't* answer, we'll be forced to look to other sources for guidance in these areas. We understand, obviously. It's not completely your fault. Your good news, your gospel of the Kingdom of Justice, and all that, doesn't really have anything to say to the physical structures or the political systems of this world. After all, all true religion is chiefly concerned with the individual and his personal, private, and entirely spiritual relationship with God. We get that. Yours is a *spiritual* kingdom. Esoteric, even. It has little practical application. We understand."

---

39. Which is not technically a gas, but is no less toxic for that.

A Life Known and Unknowable

"Obviously, you don't," Jesus said. "If you wanted to really understand you'd need to have the *Nur ad-Din*."

"Jesus, do you mean the 'Light of Faith,' or do you mean the twelfth century Emir of Damascus and Aleppo, who attacked Christian crusaders?"

"Which do you think I meant?"

"To be honest, Jesus, we can't understand why you'd be making a reference to anything in that barbaric Muslim tongue."

Well, I meant the Light of Faith, but I suppose you could do worse than Zangi's second son. He lived frugally, simply, not in luxury. For to live in luxury would be an offense to God who desires a just and equal society. He devoted himself to prayer and to study. A man of brain over brawn, he surrounded himself with scholars and teachers. Or, if you don't like the *Nur ad-Din*, perhaps you'd prefer *Salah ad-Din*, the Righteousness of the Faith."[40]

"Jesus, you're not suggesting that . . ."

"No. Of course not. But you're not really listening."

"We seem to have gotten off to a bad start, Jesus. Maybe we should start over. Let's begin at the beginning. Let's recite our catechism: What is the chief end of man? Man's chief end is to buy low and to sell high and to enjoy the profits forever."

Jesus shook his head. "I'm not sure you're remembering that correctly."

"All in all you're proving to be a rather disappointing Christ, Jesus of Nazareth. But we'll give it one more shot. Can you tell us the proper authoritarian structure for a pure American, Judeo-Christian society? One in which the state is autonomous, without concern for morality or ethics? This authoritarian structure is obvious in the godless, socialist nations, but it's still necessary in a nation like ours. We will, of course, have to rewrite some portions of the scripture. That passage from Isaiah, for example, 'All the nations are as nothing before him . . .' That's gotta' go. And the one that says, 'They are regarded as worthless and less than worthless,' that's just foolishness. We'll have to cut it out."

Jesus sighed but still said nothing.

"We are worthy, weighty gentlemen, Jesus. We are robust and rotund. If we are able to seize equality with God, why then that is our destiny. It is a manifest truth of the universe, and we will not have you disrespecting us or our leadership positions. We demand loyalty. Absolute, monetized loyalty.

---

40. Sultan of Egypt and Syria, Custodian of the Two Mosques, founder of the Ayyubid dynasty. But you knew that already.

So tell us, Jesus, here and now: What is the proper authoritarian structure for an American Christian society? And don't say socialism, Jesus. Don't even think it."

"You wouldn't believe me if I did. I mean, you didn't believe my mom when she said it. A capitalist, colonialist, imperialist Christ is no Christ."

"Well thanks for nothing, Jesus," they huffed. "You've just wasted our time."

35. A Rude Dinner Guest

Again on a Sabbath day he was sharing a dinner with a ruling member of the Pharisees. And there, among the Pharisees and rulers and lawyers was a man with dropsy.[41] His body had swollen with the buildup of fluids, and he was in continual pain. His skin was still stretched tight. He was often short of breath and he had much difficulty in breathing. He'd tried reducing his salt intake. His grandmother and other women of the village said that this sometimes helped. But it hadn't helped. He was still swollen and still in great pain.

Jesus saw this swollen man and immediately turned on his host and the lawyers and Pharisees gathered around the table. "Is it lawful to cure people on the Sabbath or not?" he asked them. But they had nothing to say, so he touched the man, cured him, and sent him away.

Notice this: it was Jesus who started the fight. It was Jesus who fired the first shot and threw the first punch. Jesus is the one who made a scene. Not the Pharisees. Not the lawyers. He is the instigator and the agitator. He is the disruptive element. And we've seen this scene before. The healing of the man with dropsy could have waited. There was nothing particularly life threatening about the condition. It wasn't a life or death, emergency situation. Jesus could have, easily, waited a few hours for the sun to set in the western sky, and then healed the man with no Sabbath day issues whatsoever.[42]

---

41. Dropsy is an old fashioned, out of date medical term for edema—an abnormal swelling, a condition marked by the buildup of watery fluids in the cavities and tissues of the body.

42. Though it's not even clear that there is a Sabbath day violation here. Jesus doesn't actually *do* any work. No work was performed. The laying on of hands is not work, not even by the most tortured definition of the word.

The lawyers and Pharisees sat in stunned silence. Jesus asked them a question, again deliberately phrasing his question so as to provoke them: "If one of you has a child,[43] or an ox that has fallen into a well, will you not immediately pull it out, even on a Sabbath day?"

Jesus was a rude dinner guest who deliberately and purposefully provoked a fight with his hosts, making an issue out of non-issues, and phrasing his emphatic question in a provocative way so as to force his audience to make a definitive answer. It was impolite. One doesn't discuss religion or politics at dinner, but Jesus does both. This, generally, is not the polite behavior of an invited guest.

36. A Pair of Parables for the Invitations

Let's say that you've been invited to the wedding reception, right. A real classy affair. None of that rubber chicken and cold, lumpy mashed potatoes. No, no, no. The good stuff: filet mignon, an open bar, and a good band[44] instead of a crappy DJ.

You wouldn't make an ass of yourself at this classy party by insisting on sitting at the head table, would you? The best man would come round behind you, tap you on the shoulder and tell you to move to the table at the back with Uncle Lenny and the mouth breathing cousins from Florida.

And when you're the one mailing out the invitations for the shindig with the tasty grub and the good liquor, don't invite your rich neighbor, the one with the new boat, or your boss with the bulging stock portfolio. You know you're just inviting them in the hope that they'll reciprocate and invite you to lunch at the country club. Instead you should invite the poor, and the crippled. Invite your disabled, veteran neighbor who's been living week to week on a fixed income. Invite him precisely because you know that he can't repay you. Take the advice of the cupbearer who said: "Eat the fat, drink sweet wine, and share with those who have nothing." This advice may come from one of my least favorite books of the Hebrew Bible, but it is good advice nonetheless. Reward will come later. What is the gospel if not good news now for the humiliated and the abused, the weak, the low and the contemptible nothings from the wrong part of town?

---

43. Or, as it is in some manuscripts, "an ass," and those two are sometimes indistinguishable, aren't they?

44. Pharaoh Necho and the Wafers is a great local band. You should check them out. They played at my cousin's wedding. Lots of fun.

Tempus Fugit

37. They Are Not My Friends

They sat together at the bar that had once been a Crusader's castle, sharing an afternoon beer. Neon beer signs and pennants for local sports teams hung on the exposed stone walls, as well as a bicycle, street signs and a pair of rowboat oars. A pair of arcade games and blinked and flashed in the corner. Strings of bare light bulbs were hung from the ribbed vault ceiling. One of them who had just passed tipsy but hadn't yet reached shitfaced, shouted out, "Blessed is anyone who will shares a friend with his bite . . . no . . . a bite with his friends in the Kingdom to come." The disciples cheered and toasted one another. Someone else shouted out, "Quiet, you *shikker*." And the disciples cheered again. Drinks sloshed. People laughed. Ah, those were good times.

"Let me tell you a story," Jesus said as he sipped his own tasty beverage. "There was this cat, a rich and good lookin' cat with reason to celebrate. So he invited his friends for a party. 'Come on up to my crib. Come share my joy. Everything's ready. Your place at my table is set.' But no one showed up for the party. Not a single one."

Jesus took another sip, and licked his lips. "Mmm. That's good. *Ein festbier in ein feste burg!*"[45] he said before continuing his story.

"The first of his so-called friends to respond said, 'So sorry, my man. I just bought a new house, and I gotta' go check it out.' Can you dig it? He bought the place sight unseen. The second friend sent him a text. 'I just bought a car and I'm gonna' take it out for a spin.' And another said, 'Dude, I just got married; I'm not going to be there.'"

The hall was quieter now. The jostling and rowdy patrons waited for the rest of the story. Jesus continued, "So this cool cat with the cause to celebrate, who was just a bit pissed that no one would come to his party, told his personal assistant, 'Bring me some guests for my party. I don't care who. Bring me anyone you can find. Bring blind junkies and crippled whores. Bring walking lepers, and lurching bravoes. Bring me some of those vermin eating saints. Bring me anyone who will come.' So the assistant went out and brought them in."

"But there were still empty seats at the table. And this cool cat was throwing a big shindig. Huge. So he said, 'Make another pass. Bring me more. More! I've got reason to celebrate and I want to party it up with all

---

45. Apparently Jesus should have said, "*Ein Festbier in einer festen Burg.*" He always had trouble with dative cases.

my friends and there's always room for another friend. There is always more in the sharing,'"

"But the so-called friends, the ones that I invited before—the ones who found excuses to decline—they are *not* my friends. I never knew them.'"

Then Jesus drained his beer, paid his tab and left a generous tip for the barmaid before heading to the restroom.[46]

38. *The Crux of the Matter*

Now this is going to piss some of you off, I'm sure. What can I say? I'll say what is true. I'll say what I know. What else can I do?

Many of you say that you are mine. But I'm sorry to tell you that it's not really true. You can't follow me, you can't be one of mine, if you don't hate your father, mother, wife, your children, brothers, sisters. Even your own life. You must hate it all. Hate Fatherland and Motherland. Hate home. Hate it all. Then you can follow me.

And if you follow me you'll carry a cross. Whole churches may have to be crucified, but this is how it goes. This is the crux of the matter: Whoever does not willingly pick up the *patibulum* cannot be my disciple. Remember, the cross is something that you carry and ultimately die upon. It has enormous weight. And remember this as well—this cross is voluntary. It's all *autothanatos* and self-sacrifice for me and mine.

39. *Consider First the Matter*

Consider: If the liar-in-chief,[47] while watching television, either in his underground Jerusalem bunker or his gold-plated New York penthouse apartment, makes an outlandish promise to build a wall or a tower—either one dubiously justified with a claim to the vagaries of that eternally sacred cow 'national security,' shouldn't you sit down and count the expense? Shouldn't you figure up the cost? How will he pay for it? Saying that 'Mexico will pay for it,' is not a realistic expectation. You've got to be smarter than that. You've got to think.

As Epictetus, with his three thousand drachma oil lamp advised, 'Consider first the matter, then what your nature can bear." Because when

---

46. Jesus turned water into wine, it's true, but he also turned beer into water.
47. Either the last one or the current one. Hell, consider the next one too...

your foolish leader is unable to complete the project (and he won't; he can't) he will be an object of rightful ridicule among the nations.

Consider also the King (who was the son of a King, and named for a leader of the Reformation) as he sat down to consider 'Can I win this war?' He realized that his army of Negros, supported by a few liberal whites, was grossly outnumbered. Even if they'd taken up arms, stormed the National Guard armories and liberated rifles and shotguns and grenades to use against their oppressors, even with ten or twenty thousand even it would be a bloodbath—with black bodies doing most of the bleeding. So the King made the moral, ethical, and eminently practical choice and went into battle with non-violent direct action and with love.

One of those obscure German philosophers said, "Thought is preceded by suffering." We might add that suffering is often preceded by a lack of thought. Another of the wisdom-loving Germans said, "It is not consciousness that determines life, but life that determines consciousness,"[48] and I know this is one is true. There are a great many individuals in positions of power who are living without a trace of consciousness—to say nothing of a conscience. Supreme authority and executive orders do not make a noble head of state. National emergencies expose the weak and reveal them to be nothing more than gangland murderers with expensive suits and bad spray tans. A life which is unlawful and lecherous, filled with old quarrels and new schisms cannot lead anything but more of the same—whether or not he manages to build his wall or his tower or his whatever.

Salt is good. 'Nothing is more useful than sunlight and salt,' said the Roman, Pliny the Elder.[49] Salt is good, but not so much when it loses its flavor, and flavorless salt is worthless, usable neither in the seasoning nor the shithouse.[50] Throw it out.

40. That's Not Fair

Meanwhile the dregs of society were gathering to hear him speak, crowding him. They were IRS agents, paperless immigrants, and high-school dropouts. Among the crowd were those discharged soldiers who'd spent their

---

48. The former was Ludwig Feuerback, the latter Karl Marx.
49. Which is a nice little play on words in Latin: *Nil sole et sale utilius*.
50. It must be conceded that this image makes no sense. Salt does not lose its flavor; neither can it have its flavor restored. Some salts are necessary to make the ground fertile, but over-salinization will destroy the soil. Take this image, as they say, with a grain of salt.

time malingering in and around crumbling VA hospitals, backbiters, along with all manner of backsliders, apostates, traitors and reprobates. They all wanted to be near him.

Meanwhile, the cultured elite, the ones with American Express Centurion credit cards and seats in the halls of power whispered amongst themselves, "He associates with vagabonds, and ex-cons, and sinners. He *welcomes* them. He *enjoys* their company. What does that say about his character? What does that say about him?"

"Ask yourself," Jesus said to them, "Which of you having one hundred sheep and having lost one, would leave the ninety and nine right there in the desert to go look for the one that was missing? And having found that one, wouldn't you pick her up and carry her home—joyfully? And having returned home with that one lost lamb, wouldn't you call up your friends and neighbors, even as late as it was, to invite them to celebrate? Wouldn't you? And there will be even more rejoicing in heaven for the one than for the ninety and the nine."

"But Jesus," they objected. "That doesn't make any sense. Don't all sheep matter, Jesus? What about the ninety and nine sheep? Besides, consider the cost-benefit analysis. Think about the risk assessment. What would the shareholders say about such reckless management? This is not a good business model. This is not prudent. And . . ." they paused with a sudden, wounded realization, "Hey! That's not fair!"

"Again," Jesus said. "Imagine a woman with ten drachma coins, and she loses one. So she lights a lamp and she sweeps the house. She spends all day, all week looking for that one lost coin. And when she finds it, she shouts 'Aha!' and calls her neighbors to join her for a party. The bright stars of heaven will bend low to the earth and rise up again with celebratory songs for this one lost and found coin."

The scribes and Pharisees responded again, "But Jesus that's ridiculous. It's bad economics. It's certainly not fiscally responsible. A drachma coin has a silver content valued at about a day's pay. If she spent all week looking for that one coin and then threw a party . . . her costs far outweigh her rewards. It's a loss. It's just plain irresponsible, Jesus."

"So you say." Jesus said with a sardonic grin. "So you say, but God is looking for the lost, and She won't stop until She finds what has been lost."

41. Gratuitously, Even

"There once was a man who had two sons," he told them. "And the younger of the sons said to his father, 'Father, I can't wait until you are dead, so give me my share of the inheritance now.'"

"Oh! Oh! Oh!" jumped up Peter. "I know this one. This is the Story of the Prodigal Son, right?"

Jesus rolled his eyes and sighed. This was his response to many of their questions. "What was the story I told just a moment ago?" he asked them all.

"A parable of a lost coin," they said slowly, hesitatingly.

"That's right. And what was the story before that?"

"A parable of a lost sheep," they cooed, excited now for they felt that they were on the verge of understanding something important.

"So," he said to them, "Let's not jump to calling him the Prodigal Son, shall we? Let's keep the connective thread between these stories. If you must call him something, call him the Lost Son. Besides, how many of you know what the word 'Prodigal' means, anyway? Anyone? Anyone?" No one answered.[51] "Shall I continue then?"

"And the younger of the sons said to his father, 'Father, I can't wait until you are dead, so give me my share of the inheritance now.' And the father did as his son demanded. This son took his money and split. He went off for the big, big city where with lots of noise and music and laughter he burned through all of his cash, spending it all on loose women and fast living. Or was it fast women and loose living? It amounts to the same, either way.

About the time that he'd spent it all, the land was hit with a famine and he, like everyone else, was hungry and in desperate need of a job, and the only job available to him was feeding swine. He took it because there was nothing else and he was desperate. Desperate enough to eat the slops with the hogs. 'How many of my father's servants are starving like this?' he said to himself. 'I should go home. My Father will take me back. He'll have to. That's what home is for.'"

"He began rehearsing his spiel, 'Father, ehem, uh . . . Father, I have sinned against heaven and against thee; I no longer deserve to be called your son; treat me as you would treat one of your hired men.' And it sounded rehearsed, you know? Practiced, like he was putting on a show, because he really was."

---

51. It means "profligate," but the disciples needed a dictionary for that word as well.

"And the boy, he returned home again, sort of like that walk of shame in the morning. You know what I'm talking about, don't you? I've seen you. And the boy, when he got home he said to his father, 'Father, I have sinned against . . .' But that's all he could get out before his father enveloped him in the biggest, full body embrace you've ever seen. The old man was weeping and laughing. He didn't care that his son's speech was really nothing but a nonpolgy. He sent his servants to fetch a robe for his son. But they hesitated. 'Ach! You take too long," he chastised them and took off his own robe. 'He will wear mine.'"

"So the servants and the staff threw a block party with roasted meats and fine wines and a local band popular with the folks at the bar.[52] They even brought in a pony and a clown for the kids. But when the elder brother heard the ruckus (and the band could really belt out the tunes) he was upset and whined to his father, 'I've slaved for you all these years, year after year, and never, not once did I disobey you. Never, not once, have you let me have a party like this with my friends.'"

"But this couldn't have been true" Jesus told them. "For, if anyone in this story is prodigal, it is the father who loves and loves lavishly, and gives and gives gratuitously. Everything he has is given to his son. But we celebrate for the lost will be found and because the dead will live again."

42. Reject Strip Regalvanize

So let's refresh: We have a Lost Son. We have a Lost Coin. And we have a Lost Sheep. But back up a bit and ask the question: How did all this begin? How did we find ourselves here? The religious center got their collective panties into a tight little twist because the dregs of society were gathering to hear him speak, crowding him—IRS agents, paperless immigrants, high-school dropouts, backbiters, backsliders, et. al.

But these stories of lost things weren't told for the dregs, or to those huddled in the margins and shadows. These stories of lost things were told for those sitting comfortably at the center. Sorry to have to be so direct about it. Subtlety is wasted on the comfortable. The lost sheep, coin and son aren't here to provide hope for the lost (though they certainly did, and they do, and they will). These stories were told to disturb and disrupt the center. They're here to make things difficult. They are here to stir things up.

Reject. Strip. Regalvanize. You've done the whole thing wrong.

52. It was Pharaoh Necho and the Wafers. I told you they were good.

43. A Small Disruptive Interruption

At this point—a small disruptive interruption:

"Did Jesus really say, 'Blessed are the Poor"?' Was he a Marxist? Was he one of those liberal, theohooligans? Was he a member of the Degradation League? Why else would he defend that most dangerous class—the casual poor? Call them what they are: AGENTS of CHAOS in the STREETS! Giving to the poor will pauperize them; it will create a dependency. They are a mass of misery festering beneath our feet. They are unemployed. They are surplus and redundant labor, breeding like rabbits and living on credit. Let the Market dictate their fate. Let Malthusian imperatives take their course."

"No! No and no, we say. Not 'blessed are the poor,' but 'blessed are the poor in Spirit.' The poor in *Spirit*! Can't you get that through your thick, libtard skulls? You've been completely brainwashed by the public school system and the liberal educrats at godless universities. Everything you support is evil; you try to flip what's good and what's evil. You try to manipulate the Bible, and the events of history to pervert them toward your own nefarious purpose. He was talking about spiritual things. Not money. Take your self-righteous bullshit and peddle it elsewhere. Or maybe you'll just like to sit back and watch as the country gets raped. Maybe you'll enjoy it even, you cuck."

Jesus himself interrupts the interruption. "Uh yeah, about that. I did say it. Blessed are the poor and the beggars too. Blessed are the children scavenging bits of tin from the dump yard, the immigrant laborers drifting from one low wage job to the next, the slave and the orphan. These are the blessed of the Lord, so stop with the righteous indigestion."

Our interlocutor scoffs, "Don't you mean 'indignation'? You stupid beta..."

"You should take notice of their misery," Jesus warns them, "before they take notice of your comfort."

He says nothing more.

44. Celebrating Incompetence and Dishonesty

He told another story, this time to his disciples. It was not an exemplary story, celebrating incompetence and dishonesty as it did. It would not be a tale told to edify. But still, he told them the story.

"There was a rich man with an accountant that he denounced as wasteful with his property and cash.[53] But really, how could the man complain of the steward's losses? The rich man himself had pissed away billions in bad investments, poor management (how do you lose money with a casino?) and legal settlements. Golden parachutes and scapegoats are always there for those at the top. The elite are cushioned against danger and risk. Their investments are insured. And limited liability? Hell, they take no liability. They've lobbied the legislature and bribed the judge so that they won't have to take any legal responsibility. "

"The rich man called his inept accountant and said to him, 'Give me an account of my accounts. Your time in my employ is at an end.'"

"The accountant panicked. 'What will I do?' He was worried and he was sweating through his shirt. 'I'm too old to start over. I've no strength for manual labor. And I won't beg on the streets like one of those hobos. Neither will I take government assistance. I'll be damned if start suckling on the government's teat.' But in a flash he had a plan; he knew what he would do."

"He placed a call to all those who owed a debt to his employer. The first owed over one-hundred-thousand dollars. 'Authorize a payment right now,' the accountant instructed him, 'of fifty-thousand dollars and I'll adjust the books to make it come out square. But remember me when I need a favor.' And he called another who owed the same and told him, "Write a check for eighty-thousand dollars that I can take to the bank this afternoon, and I'll fix it in the books for you. But remember me when I come to you for a favor.'"

"Now," Jesus said, "you might expect that when the rich man discovered the fraud his accountant had perpetrated he would be enraged, but no. He was amused by the rogue accountant's rascality. 'That's a trick I'll have to remember for myself,' he said."

"We don't understand this parable," the disciples said then. And we say it still say today. "The rich man can't be a stand in for God. And the accountant isn't a disciple. Either the lesson is obscure or we are obtuse."

"Perhaps it is both," Jesus said. "Use the mammon of unrighteousness, tainted as it is, to win friends so that when it fails—and it will, it always does—you'll have someone ready to receive you into eternal habitations. Past behavior is often the best indicator of future actions. The one who's faithful with the small, she's the one who will, as far as we can predict, be

---

53. You could say that the accountant was prodigal, even.

faithful with the big. And if you can't be trusted with mere money, with unrighteous mammon, who—besides the American voters—would trust you with real power?"

"You can't have two masters without hating one or the other or both. Especially if one of them is mere-money-mammon. Mo' money is mere money mammon," he said to them, "You've tried to replace the unseen Spirit of God with Adam Smith's invisible hand but self-interest does not, in fact, promote the common good. You cannot serve Compassion and your Total-Comprehensive-Income. You cannot serve both Mercy and the Bottom Line."

But the Americans in the crowd were covetous and envious of all the shiny things. They derided him and they scoffed. "If anyone is preaching a gospel other than the gospel of free-market-right-to-work capitalism, let him be eternally condemned. Let him be *anathema*."

45. It Will Not Go Softly

And now a word or three from our sponsors:

The Law and the Prophets have carried us all upon their shoulders and have laid us at the feet of the Baptizing John. But now it is the Gospel of the Kingdom that is proclaimed, and it is slapping everyone upside the face. It's provoking a confrontation. It will not be civil. It will not go softly.

Still it is easier for the chemical elements of heaven and earth to be consumed in the end of time fires than for one dot of the law or one stroke of the prophets to be dropped into the void. Everyone (and this includes you, unlawful and lecherous Antipas) who divorces his wife to marry a porn-star is an adulterer.

46. White Dives and Poor Black Lazarus

There was a rich white man named Dives who used to dress in tailored linen suits and who feasted every day on gourmand delights and rare, fine wines. Meanwhile, outside the gates of his palatial home, there sat a poor black man named Lazarus, covered with sores. He did not have health insurance, of course. That should be understood as a given. Now Poor Black Lazarus longed to fill his belly even if it was with even the scraps that fell from the rich man's table, but he had nothing to eat. And feral dogs came to lick at his open, running sores.

Did we mention that he had no health insurance?

Now it happened that those two men—both White Dives and Poor Black Lazarus—died on the very same day, in the very same hour. Quite a coincidence. Can you believe it? Poor Lazarus was carried away by the angels into the heavenly Bosom of Abraham, while the rich white man was buried in the family plot and descended like a shade into the shadows of the underworld.

Tormented there in Hades, he looked up into the distance and saw Father Abraham a long way off with old Black Lazarus in his embrace. He cried out, "Father Abraham, have pity on me. Please send Black Lazarus to dip the tip of his littlest pinky finger in water and let the drops of water drip down to cool my parched tongue. I am in agony here in these flames."

And Father Abraham said, "My son, remember how during your life you had your fill of good things? You lived a life of ease and privilege which is white privilege. But Lazarus lived a different life, a difficult life. Now he is the one being comforted while you are in, as you say, agony."

White Dives said, "Father Abraham, please. Father Abraham, send someone, I beg you. Send someone to speak to my five brothers. Send someone to warn them about this white privilege so they won't end up in this torment with me."

But Father Abraham said again, "They have James H. Cone. They have Howard Thurman, and Cornel West; let your brothers listen to them." The rich white man said, "No, Father Abraham. But perhaps if someone came back from the dead they'd listen . . ."

Father Abraham said, "If they will not listen to Cone, Thurman, and West, they will not be convinced even if Martin Luther King Jr. came back from the dead."

47. *What Is the Sin of Sodom and Gomorrah?*

"Sodom must be rooted out," he said to them. "It is destroying the Church from the inside out."

"Amen," they responded and clapped their hands.

"The sin of Sodom is destroying this generation."

"Preach it, Jesus," they cheered and waved their hands in the air. "Preach on!"

"The sins of Sodom and Gomorrah are destroying our beautiful country," he said.

"Come on, now!"

"And what is the sin of Sodom and Gomorrah? It is pride. It is fullness of bread. The sin of Sodom is an abundance of idle luxury, a refusal to lift up the poor. The sin of her sister, Gomorrah, is likewise. It is injustice, oppression and the exploitation of the desperate."

"Wait! What?"

48. Aristotle Was a Twat

Then she said to her disciples, "Listen. Stumbling blocks and offenses are going to hit you. They're going to knock you on your ass. Don't think of this as a prophecy or a matter of prediction; it's just a matter of fact. It's just the way the universe works. It is impossible for it to be otherwise."

"But to hell with the one who lays these traps for you," She continued. "Tie a boulder around your neck and throw yourself into the sea if you cause one of my precious little ones to fall. You'd be better off at the bottom of the ocean."

"And take care of each other," she told them. "If one of your sisters sins, rebuke her. And if she repents, forgive her. And if she does it again and again—seven times again, don't be like the ancient, Old Testament warlord, Lamech, vowing vengeance seventy seven times over. The world has enough of that toxicity already," She said.

One of her disciples interrupted her then. "Master, why is the narrator of this story using feminine pronouns for you when you are clearly a man. A very masculine man, rightfully so. It's very distracting, this *'she said,'* business."

She answered him, "What you should understand is that in the Christ there is no male or female. There is only one. You may also wish to consider the words of Julian of Norwich who will one day say of me, 'Our Saviour is our true Mother, in whom we are endlessly borne; and we shall never come out of him.'"

"But, Master," the disciple argued, "in his book *The Generation of Animals*, Aristotle tells us, and I'm quoting here, 'the female is, as it were, a deformed male; and the menstrual discharge is semen, though in an impure condition . . .' Now if Aristotle . . ."

Jesus interrupted him. "Aristotle was a twat."

". . . What, my lord?"

"Aristotle can suck it. Okay? May I continue?"

The disciples nodded glumly. "Lord, increase our faith. We've got nothing."

"Thank you," she said. "I will. But it doesn't take much. Weigh your faith against a mustard seed and you could command this mulberry bush to throw itself into the sea." But the crowd didn't respond with much enthusiasm. "And it would do it too," she added. "The mulberry bush would uprooted and flung into the ocean." They still didn't seem to get it. "Huh," she grunted, "tough crowd."

"Let's try another," she said. "Imagine that you're one of those schmucks that can afford to keep hired help in the house. And imagine that you see the maid coming in the back door with an armload of groceries. Now do you, as the high and mighty, Lord-So-and-So of the Manor say to her, 'Here, put those groceries down. Sit. Sit. Have some lunch with me'? No. No. I trow not. Of course not. You say to her, 'As soon as you've put those away, Lupita, I'd like my lunch: a toasted chicken salad sandwich with cheese, and an unsweetened ice tea to drink.' And when she's put away the comestibles and served you your repast, will you thank her? No. Why would you do such a thing?[54] She's merely done her job. Just so, when you've done all the things commanded by God, should you say anything but, 'We are unprofitable servants. We've done naught but our duty'?"

They smiled and nodded to her as if they understood everything that she was saying.

49. How's that for Gratitude?

Still on his way to Jerusalem, Jesus passed through the borderlands between Samaria and Galilee—a dangerous territory, filled with the lowest specimens of humanity imaginable. Miscegenated half-breeds lived there. Dog people. Scum. Nothing but a bunch of Pre-Adamite throwbacks. I've heard there were twenty-three registered blood drinkers in that village.[55] Seriously. These people are the worst.[56]

As Jesus entered one of their slums he was accosted by a gang of lepers with rotting skin and decrepit limbs. Some of them had lost a finger or a few toes. One had lost most of his nose to the grey-death disease.

---

54. Though, maybe you should, you bourgeois cretin.

55. Just don't ask me who they're registered with. I don't know.

56. A lot of this stuff is racist and xenophobic. Sorry. The Samaritans were hated by the Jews.

And that should have stopped him, but it didn't. Instead of shouting out the prescribed warning, "Unclean! Unclean!" to wave Jesus and his entourage away to prevent further spread of their infection, these diseased miscreants shouted out "Master! Master, have mercy on us!" They invited him closer—which was a direct, and deliberate violation of the law and cultural norms. I told you they were uncouth.

And Jesus, Jesus! He spoke to them, he actually spoke to them. He told them to go present themselves to the priests for examination. Some witnesses claim that the leprous filth that was their skin was clearing even as they departed. But who believes that sort of rubbish? The testimony of Samaritans isn't credible in court. All ten of them began running for the local priest. The doctor calls the priest; the priest calls it done.

But one of the lepers stopped and turned back to him and shouted out his thanks, "Bless you, Jesus, and the God who sent you." One. One of the ten stopped to thank him. How's that for gratitude? I told you the people who lived there were the worst. They don't care anything at all for the forms and patterns of polite society. They're ungrateful. That's what happens when you raise your children like animals.

Still, if Jesus is going to be consistent, he really can't gripe about their lack of thanks can he? If he is, as everyone seems to think, the humble, suffering servant of God, he shouldn't have even expected to receive thanks from any of them. Not if he was one of those 'unprofitable servants' who was only doing his duty after all.

50. Follow the Vultures

The Pharisees sent an investigator to him with a list of questions.

1) Where is the Peking Man? He disappeared from China during World War II. We searched for him with a wounded head and a bleeding eye, but we cannot find him anywhere. Where has he gone?

2) When shall we expect to see the coming of this Kingdom of Justice that you describe? Please describe its advent with a detailed time table.

And 3) What kind of phenomena should we anticipate before the coming of the Kingdom? What sign? Will it be dark-star disasters in the sky, comets burning through the heavens with toxic vapor tails, or four thousand horsemen shouting forty thousand blasphemies as they ride across an apocalyptic wasteland?

Jesus ignored the investigator's list of signs and demands. "The Kingdom of Justice doesn't come with timetables or checklists. Any blithering idiot could come along (and trust me, they will) and say 'Look, there it is. Out there in the desert. I'll show you.' But forget that noise. The Kingdom of Justice is within you, without you, wherever you make it."

"You'll beg and you'll plead. But, no. And no. Even so, you must not go. 'Lo, here!' or 'LOL, there!' But do not go. Do not follow. Lightning flashes and thunder follows, but not you. You will wait. Lightning flashes and thunder follows; thus for the Son of Man in those days. But first there will be suffering and rejection! Incarnation leads inevitably to incarceration."

"You'll see them eating and drinking and getting married, all the normal things. Just like it was in the days of old Noe. Same as it's always been. Same as it ever was. But then came the water. Or Lot. Remember him? Then they were eating and drinking, buying and selling, planting and building in Sodom right up until the fire fell. When the day comes and you find yourself on the roof of your house don't bother to go down to get your stuff. Just run. Run. Or if you're out in the field, don't come back into town first. Just run. Run. Try to save your life and you'll lose it. Give it away to save it. Run."

"Two men will be sleeping—one will be taken. Two women will be preparing food—one will be taken. Two men will be working the field—one will be taken."

"Taken where, Jesus," his anxious and fretful disciples asked. "Tell us! Where will they be taken?"

"It's easy," Jesus told them. "Just follow the vultures; you'll find their corpses soon enough."

51. Who's Telling this Story, Peter?

Then Jesus sat down with his friends and said to them, "Have I ever told you the one about the impertinent widow?"

Peter interrupted him to say, "Jesus, don't you mean the persistent widow?

Jesus glared at him. "I said impertinent. Listen: In a certain city there was an official, a judge who neither feared God nor had any respect for the people. In that same city there was a widow who kept coming to him, day after day, over and over and over again saying, 'Please, your honor, grant me justice against my opponent.'"

"For a long time the eminently respectable and authoritative judge refused to see the woman. But she just kept coming at him, day after day, over and over and over again. Eventually he said to himself, 'I have no fear of God and no respect for anyone, but because this widow keeps bothering me, I will hear her case so that she won't wear me out with her continual requests.'"

When Jesus stopped, Peter said, "Yeah, Jesus. That's the persistent widow..."

"Who's telling this story, Peter?" asked Jesus. "She's the impertinent widow. And blessed is her impertinence."

52. A Parable of Contempt—Two Ways

He also told this parable to some who trusted that they were righteous in themselves and regarded others with the contempt of the comfortable:

A politician went before the cameras to pray: "I'm not sure I've ever asked for forgiveness. I just try to go on and do a better job from there. If I do something wrong I just try to make it right. I don't need God in that picture. I don't. I don't think of it that way. I just try to go on. I'm thankful that I'm not like my opponents. You should see some of the things they've gotten away with. I drink my little wine (which is about the only wine I drink) and eat my little cracker. I guess that's a form of asking for forgiveness, and I do that as often as possible because I feel cleansed. My opponents and their kind have done even worse things, and thank God I'm not like them! I'll be sure to tell you about over the next several days. Amen."

I tell you this man with all the best words went up to the White House feeling justified. All those who exalt themselves won't have to be humble. Humility is for losers. And I'll tell you this as well—this man was absolutely adored by the American Evanjellyfish.

Or, to tell it again another way:

"A white man went into the church house to pray: 'God I thank you that I'm not a rapacious, lazy, lawbreaker like this colored person next to me. Sorry. Should I have said 'African American?' I don't know what the 'politically correct' term is anymore. They keep changing what we can call them. I obey the law like a good, white citizen should. I believe in Law and Order. Thank you, Lord, that I have a place in the community, a good job, and that I'm not like those hanging around on the street corners all day drinking forties or smoking dope. I rise early to go to work, and I earn my salary.'"

"But the black man said his prayers quietly and simply, 'God be merciful me; I know I screwed up. Again.' It was this man," Jesus told them, "that went home justified."

53. Bring Hand Sanitizer and Wet Wipes

The people of that place brought him their infants and squalling children. They wanted a blessing from the Master for their grubby fingered and snot-nosed brats. But the disciples ran interference for him.

"Please keep your distance from the Master. The Master is busy today. Step back. Step back; you're too close. You'll have to make an appointment. And next time bring hand sanitizer and wet wipes. And shot records. Bring your vaccination records. He won't touch any of them without proof of immunization."

But Jesus called out to them. "Let the little ones come. They're the ones who understand. Bless them heart and mind. Bless them body and soul. They are the human face of the Creator in heaven. You will in no wise find the way home except that you become like them."

54. Can Anyone Be Saved like This?

A ruler of that region who was also a brilliant young economist of the city came to him and said, "Good teacher, what must I do to inherit this eternal life of which you speak?"

Jesus rolled his eyes and sighed, "Good, Lord! There's more than one of you?[57] Why do you guys insist on calling me good? There's none good but God." The ruler didn't move, didn't blink. He just stood there like a stone. Still Jesus loved this young man. He sighed again and said, "Okay. Fine. Thou knowest the commandments: Thou shalt not bear false witness. Thou shalt commit adultery.[58] Thou shalt honor thy father and thy mother."

---

57. See page 125.

58. Whoops! Looks like Jesus was quoting from the infamously misprinted *Wicked Bible*, published in 1631 which accidently omitted a very important word. Most of the copies of the *Wicked Bible* were immediately destroyed, but there are fifteen extant copies in libraries around the world. The *Wicked Bible* had a second misprint—in Deuteronomy chapter five—which reads, "Behold, the Lord our God has showed us his glory and his

"Yes. Yes." Interrupted the young man. "I learned all that at the *yeshiva* when I was a boy. What else should I do?" He said impatiently.

"Okay then," Jesus said. "You've got everything already. Now give it away."

"What?"

"The house, the apartment, the car, the stocks, the yacht. Give them away."

"My yachts?"

"Yes." Jesus nodded. "The yachts." And here he gave a sharp eye to the inquisitive ruler. "Yachts? Plural? Really? Sell all that crap and give the money to the poor. Redistribute the wealth. That's how to find treasure in heaven. Then you can follow me." But the man from the ruling class could not follow Jesus. For all his wealth, all his money, the price was still too high.

Standing there also was a poor working man who worked two jobs but still could barely pay for rent and groceries every month. "Teacher," the poor man said, "I too have kept the commandments. Well, I've kept them as well as anyone. But, I've nothing much to sell. No land, no treasure. Only the sweat of my labor, which I sell every day, and for which I receive barely enough to feed my family. What must I do to be saved?"

Looking at him, Jesus felt a love for him also and said, "You are blessed. Learn to live in brotherhood and love."

The young economist pushed his way forward again. "Wait!" he shouted. "That's it? You demand that I sell everything I have, everything my father left me and only then I can be allowed to follow you, but this minimum wage earing high-school dropout, this illiterate gets your blessing? That's not fair!"

"What can I say?" Jesus shrugged. "Them's the breaks. How hard it is for the plutocrats and oligarchs to enter the benevolent rule," Jesus said to those who still stood around him, shocked and perplexed by what had just transpired. "It would be easier to shove a camel through the eye of a needle. And even if you succeeded, he'd be bloodied and strung out, a mess of viscera and flesh across the floor."

"But it's faith that saves us," someone in the crowd shouted back. "Right, Jesus? By grace, through faith and all that, right?"

---

great-asse," instead of "his greatness." But it should be noted that in 1631, "ass" had only the sense of "donkey" and so this misprint isn't as funny as you think it is.

A Life Known and Unknowable

"Sure." Jesus said to them. "Sure. Right. But what is faith without works? It's a camel that won't fit. Let the rich will howl for their rotted wealth and moth eaten clothes. Living in luxury is living in riot. Living in luxury is looting from the poor."

"But Jesus. Surely you're not saying that wealth is the problem? It's the *love* of money that lies at the root of all kinds of evil."

Jesus turned to his disciples. "You guys are writing all this down, right? Haven't we already had this conversation?" The disciples began thumbing through their battered notebooks and file folders looking for their transcriptions of his teachings on the topic of money. As they searched Jesus spoke again.

"Take this for whatever it might be worth: Eat the rich *is* a biblical mandate—or it will be. Just ask the vultures of the apocalypse[59] and all the birds of the midair about it when they gather for the great supper of God."

"And what can a poor boy do, if he isn't playing in a rock and roll band? What can he do in a capitalist, industrialized society to face his poverty? He can submit or he can strive to become one of the bourgeoisie himself. Or he can rebel—he can fight a revolution in the streets. Or is there another way without submitting to the crushing oppression of his poverty? Is there another way that doesn't continue the exploitation of others? Is there a way that doesn't involve succumbing to the lure and dazzle of the myth of redemptive violence? Yes. Yes. And again Yes, there is another way, but it is difficult."

"Jesus Christ," they muttered. "How can anyone be saved like this?"

55. Old Darkness for New Light

So it's up to Jerusalem now, ever forward, further on. Always up. And there, at the end, we will find the accomplishment of everything the prophets wrote concerning the Son of Man. But this is fulfillment, not an ending. Completion opens everything. So now, before the ascent, now is the time for rearrangement and reevaluation. Now before the planets fall from their

---

59. Whether these apocalyptic vultures are members of the common species of vultures (which are disgusting enough) or if they are members of the fowl breed of Gwythaint Vultures with legs like those of a man and scales like a lizard is not yet determined. Common buzzards are known to roost in trees and to urinate and defecate on anything (or anyone) below them. The rarer, but infinitely more disgusting hume-vulture Gwythaints are known to also regurgitate half-digested meals of rancid flesh in a disgusting (and dis-gut-ing) territorial display.

moribund orbits. Now before we are overwhelmed by physical action, and actual abduction. Now is the time, before we are driven into smoke.

Then he will be handed over to ungentle gentiles. I can already hear their nervous coughs and see their furtive glances into darkened corners. They are unsettled by what they will do. They know it is wrong, though they do not fully understand why it is so. He will be mocked but this is nothing new. This is the old darkness for the new light. He will be shamefully treated and treated with shame. He will be spit upon. Not the spitting three times—*ptui, ptui, ptui*—protection against the evil eye, but an intentional act of disrespect, intentional contamination in a time of disease and pandemic. He will be beaten and scourged. You know how it is. The police will slug you, and bash you about the face, they will throw you against the wall, and drag you into the court. Then they will charge *you* with assault and for creating a disturbance and for resisting arrest. This is how it will be for the Son of Man.

He will be killed.

But...

He told all of this to the twelve but it was occulted from them and they understood nothing.

56. The Permanent Midnight of the Aphotic Zone

Now he came to the oldest, continually inhabited[60] city in the world, Jericho in the West Bank. And there he met the village blind man, Mr. Ocellus. Mr. Ocellus hadn't always been blind, that I know for sure. But what was he before? I cannot say. Perhaps he was a farmer, or a craftsman. Perhaps he was a scholar, dependent on his eyes for reading and writing. And how did Mr. Ocellus come to be blind? Again, I cannot say. Perhaps he was kicked in the head by a camel. Maybe it was a fever that burned away his vision. Or apocryphal birds shat in his eyes as he slept. I do not know.

To be blind is to be held apart, removed from the source of light and life which is the sun. Unseeing is often unseen. Imagine the loneliness of deep sea creatures in the permanent midnight of the aphotic zone, creatures that have never known the Father of Lights. There may be no place in the universe that is not so dark as to hide the Father of Lights, but it is hard to see and to be seen at those blinded depths.

60. "Continuously" inhabited is a debatable claim. The village has been cyclically built and rebuilt, inhabited and abandoned for millennia.

A Life Known and Unknowable

But here, on the Jericho wayside we can see the tragic optimism of Theodicy. We can see the lamentable tangle of an unresolvable paradox: We believe that things *can* be better, but the tragedy is that they so rarely are. Theodicy is an oxymoronic contradiction derived from the Greek words *Theos*—meaning God, and *Dikē*—meaning justice, but theodicy is the absence of both. No God. No Justice. It is absurd. It is human. It is suffering. It is evil and it is cruel. Weal or woe, whatever. As the prophet Jeremiah said, "What is this perpetual pain? Why this incurable wound?" We can ask, 'Does creation prove that God exists?' And we can ask, 'Does evil prove that God does not?' But Mr. Ocellus was oblivious to this sort of question; he just wanted to be able to see again.

Sitting there wayside the road, Mr. Ocellus heard Jesus and his entourage approaching. Was this the heightened senses of the blind? No, Jesus and his entourage were just loud. But Mr. Ocellus shouted louder still, "Jesus *thou* son of David, have mercy on me! Jesus, *thou* son of David, have mercy on me!"

And the louder he shouted, the louder the crowd hooted at him and told him to be quiet. "Shut your hole!" they told him. But he kept on shouting, "Jesus, *thou* Son of David, have mercy on me!"

Figure 28–What do you see here?

Jesus advanced toward the blind man and asked "What do you want me to do?"

"Give me my eyes, Lord."

"Am I an oculist?" Jesus returned.

"I do not know, but I would have my eyes, sir," Mr. Ocellus said.

Now I have read about researchers in Houston, Texas who have discovered a way to use electrodes to electrically stimulate the billions of neurons in the primary visual cortex of the brain so that visual data can be input directly into the brains of blind individuals. They are able to help the blind to see with cybernetic prosthesis. And what they're doing is really no different than what happens with the natural eye: the eye converts light into electrical signals interpreted as sight by the brain. But this isn't what Jesus did for Mr. Occelus.

"Receive your sight," Jesus said. "Your faith has made you whole."

57. Side By Side with the Sons of Belial

Ancient Jericho—the fragrant city of palms, the city of the moon, the beautiful moon—was filled with the crush and throng of people yearning to breathe free. The city, with all its marvels, was given as a gift by Marcus Antonius to his mistress Cleopatra, along with the whole of the Arabian peninsula as trifling afterthought. It was in Jericho that Herod the (notso) Great died, and where he gave, with blackened breath, his final horrific order for murder and slaughter. It was in Jericho that his son, Herod Archelaus, rebuilt for himself a palace with gardens perfumed with the scent of roses and balsam. In the streets of that ancient city crowded together both pilgrims and courtiers. (Re)publicans and anchorites were crowded in close with fishmongers and relic merchants, as well as blacksmiths, caravanners, and Czechoslovakian mercenaries. They were shoulder to shoulder with hydroponic farmers and a few failed eremites who'd been drawn back into the press of sinful human flesh. In those crowded streets you could find musicians singing for a penny and prostitutes screwing for a pound. The sons of Abraham lived side by side with the sons of Belial.

And in this congested city lived the *architelones*, the chief tax collector, Zacci who wanted nothing more and nothing less than to see this Jesus passing through on his way up to Jerusalem. But Zacci could not see him for the press of the crowds, and because he was little of stature. Jesus, not Zacci. Jesus was short and why not?

Do we disregard what the prophet said of him, even as he approached the city wherein all that the prophets said of him would be accomplished?

Do we deny that he had no beauty or majesty to attract us to him, nothing in his appearance that we should have desired him? So let Jesus be short in this telling of the story. Why not? Let him be short with bad teeth halitosis and body odor. The bodies of the saints may have smelt of roses and lavender—the odor of sanctity—but fully human Jesus had nothing in his stature or his scent to cause us to desire him.

So Zacci climbed into a wild fig tree to get a better view as Jesus passed by. And when Jesus came to that place he looked up and saw Zacci in the branches and said, "Make haste. Come down. I will dine with you at your house today."

The tax man was astonished, but he climbed down from his perch in the branches of the Sycamore fig tree and invited Jesus—along with many members of the crowd—for a meal at his home. The crowd followed, though many of them grumbled, "this man is a sinner. He's a sinner. Jesus should know this man is a sinner!"

And all through the meal they watched and listened as Jesus ate and drank with this taxman-sinner. They listened as the disciples told jokes (some of which were a tad off color) and they heard Jesus laugh with Zacci and the other dinner guests. But as the meal progressed they grew impatient. "When will the Master speak truth to sin?" they asked themselves. "When will he preach and convict the sinner's heart and bring Zacci to repentance?"

Just then Zacci stood and urged the room to silence. "Look, Lord! Here and now I give half of my possessions to the poor, and if I have cheated anyone out of anything, I will repay it four times the amount." The room erupted in cheers and shouts of joy. Jesus smiled broadly and hugged the taxman then said to the crowd, "Today salvation has come to this house because this man, too, is a son of Abraham."

The grumblers, now past the point of all patience, sprung to their feet and exclaimed, "But Lord, excuse the interruption, but how can you say that salvation has come to him? You've not preached truth to his sin. You've not said anything to convict him. You've been the guest of this sinner, you've eaten his food and drunk his wine, but you never spoke against his sin."

And Jesus replied, "You're right. You are exactly right. I haven't, but he knows that he is a son of Abraham, and that is enough."[61]

61. ED. NOTE: I maintain that the standard Sunday school lesson readings of this story serve only to propagate stereotypes and prejudices. While Z. may have sinned and may have repented (the story isn't explicit about either), what is clear is that Jesus claims heritage and salvation for Z. regardless of either of those being true.

58. Everyone Misunderstood in Different Ways

Seventeen miles is not so far. Even on foot it's not so far. Already they can almost hear the psalms which are sung in the holy place, the strains of the temple drifting down from Mount Moriah on the breeze in the night. And now under the moon and in the cool of that breeze, Jesus tells a parable. He tells them this parable because they are nigh unto Jerusalem, and because they had begun to suppose that the kingdom was nigh as well—as close, perhaps, as the gates of that holy city on the hill. Seventeen miles is not so far.

"A certain nobleman," he told them, "went off to a far off place in order to claim a kingdom for himself." He said this as apophasis. "I will not," he winked at them, "positively name the nobleman as Herod Archelaus, but he *did* go to a far off place, one that was very much like Rome, to claim his father's kingdom. He took with him an impressive retinue of secretaries, translators, advisors, security guards, and cooks, as well as a barber, masseuse, and his personal gymnastics instructor. One seeking to claim a royal title could not travel without such an entourage. But before the nobleman departed for that great and far off city he summoned ten of his servants and gave them ten silver minas, one each, and ordered them to 'Occupy until I come.'"

"But the citizens of that country despised him and did not want him to rule over them. They hadn't voted for him, and still refused to accept the decision of the courts on the matter. So they sent a delegation of fifty of their mayors and senators to say to the Emperor, 'We will not have him as our king.'"

"Their complaints were ignored, of course, and the nobleman, who I positively will *not* identify as Herod Archelaus, was given his father's kingdom—well, part of it anyway, with the promise of more if he could prove his virtue as a king. And the nobleman, who was now a king, returned to order to rule."

"His first command was to summon the ten servants to whom he had entrusted his money. 'Tell me how you have occupied yourself with my money during my absence.'"

"The first reported that he had taken the money entrusted to him and invested it in the stock market. 'One mina,' he said, 'isn't much, my lord, not more than twenty dollars, but I was able to purchase a few shares, and those shares have only increased in value. You gave me one, I return to you ten.'"

"And the nobleman, now king, was pleased. 'You've been faithful with a little; I will entrust you with more. You will rule over ten cities for me.'"

"The second as well said, 'You gave me one mina which I used to hire a boy to fish. The fish that he caught, I sold and now have five minas to return to you, my lord.' And the nobleman turned king was pleased and appointed this servant to rule over five cities within his realm."

"The third servant stood trembling before his lord and said, 'I know that you are a stern and unforgiving lord, and that you snatch up that which you did not put down and that you will reap in fields where you did not sow.[62] So I kept your mina hidden. I wrapped it within my handkerchief. And now I return it to you.'"

"But this displeased the nobleman, who was now the king. 'Your own words condemn you,' he said to the cowering servant. 'You knew better, but you did worse. You could have at the very least put my money into the bank and let the usurers collect interest on it for me.' So he took the mina from this servant and gave it to the first. This caused the other servants (who will not get further mention in this story) to complain that the first servant already had so much. 'Everyone who has will be given more. And the one without will have what little he has taken from him,' the nobleman, now king, told them."

But no one listening to Jesus' parable understood what he meant by this. Everyone misunderstood in different ways. The capitalists grinned in anticipation. The poor looked anxiously at one another.

"To continue," Jesus said, "The king, having dealt with the servants to whom he had entrusted his silver now issued his second command. 'Bring me that delegation of traitors who refuse to have me as their king. Bring them here and let them kneel before me. Then slay them. Execute them. Cut off their heads. I want to feel their blood splash on my face as they die.'"

And as before, no one knew exactly what to make of this part of the parable.

59. Lord, I Do not Think You Understand how this Game Is Played

And the people brought their little ones to Jesus, for him to lay his hands on them and pray, and to give them a break for a few hours. The disciples

---

62. Obviously this nobleman turned king was a capitalist, taking as his own the wealth created by the labor of others.

scolded the parents, but Jesus said, "Leave the children alone, and do not stop them from coming to me. I will teach them one of the games that we play in the kingdom of God."

"First," he said, "we put out a circle of chairs—one fewer than our number—and then we play some music." Jesus winked to the kids. "Perhaps Simon Peter will sing a song for us, maybe one of the fishing songs he knows." The children giggled. They knew that Peter did not like to sing. "Then, as Peter sings, we will walk around the chairs. And when he stops singing we will all scramble to sit down in one of the chairs."

Andrew interrupted then. "Jesus. We know this game. It's Musical Chairs."

"Of course," Jesus said. "So let's play."

Jesus and the children made a circle of chairs and Peter sang for them. Reluctantly, yes, and like a trained mule, he sang. And when he stopped, Jesus and the children all clambered for a seat. One boy missed out and fell upon his butt in the dust. Everyone laughed.

"Great. Great," said Jesus as he picked up the boy up from ground. "Now in round two we add another chair."

Andrew interrupted again. "No, Jesus. No. No. You mean we *remove* a chair."

And Jesus said to him, "In the kingdom of Heaven we add a chair and a player with each new round. There is always more in the sharing and there's always room for one more."

But Andrew said, "Lord, I do not think you understand how this game is played."

60. I No Longer Believe in the World

The road from Jericho is short but steep, uphill all the way. So Jesus and the disciples were sweaty and tired when they arrived at the gates of Jerusalem. Tired as they were they were still filled with the pilgrim's eager anticipation at having finally arrived at the holy city. And in this they were no different than the thousands of other pilgrims who were also making their way to Jerusalem for the Passover celebration and who were also waiting in line to enter the ancient city through the security check point. Barbed wire posts and stanchions cordoned off restricted areas and kept the pilgrims in single file lines.

"Get back!" shouted the Roman soldiers carrying large caliber ghettoblasters who were positioned among the crowd. "Get back or you'll get it in the back! Have your identification papers ready." Large signs posted in three languages: Greek, Latin, and Aramaic, warned the pilgrims that no weapons would be allowed into the city. "This road leads to area 'A' under Roman authority. Entrance for any *Sicarii* is forbidden. Dangerous to your lives. Have all bags open for inspection." The eager pilgrims shuffled along together, glancing nervously at the gates, at the soldiers, and the weapons they carried. Mothers and fathers held sleeping infants in their arms, while their older children huddled together giggling and eating oranges.

Entertainers circulated at the edges of the crowd, singing songs for a coin or selling prayer cards and beads and postcards. One of the performers amused the crowd with a trained monkey dressed in a red fringed vest and a monkey sized *keffiyeh*. He wore curled slippers on his feet and a slightly oversized fez on his head. "Show us, Aziz," the performer called to the monkey as he tossed him an apple. "Show us how the Samaritans eat."

The little monkey snatched the apple out of the air and immediately began devouring the apple, biting, and gnashing the fruit, sending bits of peel and pulp everywhere but down his throat. The crowd laughed. The entertainer called to him again, "Aziz, show us how the Samaritans pray." On command the monkey defecated on the stone cobbles of the street, then he scooped it up and began flinging it at members of the crowd. The crowd laughed and cheered and tossed coins to the entertainer, all of them except the ones who'd been pelted with feces.

Meanwhile Jesus and his followers had inched closer and closer to the front of the line. Jesus made eye contact with a young Roman soldier standing at the checkpoint. And although he carried an M4a1 carbine over the bright orange safety vest that he wore over his military uniform, he was scared. His eyes darted back and forth, scanning the faces of the crowd, looking for the terrorists and malefactors that his superiors told him would inevitably be there.

Jesus spoke to him. "There is no cause for fear. I no longer believe in the world. There's nothing to fear here." He presented his identification papers and his photo ID. The guard looked at them, then at Jesus and back to the papers before nervously waving him and his disciples through metal detectors at the gate.

The Argument

I Feel Pretty Shattered Most of the Time

There is a Jewish tradition originating in the Kabbalah of the sixteenth century saying that when God created the universe he put part of himself into vessels of light, but then something went terribly, tragically wrong and those vessels of light were shattered, trapping the light of God within the physical material of creation. This tradition also says that it's up to us to restore that light. This is called *tikkun olam*, "the repair of the world."

It's a late tradition, yes, and it has gnostic affinities, but I rather like the idea that we, each one of us who are created in the image and likeness of God, have a splinter, a shard of God's eternal light hidden within us. And I like the idea that we can do something to fan the flame of that light in others. Even more, that we are obligated to partner with God to restore the goodness of the world. I *want* to believe that.

But, light of God hidden within me or no, I feel pretty shattered most of the time. It's been a rough year and it hasn't been a good day. Admittedly, there haven't been many good days this year but today, while it hasn't been particularly or specifically worse than any of the other rotten days thus far this year, I am not doing well.

I feel like I'm falling apart. I cry for no particular reason. I have no patience for anything or anyone. I curse and I swear at everything—not every*one*, mind you. Not yet, but I can feel that it is close. It may be that the candle delights to burn, but I am sincere and wickless. I desperately want to believe that the light of God can be restored. I want to believe that I can be restored.

I've also been thinking about something my friend, Rizwan once told me. He said, "We thank Allah that death comes, not at the beginning of life, but at the end." I think about that a lot. I don't know what to do with it, but I think about it. It helps when I think about the fact that the universe is running toward death and chaos, running down to heat death, entropy, disorder, decay. This transient existence of darkness will someday be dispelled by broken shards of light.

VI

Dum Spiro Spero

1. A City of Death and Devotion

HAVING SPOKEN AND SAID all that he needed to say, Jesus went up to the city of Jerusalem, the City of Peace, Zion, to Mount Moriah. He went up, for it is always up, to the City of David which was once the City of Jebus. He went up to the city that is called the Lion of God, to Iliya, to al-Quds, a city both beloved and condemned. A city of both prayer and of blood. A city of death and devotion. A city of dreams and hopes and rising aspirations as well as cascades of failure.

My friend, Amartyros went there some years ago, but no one has seen him since. He disappeared. Was he absorbed into a holy vision there or was he swallowed up by violence? No one can say. No one can give testimony; there were no witnesses.

Jesus went up to the city under bold beautiful skies, gravitationally bound, drawn there as if in a dream. Measure for measure, step over step. He had to go there. But first he drew nigh to Bethphage[1] and Bethany[2] at the Mount of Olives.

He sent two of his disciples[3] to the village with instructions to find a donkey that had never been ridden tied up there. "Bring it to me," he told them. "And if anyone asks, tell them 'the Master has need of it.'" They went and they found the unbroken colt, just as he'd said.

---

1. Which is the House of Figs.
2. Which is either the House of Affliction or the House of Obedience. Take your pick.
3. Let's call them: Who Are We? and Where Are We Going?

A Life Known and Unknowable

And, indeed, the owner burst out of the barn yelling, "What in the hell is going on here?"

When the European knights of the first crusade had their horses killed beneath them they sometimes resorted to riding oxen that they pillaged from the towns they'd raided, or riding donkeys, or goats. Even, if you can believe it, large sheep. They were humiliated by the loss of their stallions and war-horses. They were embarrassed to be forced into the ranks of the common foot soldiers.[4] For them, riding stolen farm animals was preferable to riding nothing like the peons and the *hoi polloi*. For what is a knight without his steed? Nothing. But for the master, the donkey wasn't a humiliating second choice. It was part of the pattern and the plan.

But was it a prearranged act, or a bold presumption? Was it divine omniscience or a negotiated transaction? This is the mystery. Whatever the case may have been, the disciples brought the animal to him, and he rode it into the city. And the disciples and the people of the city spread their garments on the road before him as he rode in lowly pomp. They shouted for him. "Blessed be the King. Blessed be the one who comes in the name of God. Let the peace of Heaven and the glory of God be seen among us!"

2. Order Must Be Maintained

The Pharisees of Jerusalem stopped him and said, "Jesus, we've heard that some of your followers are communists and Marxists and that they're demonstrating in the streets. We've heard that now they're weaponizing bees, and flies, and mosquitos—using them to spread viruses and to implant microchips in our children as part of the Mark of the Beast that will prevent us from entering the gates of heaven."[5]

"We've seen flocks of murder-crows attacking people in Wal-Mart parking lots. We've seen swarms of jellyfleshed jellyfish on the shores of the Great Sea. What do you have to say about all this, Jesus? We've seen your protestors pulling down statues in Capernaum and Bethsaida of revered generals like Judas Maccabeus—who took Apollonius' sword and used it ever after. Those statues are part of our heritage, Jesus. What are you going to do about it?"

---

4. But they weren't embarrassed to ride an outsized sheep? Fragile masculinity is fragile.

5. Obviously they, like modern American Evangelicals, subscribed to some of the more fantastical theories produced by QAnon.

"And now your followers are rioting here in the streets of Jerusalem," they continued in a huff, nearly out of breath with such an extended tirade. "We're all for justice, Jesus. We can even tolerate some of this 'social justice' stuff you've been spouting recently, but you've got to get a handle on this. Your followers are out of control. You can't just go around shouting 'Hosanna!' in the streets, blocking traffic, waving palm branches and making a nuisance. The Romans will not take it lightly. The Romans take nothing lightly."

"But," Jesus tried to interrupt. "There are no hosannas or palm branches in this version of the story. It's a strange elision, I know, but here we are. Check the source material if you don't believe me," he said to them. "Perhaps we could wave chrysanthemums like the Hungarians did after their short lived revolution in October of 1918."

But the Pharisees ignored him; they rolled right on without even hearing him. "We'll tell you this for free—if you won't yank on their leash, Jesus, we'll start running them over in the streets. We'll plow them under our SUVs. We'll turn the dogs and the firehoses on them. We'll bring out the flashbangs and shock-batons for all of them. Law and Order, Jesus! Law and Order! Clear and precise. As clear as the present danger. Law and order with measurable standards. Our standards for your protection."

"People should be treated like objects," they continued, "To be sorted, and ordered, and controlled, and, when necessary, terminated. It's just another NHI—sex workers, drug addicts, indigents, coloreds—As they say, 'no humans involved.' We have no time to treat them like human beings. Human rights are a luxury in times of political crisis. So rebuke your obstreperous mob before we have to do it for you."

Jesus was silent for several seconds before he spoke.

"What do you expect me to say? How should I respond to all that, except to say that if these rowdy friends of mine were silent, if they stopped their chants, put down their signs and went home, then the lithophonic stones on the ground would take up the cry for justice. And the lapidaries among you would be the ones to record their songs. You guys should turn off Herod's Fox News every once in a while. You're rotting your brains."

"Order must be maintained," the Pharisees insisted, "and it's up to you to make your followers docile, Jesus. You need to keep them servile. Tell them to quiet down. Stop their whooping and shouting it up. Make them stop their protestations and their agitations. You are a rubble-rouser. You are a jacklegged demagogue, and loud. You are untimely and unwise. You are an unwanted extremist. You are nothing but an outsider, and your followers are outside agitators. Can't you and yours just be civil?"

Jesus responded to them, "No. It is not enough to know what *is*—it is necessary to overthrow the existing state of things. It is necessary to *wreck* it. The *status quo* is not immutable forever. It is malleable and changeable. It is breakable. It is not enough to interpret the word and the world, the theologian's task is to smash it. Truth is not merely what *is* but what *should be*, what *must be*."

"Rabbi, we've heard that you . . ."

"I'm going to stop you right there," He told them. "Hearsay heresy is the lowest form of heresy. You know that this is not a refusal to speak the truth, or live the truth in light of the One who is Truth, so why do you pester me and mine with this pettifoggery?"

3. How Often Must I Weep for You

Oh Jerusalem. Woe Jerusalem. Do I really have to say this again?[6] How often must I weep for you? How often must we sing these muted hosannas? Beat the drum slowly and play the pipes low; the king is on the way. If you only knew. If you only knew all the ways that would lead you to peace.

They're hidden from you. Or you refuse to see them. Either way, it is all the same. All your noonday brightness is lost in blindness. All your genius, all your grand achievements will be burned to dust and rubble and soon. Your enemies will be kicking down the gates. They'll be digging trenches and raising walls around you before you can open your eyes. Then they will throw you to the ground and smash your babies against the rocks. And none of the stones will be left in place.

This vision will be removed from your unbelieving eyes. And all of this because you did not know, and would not learn what you should have known. All because you did not know all they ways that could lead to your peace.

4. A Bazaar of Filth and Flies

Straight to the temple he went; the pilgrim's deep seated longing drove him into the holy precincts. But there, where he expected to find the faithful at

6. See page 153.

Dum Spiro Spero

prayer, he found the stalls and thralls of buyers and sellers. The courts of the temple were overrun with traders and merchants. The sound of psalms was dinned by the clink of coin. What had begun as the sale of sacrificial animal-victims and the helpful exchange of foreign currency with idolatrous engravings for pure and acceptable Hebraic coinage had become nothing more than a secular exchange of cash for goods and services within the temple courts.

Under the garishly colored canopies of squalid stalls they bought and sold sheep from Bethlehem and doves from Tel-Aviv. They bought and sold Egyptian cotton alongside Ethiopian slaves. They bought and sold beeswax and cedar from Lebanon, almonds, Brazil nuts, macadamia nuts, walnuts, and olive oil. They bought spices like pepper, cinnamon, nutmeg, coriander, aloe, cloves, mace, ginger, chocolate, and saffron. They sold silk and velvet lingerie, and sackcloth. Cuban cigars, cotton T-shirts, Florentine cloth, Balkan lead, and Flemish wine. Breakfast cereals, soap, imported CDs, and refurbished two stroke boat motors. Taxidermied monkeys, peacocks, jackalopes, and camels, along with all manner of exotic birds and cats. They openly bought and sold illegally modified firearms alongside DIY personal stigmata kits. They sold tripe, and cow's tongue, and oxtails. They bought and sold glass vessels and brass basins. Damascene metal and lace-works. Aromatic gums and resins. Ostrich eggs, pearls, rubies, diamonds, jade, and cheese. Apples, violets, and rosewater.

There were fire-dancers, wind-talkers, dog groomers, private detectives and oddsmakers offering their services to anyone with an interest and a coin. Travel agents booked discount tours to shady Cyprus and shady modeling agencies looked for the next beautiful face to sell perfumes and cosmetics.

They played games of chance with dice and cards and little wooden pins. They traded fur coats, and gold rings for used books, cocaine and methamphetamines. They drank English gin, Scottish whiskey, and vegan, microbrew craft beers from central Iowa. They traded in land grants, pork futures, stock options and golden parachutes. There in the temple courts you could even buy snow, painstakingly packed down from the mountains in sawdust and straw. Anything and everything was there if you had the cash.

Jesus shouted over the din of it all. "It is written in the prophets that this house, my house, is to be a house of prayer. But you! You have made it the lair of liars, a den of thieves and cutthroats. You have transformed it from the habitation of God into a common bazaar of filth and flies. Your service to this false god, Mammon which is the spirit of all your capitalist drive, does not become holy when given a religious veneer, neither when it is proffered in the holy courts. Wealth is no indicator of divine approval.[7]

You are a handful of burnt out coal. You are old women walking in the snow. Double-limbed, bristle-haired barbarians, you reek of onions and garlic and locker-room funk. Your god is your belly and your courage is broken wind. You are brothers to lice and vermin and the fathers of all manner of parasites."

And he cast them out—both them that sold and them that bought, merchants and consumers alike.[8]

5. Wait and See what Tree We Will Hang Him From

Every day he taught in the temple courts. Now that the merchants had been driven out the place could be the habitation of God once more. He taught them there by the wall where some juvenile but literate delinquent had spray painted rude graffiti. It had been scrubbed away, of course. It wouldn't do to allow the defilement to linger, but faint as it was, it was yet legible (though probably meaningless. Probably.) *"Epidemic! Endemic! Pandemic! Ipecac!"*

Every day Jesus taught them, speaking the words of truth and peace. And this, this is precisely how the lawless one is conquered. Not with swords. Not with tanks and unmarked helicopters. Not with whips and scourges. This is how the lawless one is slain, by the breath of Jesus' mouth. This is how the kingdom of God comes, with words of truth and peace.

And every day the chief priests and the scribes who were the principal men of the city, along with all those who belonged to the Sanhedrin sought to kill him. The Sanhedrin ruled as the final court of appeals in all religious matters, and in the affairs of the temple. And Jesus' outburst in the temple challenged their position and their place. And in that place there could be no conciliation—only feuds and intrigues. No one would be given praise except that it came blunted and backhanded. Animosity was masked

---

7. Say it again for the folks in the back: Wealth is no indicator of divine approval!

8. Many contemporary Christians will tell us, of course, that the Bible should be read literally—except when it condemns wealth and consumerism. Anything else would be a wicked, and unAmerican reading of the scriptures. Anyone preaching it should be condemned as a heretic or as a traitor or both. But don't let them tell you that destruction of property isn't a valid form of protest and religious reform.

as friendship and rivalry as partnership. There were no friends here, only temporary allies, and only so long as they could prove themselves useful.

No one would be allowed to disrupt their patch. Before, when he traveled up and down the green hills of Galilee, he'd been in Herod Antipas' shrievalty—and free to do and say as he pleased. But now that he was poking about where he wasn't wanted, here, in Jerusalem, here in their home courts, they were compelled to take action against him. "His views are so twisted, he's so far down that dark hole," they exclaimed to one another with a grimace, "that he's actually rooting for the destruction of Israel. If it weren't so blasphemous, we might laugh. It's comical. He fell out of the stupid tree and hit every branch on the way down. But just wait and see what tree we'll hang him from."

But, seek as they might, they could find nothing to do; the people hung on his every word.

6. A Chance To See these Holy Places

The disciples approached their rabbi with a request. "Master, while we're in the great city of Jerusalem, we'd like to visit some of the spectacular sights like the threshing floor of Araunah the Jebusite, and the Dung Gate. Oooh, ooh and Hezekiah's tunnel. And the valley of the Cheesemakers!"

"We won't have time for all of that," Jesus told them.

"But, Jesus," they pleaded. "We've come all this way, how often will we get a chance to see these holy places?"

The master saw their earnestness and relented somewhat. "There may be time to see the *Via Dolorosa*," he told them.

"The Sorrowful Way?" they translated. "What's that?"

"You'll see," he told them. "You'll see it soon enough."

7. The Cut and Thrust, Jab and Parry of Reasonable Dispute

One day as he taught them in the temple, as he preached to them concerning the arrival of the kingdom of God on earth, members of the Sanhedrin came to him. They were the chief priests, scribes, and elders all dressed in finery and each one speaking with refined eloquence.

"Tell us and be precise, if you please," they said, "by whose authority do you do and say these things? By whose authority to you speak thus and teach thus? From what school did you graduate? Under which rabbi did you study? What articles have you submitted for publication, and in what peer reviewed journals? What are your credentials, please?"

And like any good rabbi, engaged in oral debate, he met question with counter-question. This was the cut and thrust, jab and parry of reasonable dispute. "Tell me yourselves: Was John's baptism authorized from heaven or by mortal men?"

The deliberate members of the Sanhedrin deliberated amongst themselves. "If," they reasoned, "we say from heaven, he will ask us why we failed to believe. And if," they adduced, "we say it was by men, the mob will riot for they actually believe the Baptist was a prophet and that the Baptist's life mattered." They anticipated violence, it's true. Not that they disdained violence, but only their own violence would be judged acceptable.

They answered finally, "We don't know."

Jesus said, "Neither then, will I tell you." The members of Sanhedrin slunk away in discomforted silence. His disciples gawked at him. "Are you writing this down?" he asked them. "Have you got all this?"

"Yes, lord." they answered. Though, in truth, they'd only noted down the gist of what he said and not his words verbatim.

"Good," he told them. "Throw it out."

"But . . ."

"These words can be recreated, drawn back from the air. They can be pulled from the void and put back into place once more, but will they be the same? Will the message remain the same? It's a risk. Still . . . I said throw it out." They complied with his demand, but later they attempted to copy it down again from their combined memories.

8. Have No Illusions about the Cause of Human Strife

You read a lot of history, do you? I do too. But have you ever read this?

A man planted a vineyard.[9] A man planted a vineyard and leased it out to some tenants before going away to a faraway country for a long time. But do not think, as the premillennial dispensationalists with their well-thumbed Scofield reference Bibles and their autographed photos of Tim LaHaye and Jack Van Impe think, that this is a long time into the future, and that we are still to be waiting. They have a rented eschatology that they can't really afford—and still they continue making payments. "Soon," they

---

9. This is not a new story. Jesus himself read it in the pamphlets of the prophets and retold it as his own in much the same way that I am doing now in this novel.

say, even in the twenty-first century they're still insisting that it is, "Soon." It's always "Soon." It's always, "Maybe even today," for them.

Instead, think backwards, think of the long relationship through time culminating in the arrival of the son. But I'm getting ahead of the story.

During the first three years, there was no fruit from the vineyard. No fruit for the eating. This according to the Levitical law.[10] The fruit of the fourth year was held as a holy celebration for the Lord. But the fruit of the fifth year was to be finally harvested and enjoyed. This is not only the law of the Lord but it is also good husbandry. In that fifth year the owner of the vineyard sent his servant to collect a portion of that fruit from his tenants as his due.

But they beat the servant and sent him back shivering, sweating and empty-handed. So the owner of the vineyard sent another, but the husbandmen beat the second servant as well as the warning wind picked up swirling dust all around them. The owner then sent a third servant who they also tortured. Shapeless and broken, they cast him out. They would have none of this talk of brotherhood, and peace and love

So the owner said to himself, "What shall I do? What is left? What more? Shall I send them this at last, my first, and my beloved, my only? Indeed, I shall send them my son."

And the tenants, seeing the son, conspired together. "We will kill the lad," they said and then, proving themselves woefully ignorant of inheritance law continued saying, "and then the vineyard will be ours. All ours." In their final mad act of war they cast him out from that empty place devoid of stars, devoid of light, devoid of love. And they killed the owner's son, left him bloodied and battered in the dirt outside the walls. Dead.

So, a question: What will the owner of the vineyard do now? Have no illusions about the cause of human strife in this post-apostolic wasteland. You know the rules. I sent you scribes and wise-men, professors and scientists, educators, engineers, scholars, theologians, translators and historians. I sent you my servants the prophets, and some of them you hounded, some of them you hunted, and haunted. You hurt them. Some of them you labeled as traitors and deported them as malcontents and heretics. They're all dead now, of head wounds and gunshots to the chest, but seldom buried. So now a question: what will the owner of the vineyard do to the sons of those who murdered the prophets and assassinated his son?

---

10. You can look them up for yourselves in Leviticus 19:23-25

He will destroy them. Of course that's what he'll do. And he will take the vineyard away from those wicked tenants and give it to others. Is this supersessionism? Is it replacement theology? Perhaps. But don't let later Christian anti-Semitism and replacement theology nullify the story. The first Christians were, like their master, descendants of Father Abraham.[11]

The scribes and priests objected. "Heaven forbid!" they exclaimed. "We only wanted to entertain an exchange of ideas, Jesus. There's no call for censorship or judgment like that. You can't just go around condemning everyone who disagrees with you."

But Jesus said, "No. It's all there. You've read it. *'The stone that the builders rejected will become the chief cornerstone.'* And when that stone falls on someone it will crush him to powder. Dust he was; dust he shall be." And because they recognized that the story was about them, the scribes and priests tried to seize him. But they held back. They were too afraid of the mob to attempt any direct action against him at that time.

9. Pretending To Be Sincere

So they watched him. They stared at him and they followed him. They sent spies and Pinkerton detectives[12] with covert recording devices strapped to their chests who feigned themselves, pretending to be sincere in order to monitor his activities and to mark his motions through space and time.

They wanted to twist his words, to fold, spindle, and mutilate them before reporting him to the authority and jurisdiction of the governor—even if the Roman governors themselves were only amateurs playing at Roman law. This is how the world works. This is how the world has always worked. The wicked walk on every side and the lowest of men are lifted up. It was thus when Nebuchadnezzar spies lurked in the back allies of Babylon. It was thus when Allen Dulles and George H. W. Bush skulked around in the shadowy basements of the CIA. And thus it will be for every strong-armed ruler everywhere. Scoundrels will enjoy their peace and the wicked will

---

11. Maybe now's a good time to quote the Jewish Christian Prime Minister of England, Benjamin Disraeli who said in a speech to the House of Commons in 1829, "Where is your Christianity if you do not believe in their Judaism? . . . All the early Christians were Jews, every man in the early ages of the Church by whose power or genius the Christian faith was propagated was a Jew."

12. And the Pinkerton agents were a good choice for this work, experienced as they are with both union busting and skull cracking.

swallow up the righteous. It may have been an obscene affair, but it was their affair and they were committed to it.

10. Gross Nationalism Masquerading as Piety

"Rabbi," they said. "Teacher," they said as they grinned. "We know that you are honest. Honest to a fault. And we know that you show no undeserved favoritism." They said these things with a salute on their lips and a sneer in their hearts, "We know that you teach the true way to God."

"What do you want?" he asked them. He was getting bored with their faux civility and their phony courtesy.

"Tell us, is it lawful for devout and patriotic Jews to pay the annual poll tax of our Roman overlords?"

And, oh, what a clever trap it was. Say "YES" and he would alienate his base with accusations of antinationalism and a lack of patriotism. They would never willingly pay that tax. The humiliation of subjugation was too great. But to say "NO" would leave him open to charges of treason to the Roman Empire. What would he do? What could he say?

"Bring me a denarius; bring me one of those silver pennies," he said to them.

Someone in the crowd fished a coin from his pocket and flicked it to him. Jesus caught it deftly and examined it, both obverse and reverse. "Whose image and superscription is here? Whose likeness and inscription is engraved upon it?"

"Caesar!" they said, "Obviously." The image of the deified Caesar stamped upon the coin was offensive to all law abiding Jews as it violated the commandment against graven images.

"Well then," Jesus told them coolly, "render unto the Caesar in Rome all those things that belong to the Caesar. What is due to him? Money? Maybe. Loyalty? Some, perhaps. Honor? Give whatever honor may be due to dishonorable men. But give to God, and only to God, those things that belong to God and only to God."

Do not be fooled by this. Do not misunderstand. This is no tactful, noncommittal non-answer. This is no skillful evasion; he has taken sides. There is no apolitical preaching. There never was. There never could be. Pay the poll tax; support the state, he tells them. And this in no way violates your loyalty to and worship of God. Is it treason? Is it insubordination? Very well could be. But it is not, in any way, civic camouflage.

Do not give in to gross nationalism masquerading as piety. Don't be taken in by appeals to our so-called 'Judeo-Christian heritage.' This is a spurious credo and a vacuous faith. Religious nationalism is a desperate void. Blood and soil populism is the dust of the devil and the fear of *überfremdung* is not restricted to Nazi Germany. You can find it just as easily in the United States of America where they wholeheartedly believe in the inadequacy of reason. Children in cages at the border, forcible hysterectomies, race riots, viral racism, police brutality, the exploitation of the two-thirds world and rampant poverty—none of these can be severed from the passion of the self-righteous nationalist. Your plutocratic oligarchs holding Bibles and posing for pictures in front of the Temple while their riot squads fire tear gas at the priests do not fool God in heaven. "Give to God what belongs to God!"

"Why aren't you writing this down?" he asked his disciples.

"Master," they whined. "You told us to toss our notes out last time, so we've hired a professional rememberer."

Jesus gave them this warning: "In the paraphrased words of the Jewish carpenter who renounced his father's name to sing the blues out on Highway Sixty-One, be careful of your memories. You won't be able to relive them after they've gone."[13]

11. No Mere Absurdity

Next with questions came the Sadducees. The Sadducees believed neither in angels nor spirits, nor in life after death.[14] They rejected these beliefs as the newfangled, modern theological inventions of the preceding two hundred years and not explicitly described in the *Torah*. They drew their faith from the books of Moses, and rejected the oral law additions created by the pharisaical rabbis, just as they also rejected a fatalistic attitude believing instead that humans have a free will to do good or to do evil. They were aristocratic and educated, landowners and rich, but they weren't necessarily more (or less) influenced by Greek culture than other Jewish groups of the day.[15]

---

13. Either Jesus was paraphrasing or was quoting from some now lost translation of a song by Bob Dylan, born Robert Zimmerman—Zimmerman being the German word for 'Carpenter.'

14. Neither did they believe in life after life, as you and I do, Theo.

15. And it's certainly not at all true to say that they were the "secular branch of

Dum Spiro Spero

But it's true that they also did not believe in the resurrection of the dead. And why would they? There is little in the *Torah* that can be read with an eye to the resurrection of the dead, and what is there is rare, obscure, and late. In the *Torah* there is no resurrection, only the grave, the pit. There is only the hungry mouth of *Sheol*. Everyone—good, bad, or indifferent—is swallowed up by the grave. This is why they came to Jesus with their particular question.

"Master," they began, "Moses instructed us that if a man's brother should die without children, that he should marry his dead brother's wife and raise up seed, that is to say have children with her for his dead brother's name."

"Yes," Jesus agreed. "The levirate marriage ensures the continued legacy of a good man's name. Even in death, he should not be forgotten."

"To be sure. To be sure," the Sadducees acknowledged, "but imagine a hypothetical situation if you will. There is a family of seven brothers, and the first of these brothers marries a wife, but dies without a son. The second, in obedience to the law, takes her to wife, but he also dies. The third brother, and the fourth likewise, and in the same manner all seven brothers marry her and die without producing an heir. Finally the woman dies as well. So now, in the resurrection life that you and the Pharisees and so many others believe, whose wife will she be for she married them all?"

This is no trick question. There is no trap here. It is honest theological debate. Though somewhat ridiculous, their hypothetical example is no mere absurdity to make Jesus look foolish. They presented him with a perfectly logical syllogism:

MAJOR PREMISE: Polyandry[16] is ridiculous.

MINOR PREMISE: The resurrection of the dead will lead to polyandry.

CONCLUSION: The resurrection of the dead is ridiculous.

Jesus could have cited the writings of Daniel to refute them, ". . . of those sleeping in the Land of Dust, many will awaken, some to everlasting life, some to shame and everlasting disgrace," but he didn't. He knew they'd already rejected that text as a modern invention unworthy of their consideration. Instead he gave his own answer. An answer in two parts.

Judaism," so stop spreading that particular ill fitted slander.

16. A woman marrying more than one husband. Technically this is covered by the term polygamy, but we usually use that word in the traditional sense of a man having more than one wife. The more specific term for having more than one wife would be polygyny.

"First," he said, "you don't understand the nature of the resurrection. The sons and daughters of this age are married and given in marriage. They procreate and produce children. This is all perfectly natural. But in that age, the age to come, when they are equal to the angels,[17] they will not need marriage or procreation as they will not die anymore."

The Sadducees began to object, but Jesus cut them off, "Second," he said over them "Even Moses demonstrated that the resurrection of the dead is a thing to be believed. Do you remember how, at the burning bush, he heard the voice of God calling out from the flames, 'I am the God of your father, the God of Abraham, the God of Isaac, and the God of Jacob,'? If they were dead and gone, with their lights snuffed out by the darkness of *Sheol*, then God would have said, 'I *was* the God of Abraham, Isaac, and Jacob.' Right? For he is not a God of the dead, but of the living, and all live to him and in him. But if he *is* the God of Abraham, Isaac, and Jacob—in the present tense, and *if* they have died (as all men do) then they must live again in him."

12. Double Damnation

Now some of the scribes and seminarians were there that day, and they were delighted to hear Jesus take down the proud Sadducees this way. They applauded as the Sadducees drifted off. "Well spoken, Master Jesus. Well done." But Jesus pushed into them as well.

"How can they say that the Christ is David's son?"

Caught off guard, they stammered. "What?"

"It's a simple question. How can they say that the Christ is David's son? How can the Messiah be lesser than David, when David himself says in the *Tehillim* 'The Lord said unto my Lord, sit Thou on my right hand till I make thine enemies thy footstool,'? If King David calls the Messiah Lord, then how is he his son?"

But the scribes couldn't answer.

So Jesus turned to his disciples and the rest of the crowd and said, "Beware of the scribes with their soft, effeminate robes, with their long-sleeved, bejeweled amaranthine robes. They're eunuchs and liars who love going about dressed in purple and hearing greetings and salutations from the people as they walk through the markets. They snatch up poor widows'

---

17. Like the Australian singer and bad seed, Nick Cave, the Sadducees didn't believe in the existence of angelic beings but that's not really important to Jesus' response.

houses when they can't pay their debts and make pretentious prayers in the temple courts as if they could stand before God. They will receive double damnation."

13. Everything Comes from Them

He looked up from there and saw the rich, in their finery, in their plum and gold colored finery. He saw them pull up to the Temple in silver Mercedes driven by liveried chauffeurs. He watched them cast their gifts into the trumpet shaped treasury jars.[18] After they'd waved to the crowds and returned to their cars, Jesus saw another putting her treasure into the treasury containers—a poor widow woman. She put in two mites,[19] tiny Roman *leptons,* copper coins worth all of maybe two dollars.

"Of a truth," Jesus said. "Forsooth and verily I tell you, she put in more than they."

The universe is composed mostly of hydrogen and the poor. And these things themselves are composed of further smaller pieces: protons, electrons, quarks and leptons. Little things that may be elementary and incapable of further division. It's the little things that make so much. They may be the wretched and despised of the earth, but they are blessed too. Everything comes from them.

"The rich ones gave from an abundance." Jesus told his followers, "They give from an overabundance, a superabundance, which is a surplus value equal to the value created by the labourers and workers in excess of their own labour-cost, and which is appropriated—that is to say, stolen—by capitalists as profit. So they give, as they say, from their abundance.[20] This is how they devour widows' houses. This is how they turn aside the needy from judgment, make widows their prey, and how they rob the fatherless. Those that devour the property of widows and orphans swallow coals of fire into their bellies. This is how they shall burn. But the widow woman gave from her penury."

---

18. There were thirteen of them, one for each of the categories of the annual Temple budget. Donors contributed to the budgetary item that they felt most dear to their hearts by tossing their coins into the appropriate jar.

19. It might have been good ole' Willy Tyndale who first called them mites, but he was remembering an unfinished poem by Geoffrey Chaucer that spoke of *mytes.* Divide and subdivide, push it further back.

20. Does Jesus sound like Marx or does Marx sound like Jesus?

"Hear this: Praise the widow and her giving we might, and she deserves our honor, to be sure. So praise the widow woman and her mite, but we must also condemn the system that created her. Moses told us clearly, 'There must be no poor among you.' He couldn't have said it more plainly than that."

14. Cry Terror in the Sky

We sat there watching the people moving in and around the temple for a while longer. Many of the pilgrims sang as they moved in and out of its courts. "This is the temple of the Lord, the temple of the Lord, the temple of the Lord."[21] The pilgrims chanting the song were led by the Levites who accompanied them with harps and trumpets and cymbals. "This is the temple of the Lord, the temple of the Lord, the temple of the Lord. See how nobly adorned it is, with goodly stones and holy offerings. See the marble of its stones and its gold and golden glory."

"But all these things," Jesus told us, "all these things and more, things seen and things still unseen, will give way in days to come. They will collapse and they will fall. One stone here will not remain upon another. Do not say 'The temple of the Lord, the temple of the Lord, the temple of the Lord.' Don't trust in deceptive, worthless words, even the ones that sound religious enough for family friendly radio."

"But, Master!" we exclaimed. "Master, when and what sign? How will we prepare?"

"There is no preparation," he said flatly. "Take heed and do not be deceived by the smooth words of claimants to my name. 'I am the Christ,' they'll say, and 'I am the real thing. Lo, here!' and 'LOL, there! The time is now.' But do not go. Do not follow these wretched things."

"What will account for the bursting gamma rays of those days? An exchange of nuclear weapons? Terrorist attack? Magnetic pole swap? Gravitational collapse? There will be wars and commotions. There will be tumults all around you and raging infernos, like that of Vesuvius, of Krakatoa, of Lawetlat'la. Do not be afraid. These things must be, but this is not the end."

"The blood circulates through the body as a continuous stream. Round and round. Russia attacks Israel. Israel attacks Palestine. North

---

21. This was a popular praise and worship song, composed in the time of the prophet Jeremiah.

Dum Spiro Spero

Korea attacks South.[22] And the United States attacks everyone. Oxygen in. Carbon Dioxide out. It circulates. It breathes. It burns, but this is not life. And this is not the end."

"Look also for landslides, earthquakes, and famines, for all manner of peculiar pestilence and disease. Look for landmine gardens and jackals in the hills. Look for lightning flashes over the heads of border patrol guards armed with 6.5 mm Mannlicher-Carcano rifles and Smith and Wesson .38 revolvers.[23] There will be strange sights in the sky and terrifying signs in the heavens. There will be plenty of these, and still this is not the end. Do not panic."

"History is little more than a record of burning and ignorant men. Fire and ashes and dumb-asses. Rinse and Repeat. Evil and ignorant men will deliver you up to like coals to their synagogues and embers to their black-iron prisons. That will be the time to speak. But don't worry about it. You will not need radio waves, ultraviolet, or infrared. I will give you a mouth which is my mouth. And words which are my words. I will put my words into your mouth and in your bones like a fire. I will give you a wisdom that no one can gainsay or resist."

"You will be betrayed, but aren't we all? You will be betrayed by your parents and your brothers, by so-called friends and once-loving wives. Some of you will die. But don't we all? Some of you will burn. You will be despised, but not a hair of your head will perish. Not a molecule will be lost. In patience you will possess ye your souls."

"Watch for the circumscribing of Jerusalem; that is when the desolation is nigh. When you see al-Quds surrounded, everything written in the *Tanakh* will come true. Surrounded by the *goyim! Oy vey!* The Romans will raze it then raise it as *Aelia Capitolina* and there *will* be no more *Aliyah*. You may go up, but it will not be there.

"Cry treason! Cry thief! Cry terror in the sky, but you will cry."

"Those in Judea should flee to the mountains. Those in the city should flee forthwith. These are the days of vengeance and desolation. It will be hardest for those with child, for those nursing and those giving suck. The great distress of the land will be heaped upon them. It's always that way. They fall by the edge of the sword, by the bullet of the gun. They will be

---

22. Or maybe it will be the other way round this time.

23. All purchased legally through mail order catalogue from Klein's Sporting Goods Company in Chicago, Illinois.

beaten with clubs and kicked with boots. They'll be led away as slaves when Jerusalem is torn down and Aelia built up."

"Look for signs in the sun and visions in the moon. Look for solar flares and nightmares. There will be distress among the nations and on the surging seas. Men's hearts will war with themselves and fail for fear. From the realm of atoms and elementary particles to the realm of galactic clusters, the very powers of heaven will be shaken."

"There are four fundamental, elementary forces that shape the universe, motivating every action and interaction in the universe as we know it.[24] None of them have any bearing on this but all of them are involved. It could not be otherwise. These are the physical forces that shape and direct every action and interaction in the known and observable universe. How could it be otherwise? What we have is a kinetic theory of gases. What we need is a kinetic theory of people that considers people as a collection of widely spaced individuals, moving in random directions and at a broad range of speeds. This is how to predict the future."

"Fainting men will watch the falling sky. *Cecidit de coelo stell magna!* Then they'll see what they missed. They'll see the one they were waiting for in clouds of power."

"Behold the fig tree!" he announced with a flourish of his arms, "and all the varieties of trees—the palm, the oak, the juniper, the larch, even the Zaqqum tree that blooms in hell. You know that when the trees shoot forth in leaves it is nearly summer. The signs are there for anyone to see. Observable. Predictable. When you see them, you should understand. This generation—this very generation—in a real and perfectly normal, un-metaphorical way of speaking, literally—this generation will not pass away before the end. Why's that so hard to comprehend? Heaven and earth may pass away—and maybe sometimes we wish that they would. But my words are forever. Listen for them in the eternal vibrations of the strings of our twenty-six dimensional universe."[25]

"Don't let your hearts be troubled. Don't be weary even when your hearts are chipped and broken, when they are numbed by the tremendous weight of this world. Don't be dulled by drink, or wine or strong beer. I know. I know. The Proverbs tell us that wine and strong drink are appropriate for

---

24. They are: Gravitation, Electromagnetism, and the Strong and Weak Nuclear Forces.

25. In Bosonic superstring theory there are twenty-six dimensions. In other string theories there are ten or eleven, meanwhile Bob Dylan had numerous red, white, and blue shoe strings and silent telephones. Either way, the universe is weird.

Dum Spiro Spero

those with heavy hearts and Paul says it's good for your stomach, but drink responsibly. The day will come unawares. Like a snare, like a tripwire surprise. Whoosh! Bang! There it is. Watch and pray. Always. Perhaps you'll be counted worthy of an escape. Maybe, but maybe not."

"You will see racist kings railing at hurricanes, threatening them with nuclear weapons. They are vulgar trumpets of doom. Is it King Lear? No. King Leer. Reason is dead and truth with it. The only way forward is to ride the hobby horse of insanity. Dada was right. Qoheleth was right. Everything is meaningless. Look for all of this. Look for it because an invisible, unseen apocalypse is a contradiction in terms. But remember and keep this clear in your mind: Everything is wasted vanity."

All of this he said to us, and a little more, while he was in the courts of the Temple. Then, every night, he left the temple to camp in the garden on the Mount of Olives. Every morning, as early as the dawn, we gathered in the temple courts under the fading, scrubbed out non sequitur graffiti to hear what he would say to us.

15. How To Destroy a Prophet

It was time for the Festival of the Unleavened Bread and the cramped and twisting streets of Jerusalem were thronged with crowds. National Guardsmen stood on the corners armed with automatic rifles and rocket propelled grenades. Tanks and armored personnel carriers rumbled up and down the streets. Even the traffic police were out in multiplied force wearing body armor and carrying m249 SAW machine guns.

And the top priests and *Torah*-teachers were looking for a way to kill the prophet.[26] They met in the shadows as they always do, in the hidden chambers of forgotten caves beneath the city. They whispered the secret words of greeting—words condign to their clandestine concave—secret words kept guarded from public exposure. And, having acknowledged one another in the manner prescribed by the honorable elders, they pulled back the hoods of their heavy, woolen cloaks. Even uncovered however, their faces remained obscured by the shadows of the underground Star Chamber. Secret tribunals and shadow governments can always be found under the same stones. Lift the rock and watch the centipedes flee.

---

26. It shouldn't have been too difficult to find one, after all, he was looking for a way to die.

They said, "Come! We'll devise a plot against him. And come! Let us strike at him with our tongues. We will wound him with our words. We'll release a torrent profanities—both pious and polite. We will use both slander and libel against him, and then we'll no longer have to endure with him.

"We will use public humiliation coupled with oft repeated lies. We will isolate him from resources and from his comrades. We will threaten him with termination for even minor faults. Let us set impossible goals so that we can mock his inevitable failures. And if he should approach something like success, we will sabotage his work. If he should find victory in some small thing or another we will be there to claim the credit and the reward for ourselves."

This is how to destroy a prophet. This is how to break his spirit.

Dig a pit for him to fall in and let it be filled with slime so that he cannot escape. Let it be filled with mud and mire for his feet. Ready a stone to crush him. He will fall into the pit. Destruction from above. Fleeing terror on every side. We've spread our nets to capture him. Like an ox to the slaughter, like a deer in the headlights, or a bright little bird darting into the snare, he is waiting for the arrow that will pierce his heart.

This is how to break a prophet. This is how to destroy his spirit.

We have heard it was said, "You will not harbor hatred for your brother," And this is holy and just, but it does not apply to us for he is no brother of ours. And we have also heard, "you will not exact vengeance, or bear a grudge of any kind against the children of your people," but he is not one of our people. He has been banished. He has been stripped of his uniform and his rank. He has been removed from the rolls, his words struck from the scrolls. Send him out into the cold; let him suffer the wind. Let him be crushed by immediate and unmerciful hands.

As Moses' own tribe rose up against him, so do we rise up against him.

As Moses was cast into the water, so do we thrust him into a pit.

By the decree of angels, and by the command of holy men we excommunicate, expel, curse, and damn him, with the consent of God, Blessed Be He, and with the consent of all the Holy Congregation, in front of these holy Orders and Regulations, with the excommunication which Joshua banned Jericho, with the curse with which Elisha cursed the boys, and with all the curses which are written in the Book of the Law. Cursed be he by day. Cursed be he by night. Cursed be he when he comes in and when he goes out. The Lord will not spare him. The anger and wrath of the Lord will not depart from him. And his name will be blotted out from under heaven.

We here do order that no one should communicate with him orally or in writing, show him any favor, or stay with him under the same roof. Neither should they read anything composed by him. Now and forever. Amen.

16. Whatever His Appearance, Whatever the Motive

Then Satan entered Judas, being a number of the twelve.

Speak to me now of motive. Describe his intent, if you can. If you can read the heart, tell me—was it avarice? Was it wrath and pride disguised as noble idealism? According to our source, it was none but Satan. Though, for what it's worth, avarice, envy, and pride are often indistinguishable from satanic possession. Even so, we shouldn't discount the complex, multivalent tangle of human motivations. We cannot ignore emotional, psychological motivations or personalist philosophy. We will accept the story as it is told, for now. Let him be polysemous and we will keep the ambiguity in mind.

But other questions arise: Did Satan assume a pleasing shape or appear in the traditional trappings? Was he wearing an Armani suit or did he sport the customary goat horns, tail, and hooves? Did the scatological prince wrap himself in leprous skins? Did he carry red hot tongs? Or perhaps that old stand-by, a pitchfork? Did he bring along his big black book of names? And if so, did he ask Judas to sign it in blood?

Did Satan leave a mark upon Judas? Did he brand Judas the way that runaway slaves were branded? Was Judas marked as cattle are—with a bar sinister to demonstrate his position as property and chattel? We have so many questions. Was Satan's presence announced by a murder of crows on a high tower? Did he arrive with iron or in fire? Or perhaps with neither iron nor fire, but with the oil of an unctuous tongue? Was there blood? Was there heat? Was there ash or smoke? Did the Prince of the Air leave his nest of intrigues to make feints and false thrusts upon the earth? He does oft times appear as an angel of light. Did he do so at this time?

And on this occasion, on the entering of Judas Iscariot, did Satan introduce himself as Outis? As Nemo? As Nobody? Or did he come in the full regalia and power of the Lord of the Flies, Beelzebub?

Whatever his appearance, whatever the motive, Judas went and communed with the chiefs and leaders and captains, seeking a way to betray Jesus. He promised to find an appropriate opportunity to give him into their hands without the surrounding crowds. And they were pleased to pay him for this exchange.

17. *A Memento Mori for Those Who Would See*

Dawn broke over the eastern hill on the Day of Unleavened Bread. In the temple, priests prepared for the slaughter. Hearts like stones, in time, may change the course of rivers but who, in the light of that new dawn, could have charted the course of that day? Who, even with the prophets' foreknowledge could have felt the pulse of those hearts and the progression of those hours?

To Peter and John Jesus said, "The water is now drawn. The room has been swept with a feather and the leaven removed. Even as we speak the lamps are being filled with new oil and in the kitchen, bread is kneaded and ready to bake. The day has arrived. The time is now. Go into the city. Find the Aquarius man who will lead you to the room of the Goodman. Say to him, 'Where is the chamber in which my friends and I can celebrate?' He will show you our high-ceilinged cenacle for the evening. Tonight we will try to forget the torture raids and peasant liquidations. We will forget for a time that Relocation Camp Number 517 has been relocated, and that no one can, or will say where. We will forget, to what degree it is possible to forget such terrible things, the barbed wire compounds that surround immigrant families, and the torched olive groves behind concrete walls in occupied lands."

Peter and John stared at him without comprehension. "What?"

"Go into the city. Find the man carrying a jar of water. He has a room for us."

"What?"

"Go!" he said, exasperated. "Go. Get. Gone."

They went and found it just as he said. What a mystery is life. What a mystery love. Time and space are mysteries too. The winds blow; rivers flow into the sea. The core of the Earth is a spinning liquid ball of iron that produces electrical currents and magnetic fields. There are traces of life in the Sulphur hell that is the planet Venus. The sun sets, the sun rises. All of life is a wonder and a mystery. All of life is a *Memento Mori* for those who would see.

18. *All the Tormented Souls*

Before smallpox pustules, before the armpit buboes of the plague, before the all variable symptoms of Covid-19, before the collapse of unstable plasma, before terrorist attacks the hour had come and Jesus sat down with his friends.

"I have desired to celebrate this Passover with you," he said. "This life that we have right now will last forever. At least that's what we tell ourselves. And we have to believe it. Consider the source, right? We tell ourselves that we will endure. We tell ourselves that it will all be okay. We tell ourselves that next year will be better. And we find comfort in that dangerously threadbare statement. "With great desire I have desired to celebrate this Passover with you before I suffer."

"This would have been my last Passover," he went on, "but I'll not eat the unleavened bread and I'll not drink from the Paschal wine until the ancient feast has found its glowing fulfillment in the coming Kingdom of God."

This would be the Last Supper. But we can call it by other names. Call it The Lord's Supper. Or call it Communion. The Eucharist. Call it the Mystical, Secret Supper. He shares this meal with all the tormented souls, the *écorché vif*, and *les damnés de la terre*. He shares the meal with the apostles and with his friends. He shares the meal with us. The anonymous author of the Didache wrote, "There are two ways, one of life and one of death; and between the two ways there is a great difference,[27] but there is one meal to share with one Lord."

Figure 29–Do this in the losing of forgetfulness.

So share with me the medicine of immortality. The heart pumps blood and the lungs fill with oxygen. Inhalation. Exhalation. Blood through the coronary arteries. Blood through the kidneys. Oxygen in. Carbon Dioxide

27. Didache 1:1

out. The body breathes. The body lives. But not for long. His back is already to the wall; the knife is already at his throat. The electrodes are already placed to his genitals for torture. He does not have long now.

Later they will say that the Eucharist must be preserved and held special, holy. The author of the Didache will say that only the baptized should receive the bread and the wine that are the flesh and blood of our Savior.[28] And mostly I agree. But remember that Jesus shared this last supper and first communion with Judas, whom Satan had entered. "The hand of my betrayer is here among us," Jesus told them. "He is eating my food and drinking my drink. I will go where I will go. I will go where it is written that I must go. But for the one who is drinking my drink and eating my food and will betray me anyway, there is only woe. You may count him among the two-headed horse corpses and with the malevolent leopard men. You may list him with the six-legged snakemen of the wild Amazon, with zombie dogs and transnational corporation spiders. He is one of them now.

19. Space may Be Curved but the Heart of Man Is Bent

This is now the war of everyone against everyone else, the struggle to conquer and to control, to stand atop the heap. This is the time to shout the words of Ozymandias to the world, "Look on my Works, ye Mighty, and despair!" There was strife among them, even among his friends at the table, to determine who would be credited as the greatest. Space may be curved but the heart of man is warped. It is bent.

"Kings and gentiles, and the kings of the gentiles like to exercise their lordship over others. They demand the pride of place and enjoy all the prerogatives of power. They will expect you to call them benefactors and to thank them and bless them for their great benevolence. They will expect you to bless them for their kindness and their generosity which falls like rain from heaven upon all the little and insignificant people of the earth. But not you jackasses. There will be no onolatry in my kingdom. If you want to sit at my table, and want to eat my food, drink my drink, you cannot be one of those. The Porsche, the Rolex, the Stuart Hughes Diamond Edition suit, the sun, the moon, the stars—these things are not for you. We've said it before: flesh takes motion to make motions. Ambitious will does what it will. But not among you. Among you, less is more. Do you understand?"

---

28. Didache 9:5

Dum Spiro Spero

"You should be like the youngest, like the youth. You should be the least, like the guy polishing boots in the closet, like the woman gathering twigs for fuel. You know that the optimates will sit at tables with Damask cloths and bone china waiting to be served, waiting for someone to bring them silver forks and sharpened knives. They enjoy the perquisites and privileges. They enjoy all the dignity of their rank, all the prerogatives of power. But look. I'm a servant and not one to seize or to grasp. I will not exploit."

"My father's given me a kingdom that is mine to share and I will share it with the ones who've stayed with me through my trials, through my temptations and my vexations. If you want to eat and drink at the table in my kingdom, if you want to sit on thrones as judges for the twelve tribes of Israel then you'll understand what I'm saying. I will let him who wins the victory sit with me on my throne. And the victor won't be the obvious winner. Listen. 'Victory or Death' is not a new or radical military policy. The wives of Sparta on the eve of battle told their husbands, 'Come home with your shield or on it.' This is nothing new. But in my kingdom, in the new heaven, victory will be something different. You must learn what I mean."

20. The Crepitations of Your Weakness

"Simon. Simon," Jesus sighed. "What can I say? Ready yourself. Feel your pulse. Test your vision. Listen for the crepitations of your weak knees, the grating, cracking pop of bone on bone. Look, Satan has desired to have you. He wants to own you like Job. The four-horned head of hell has made demands upon your life. He has made four thousand and nineteen hundred steps across the graveyard. He has traced his hand across the stone and said the words, '*Da mihi, quod cupio.*'[29] He has summoned the celestial court of Oyer and Terminer to condemn you and to bind you heel to neck until blood gushes from your nose. But Simon, Simon, I have prayed for you. I have prayed that your faith will not fail, even when you fall. And you will. And that later, when you've turned yourself around, you'll be able to give strength to your sisters and your brothers."

"*Quo vadis*, Lord?" Peter said. "Where are you going? I'll go. I'll go. I'll go into exile. I'll go to prison for you. I'll even go to my death for you. I'll go anywhere. I'm all yours. *Totus tuus sum.*"

---

29. This is the demand of terrorists and toddlers around the world, "Give me what I want!"

"Peter, Peter," Jesus sighed. "You won't get through this day without failing me. Before the rooster wakes the dawn you'll have denied even knowing me. A crisis of faith like a seismic terror will leave you waving your little white flag of surrender."

Jesus looked around the table at them all and sighed again. "I'm so tired."

21. More Than Enough

"Sell what you have and buy a Buick-knife," he said to them quietly.

"Uh... Lord, do you mean a buck-knife?" one of them asked cautiously.

"No. Bigger. A Buick-Knife."

"We've got a zip gun that Andrew made out of a mess of scrounged up plumbing materials and a rubber band on the firing pin. And," they added with a sly grin, "we always have Peter's foil."

"Well, that's enough, I suppose."

"And my cousin's got a line on twelve unexploded sticks of dynamite. We can..."

"Stop. No! This is enough," he told them.

"But the ideas of the ruling class are the ruling ideas," they shouted over his objection. "Always, Lord. Neither Martin nor Malcolm has had a lasting effect. It is still business-as-usual on Wall Street, Main Street, and Pennsylvania Avenue. What we need is a more aggressive, more violent kind of faith. Let us bring back the blade. Let us wield the sword of the flesh in one hand and the sword of the spirit in the other. Then we'll show you how we can win the world."

"I said that's enough!" Jesus shouted. "That's more than enough. Let it go! Our fight is just; our cause is pure. If we adopt their rules and tactics, if we take up their tricks we may win the battles, of course, but we will have lost the war. We will lose. And we will lose everything. Taking up arms of our own would give them excuse, would give them cause and justification to make a righteous killing of us all. Watch for them to stir us up to violent action. Beware of their provocations. They want us to react with violence so they can unleash the wrath they've been stockpiling since the beginning. Look for them to lie and to twist so they can put off the mask of civility and strike with impunity. They're going to malign me," he continued. "They're going to label me as a traitor and my followers likewise. But this was expected. It was written down; don't let it get you down."

Dum Spiro Spero

The disciples grumbled.

"Let's go out to that place on the Mount of Olives," he said to them. "You know the one I like. Let's go."

22. I Don't Want To Run with the Horses

A woman old enough to be his mother stopped him then on the street outside the upper room. "Son," she said in that tone that only deeply concerned mothers can fully master, "what's wrong with you? You sigh too much and too often. You didn't speak strong tonight."

"Nothing is wrong, mother," he answered with a weak and trembling grin.

"You can't fool me, Jesus. I know you. I've known you since you was a boy. Something's bothering you and I can tell."

He tried the smile again and patted her shoulder. "Everything will be fine. I promise. I'm just tired."

The woman shook her head and reached out with both of her substantial arms to pull him into a fierce embrace. "You listen to me, now, son. You listen, and you hear me true. You know that we're with you. All of us. We're all behind you, every step. But even if we weren't, even if we all fell aside and fell away, God is still with you. The Lord is with you, and he's going to take care of you."

"The footmen have worn me out, mother," he said, his voice breaking, "I don't *want* to run with the horses." Then Jesus wept on her great, matronly bosom.[30]

23. Silence in the Garden

He went off about a stone's throw away—but who threw the stone? And how far? Not far. But far enough to be alone, but not far enough to be isolated. He went off to pray.

"If you are willing," he began his prayer, an orant in the garden with his elbows close to his side

---

30. Yes. You are certainly correct. I've borrowed this story from the life of Martin Luther King Jr.

Figure 30–Prayer is danger.

and his hands in the air. And don't let the sentimentalists among us confuse you here. Prayer is danger. Prayer is hurt and prayer is desperation. Lift up the hands which hang down and strengthen feeble knees. He prayed in that garden for a way to move forward. He prayed for a way out. Ignatius may have prayed to become food for the wild beasts so that he might be ground by their teeth and become the pure bread of God in a beautiful act of martyrdom, but Jesus prayed, "Remove the cup," because he was terrified. "If you are willing, remove the cup. But not my will, only yours. On Earth as above."

Sometimes prayer is resignation and self-sacrifice, but it is always dangerous.

And in the garden, a stone's throw away from his sleeping friends, surrounded by olive trees and imminent mortality, Jesus began to sweat great drops of blood. Hematohidrosis is a thing. You can look it up. The small blood vessels that fed into his sweat glands burst under the stress of his stress and anxiety.

Dum Spiro Spero

Figure 31–A comforting angel.

And he sweated great drops of blood from his forehead, and fingernails. His tears were scarlet tinged. He doubled over with stomach cramps and a ringing headache. But an angel from the realm of light appeared in the garden to give him strength enough to carry the sorrows and solemnity of that night into the soon dawning final day.

Polycarp,[31] tied to the stake with the flames rising around him, heard a voice from heaven encouraging him toward his death: "Be strong, Polycarp, and act like a man." But what does Jesus hear from heaven? Nothing. Jesus hears silence. The voice of his encouragement came during his baptism, back when everything was easy and clear. But now, in the dark, on the cusp of blood and vicious viscera, there is only silence from heaven and nothing more.

Some of the details of this story are missing from our earliest copies of the bible. It is missing from the Codex Vaticanus and other important, early manuscripts. So we might ask: Is the hematohidrosis a later embellishment? Is the strengthening arm of an angel a bit of colorful folklore that was later added to the story? Is it an unnecessary supernatural expansion? Were the great drops of blood thrown in later to combat the Gnostics and the

---

31. Bishop of Smyrna (modern day Izmir, in Turkey) A.D. 69-155. The right hand of Saint Polycarp was kept for many years at the Holy Monastery of *Panagia Ambelakiotissa* until it was stolen in the spring of 2013. The Albanian thieves were apprehended, but the arm of Polycarp is still missing. The vaguely disreputable, Jacob Spatharios may have a line on it, but this is not the time to talk about that shifty relic merchant. Look for him in the sequel.

Docetic heretics who argued that the Nazarene's body wasn't fully human but was only a phantasm? Was the strengthening angel added to muffle that silence from heaven? I do not know and couldn't begin to say, but it's not the potentially missing details of this pericope that frighten me. It's that silence in the garden, that unendurable silence from heaven.

24. Meacocks and Cowards

Ever notice how Roman soldiers won't do anything to you if you're obeying the law? Ever notice that the Temple guards won't come gunning at you if you behave and don't break the law? If you don't act like a terrorist they won't arrest you. Don't act like a terrorist and you won't get treated like a terrorist. Destroying private property or riling up dissent against the authorities will get you put on a government watch list. That's why they came for him in the garden at midnight. Law and Order must be maintained, right?

The soldiers marched into the garden in tight formation, dressed in full riot gear. They came with torches and swords but without their megaphones. They intended to keep this arrest secret and quiet. Journalists with their cameras and microphones had been kicked to the curb before they could follow the soldiers to the garden. Law and Order does not require transparency, after all. It usually functions better without.[32]

They were led by Judas, who was one of the twelve. He was one of us; even then, he was one of us. God help us. Then Judas drew near to Jesus to greet him with the intimate touch of trust. "With a kiss, Judas? Is that how you betray a friend?"

And suddenly there was a tumult of shouting and shoving. The disciples were screaming in panic and in pain. "Should we draw our swords? Should we run? Should we fight? We'll fight, Jesus. We'll swallow stones! Tell us what to do!" The soldiers swung their clubs and their swords in great arcs. Their truncheons smashed against the disciples bodies and turned their shouts of support to groans of pain.

"*Mani in alto.* Hands up! Don't Shoot!" Jesus said to his followers and to the chief priests and the captains of the guard, but it was too late. Peter, more zero than hero, more zero than Zorro, had already swung his blade and sliced off the ear of the high priest's servant. The soldiers responded by clubbing him to the ground along with Jesus and the others.

---

32. The fascists tell us this is so, and they're very fine people, to be sure.

"You come at me with carbon-fiber batons," Jesus said between blows, "You come at me and my friends with CS tear gas, which you know full well was banned by the Geneva Protocols. You come dressed in Kevlar armor and carrying riot shields. You come swinging truncheons at me as if I were a thug in the street. As if I were a back alley criminal. You could have come when I was in the open, in the light of day. But now you come. Now, in the dark. This is the power of darkness. This is your hour of power, you meacocks. You cowards."

"No more of this," Jesus told them, the riot guards and his disciples, all. "Enough," and for a moment the thrashing subsided. He touched the wounded man's ear and restored him. Healed him. But that action was lost in the shuffle as the guards seized him up, zip tied his hands, and dragged him to the high priest's house and the disciples scattered into the darkness.

25. Contradictions Are Revealed

Prick the conscience and contradictions well up to the surface—like pus, like blood. Prick the conscience and the gap between the value and the practice is exposed. Peter followed at a distance as they dragged Jesus, bound and gagged, through the twisted and tenebrous streets of Jerusalem. Peter stayed in the shadows, passing beneath balconies and overhanging canopies. He knew there would be police drones in the sky above, watching, tracking known terrorists, recording conversations, and identifying faces, scanning official databases for a match. He passed clusters of ragged homeless men and women gathered for warmth around trashcan fires. He did not wave and they returned the favor. He passed heaps of vomit and excrement and the corpse of a feral, mangy dog which was covered in flies. Puddles of stale wine and urine filled the gutters. Ants in the cracks between the pavement stones fed on clotted blood. Peter passed frightened pilgrims, shoved to the ground by the heavy-booted guards escorting Jesus to the home of the chief priest. Hearing the rumble of tanks, he paused briefly, beneath a poster featuring a smiling blond girl extolling the benefits of the German made, Doramad Radioactive Toothpaste.

Someone lit a fire in the brazier in the courtyard of the chief Priest's house. And as the staff and hangers-on in the chief priest's house gathered around it to warm themselves in its heat, Peter skulked close. One of the priest's maids gazed at him in the light of the flames. "This man," she shrieked and pointed, "This man was with him!"

A Life Known and Unknowable

Peter backed up rapidly. "Woman, I don't know him!" he croaked, laryngitic with fear. He shrunk back into the shadows as if he could melt and disappear into a puddle, seep into the soil. He would, if he could have, slipped through the cracks of the world into oblivion.

Later, a man saw him shivering in the shadows. "You! You are one of them, aren't you?"

Peter threw his arms in front of his face. "Man! I don't know him. I don't know him!" huffed as he dodged further into the shadows. "I don't know him." A great ruin was not far off, a vexation unto death. Great damage and great fear were now as near as the yawning sepulcher.

About half an hour later another accuser, a squint-eyed woman this time, confronted him. "This man is a Galilean! You can hear it in his voice. He's a Galilean! Either that or he is one of the *Galleanisti*, one of those followers of the Italian anarchist, Luigi Galleani. You can't trust any of these radicals, with their foreign accents and their 'direct actions.' Galleani looked more like a lawyer than a bomb throwing radical, with his balding pate and his beard. This one," she said motioning at Peter, "doesn't look like much either, but as my dear, departed mother used to say, 'you can't tell by lookin', can you? But just listen to his words, his accent. He's one of them. I'm sure of it."

"Who are you talking about?" asked a servant standing nearby.

"Galleani."

"Never heard of 'em," said the servant and went back to his duties in the house.

"But this one's one of them, I tell you. He's probably carrying a bomb right now," the squint-eyed woman shouted. But no one paid her any attention, and Peter slipped further into the shadows.

At that very moment Chauntecleer crowed clear and loud as if to cower that ancient serpent, Wyrm, back into the abyss beneath the earth. The cock crowed; the crow cocked. Jesus turned and locked eyes with Peter across the courtyard. Had he been there the whole time? Had he heard every dismissive word Peter spoke, every curse and curt denial? Peter remembered the prediction: "Before the rooster wakes the dawn. Before the coming of the light you will face a great shaking of the earth, a seismic terror, a crisis of contradictions." Peter ran sobbing from the courtyard in desperate anguish.

Dum Spiro Spero

26. *Status Quo Quotidians*

The generation of the Messiah, the Talmudic rabbis tell us, will have the face of a dog. And the people of that generation will smash that impudent and shameless face. Repeatedly. They will kick it in the jaw just to hear it howl. They will blindfold that face then strike it—first with a fist from the left, then a fist from the right. "Prophesy," they will guffaw. "Prophesy and tell us who struck you."

His trial is chaotic, disjointed and anarchic. It's a Marx Brothers riot without the slapstick, but plenty of slaps. It is perfunctory, but hardly routine. And those in charge are hardly indifferent. They blaze. They burn to see him sentenced. They are scribes and doctors and lawyers, but they are still amateurs at the law. They are *status quo* quotidians. His trial is not the result of the failures of great men, for they are not great men. They are weak and the poet rightly condemned them as men without conviction. They are mediocre personalities straddling the gulf of arrogance and stupidity and inflexibility. It is not forced. It is not inevitable fate. But here they are.

"We are noble men," they say when the light of the sun has crested in the east. "So tell us, Jesus, are you the Messiah? Are you the Christ?" But Jesus says nothing; he keeps his tongue and keeps his silence. "It is good that you are quiet," the elders tell him. "Messiah's have an unfortunate tendency to die young. And you don't wish to die do you, Jesus? But we are noble men, so you can tell us. Are you the messiah?" The sun is too hot. The moon is too cold. The pressure here is too great. He will be crushed beneath their cruel gaze. "Do you require a strengthening of memory, perhaps, Jesus? Have you forgotten? Are you the one?"

A quiet voice. A pleasant voice, even now. "If I tell you," he says with his eyes to the ground, "if I tell you, you will not believe. This ground is fruitless. There is no fecundity found in it." He raises his eyes to the sky, "And if I question you, you will not answer." He sighs before continuing. "But from this point forward, the Son of Man will find a seat at the right hand of Power."

"No more riddles, Jesus," they harrumph and they spit. "Speak plainly and to the truth: Are you the Son of God or not?"

"You say so, boss." Jesus says in reply.

The elders and captains, priests and lawyers howl now. "Strike the pages and burn the books!" they shriek. What further testimony would be required? He speaks the words himself. We are noble men," they say.

"Honorable. Virtuous and manly.[33] Pure," they say. "We have heard his words."

27. We'll Have Time To Sort out the Details Later

The priestly Deputy Director of Communications stood at his podium in front of a velvet blue curtain emblazoned with the great Star of David. "Ladies and Gentlemen of the press, Jesus of Nazareth, the radical dissident from the Village of Nazareth, in Galilee, was arrested and taken into custody early this morning."

Immediately the reporters began shouting questions. The priestly communications officer continued to read from his prepared statement. "He is currently charged with violating an unspecified city ordinance, but other charges are pending."

"What charge?" the reporters shouted. "Which ordinance?"

"Does it matter?" the priest replied. "He's in our custody now. We'll have time to sort out the details later."

"But sir, haven't police investigators . . ."

"Newly discovered evidence has come to light, it's true. But this does not necessitate a new trial, especially one likely to have a different outcome. Our juries must not be confused with facts or, rather, with these alleged, so-called facts."

What the priestly Deputy Director of Communications didn't tell the reporters is that officials were already manufacturing the necessary evidence. He knew, though he did not say, that it is sometimes necessary to commit ignominious acts in order to protect one's dignity.

28. A Word of Advice to the Author from a Concerned Administrator

Who are you? You with your low utopianism, you cannot dismantle power. You cannot rewrite history. You cannot change the trajectory of the future. Who are you? With your liberal-humanistic hand-washing, your cheap ideology, your perverse intent to change the world, to change the times and seasons, who are you?

---

33. Which is a repetitive redundancy, of course: "Virtue" is literally "manliness" in Latin.

You would shake down the present to find a new future, but this is wrong. You must keep the past; there is no other future than that. Maintain your place within the structure, within the *status quo res erant ante bellum*.[34] Forget your crude great harmonies. You are aggressively ill dressed. You are not merely untrustworthy, but boring as well, which may be worse. You are a used car: irrational and dangerous. Do not force us to make a recall.

You write false fables and delusional dreams. You say Marxism is Christianity without God like that's a good thing. Your illusory, leftist, blissninny idealism is evidence of your pathetic delusions. You must learn to inhabit the realms of necessity and realism, just as we have. Utopianism is willful thinking, and you are a willful stubborn child. Nature is hard, but we will be harder. Nature is strong; we will be stronger. We will be indifferent to the weather, to hunger and to thirst. We will be indifferent to you. This is the way the world is,

This is the way the world is,
This is the way the world is,
Stop your whimpering.

28. Both Blasphemy and Treason

There was, for the cantankerous philosopher Friedrich Nietzsche, one and only one solitary figure in the gospels that one is obliged to respect: the fifth governor of the Roman province of Judea, Prefect, Procurator, Viceroy, *Epitropos* Pontius Pilate. Drinking wine and eating sweets, observing neither the order nor the time, with inflamed eyes he levied taxes on a whim, arresting one and now another for a caprice. One or maybe the other released for ransom. Or not. It depends on the day and which way the wind is blowing. Pontius Pilate may not have been a philosopher king, but he was an ironist. He asked questions without expectation of answers. His tolerance was mingled with and mitigated by his indifference. What answers could there be? What *is* truth? So maybe we should raise a glass with Nietzsche and have a drink in honor of the Antichrist and *Übermensch*.

Jesus was shackled and dragged from the high priest's house to the court of Pilate where the authorities piled accusations upon him, one after the other.

---

34. "The situation as it existed before the war." Paradoxically, it was both better before the war and we went to war to make it better. Always.

One: He has, with deliberate intent, set out to pervert and debauch the nation and its youth.

Two: He has, on many occasions, both public and private, spoken against the paying of lawful taxes.

Three: He has done what it is forbidden to do.

Four: He has unlawfully and without warrant mixed the *ora* with the *labora*.

Five: He has claimed, falsely, to be both Christ and king, which is both blasphemy and treason.

"Welcome," the governor said to the bound man before him. "Who the devil are you? Are you, as they say you've said, a messiah? A king?"

"Would you take my blood? You've said it, not me."

Pilate stared hard at him for several seconds before turning back to the members of the Sanhedrin. "I am not persuaded by your sham celebrations and false denunciations. I find no fault with him."

"But your majesty," they exclaimed. "He is a scoundrel and dissenter. He stirs up unrest wherever he goes, here in Jerusalem and Judea. He's created nothing but riots and discord ever since he left Galilee."

Pilate seized on their words, "Galilee? He's a Galilean? Well that changes everything, of course. If he's a Galilean, then he belongs to Herod and to Herod's jurisdiction. And, providentially, Herod himself, my informants tell me, is here in Jerusalem even now. So you're in luck." Pilate the procurator, now played the cunctator and sent Jesus off to Herod.

29. Some Sort of Representation

"Jesus, you're entitled to some sort of representation. Do you want us to call your lawyer? Do you even have a lawyer? Maybe you can't afford a lawyer. Should we call a public defender for you? Perhaps we can call your union rep? I think we can get you in with the Prophets' Union. If they let in that fig-plucker from Tekoa, they should let you in, right? How about an ombudsman, at the very least? Let us look into those governing officials that are responsible for this kangaroo court, Jesus. They're all a bunch of bungling baboons. Jesus, Jesus! Say something. Please."

"God protects me against all danger, shields and defends me from all evil. God does all this because of pure, fatherly, and divine goodness and mercy, not because I've earned it or deserved it. For all of this, I must thank, praise, serve, and obey God."

Dum Spiro Spero

"No, Jesus. You don't underst . . ."

Yes, this is true!" He said. "This is true."[35]

30. It's a Display of Power

Herod Antipas was busy working at his desk when Jesus was escorted into his office. He looked up from what he was typing. "Jesus, excellent! I'm very glad you're here. I've wanted to speak to you about a few things. Have a seat," he said indicating a chair. He continued typing at his typewriter for a moment, then looked up again.

"Gladiators are expensive, Jesus. Did you know that? They have to be trained, and fed, and equipped. They must also be housed and entertained, if you know what I mean. And if they die, well, all that money is lost, isn't it? Wasted. It's all flushed right out the vomitorium and poured down the sewers. It's very expensive and wealthy citizens all across the Roman Empire are looking for a cheap source for new gladiators. So I'm proposing a measure to present before the Imperial Senate to relieve landowners of the burden of financing the gladiatorial games. It's my idea that we should allow condemned criminals to be conscripted to fight in the games. They'll fight, and die, I suppose. Everyone dies eventually. Why not sooner than later? They'll fight and die at a fraction of the cost of professional combatants. And we'll have the added benefit of ridding our society of all manner of undesirables. We can use thieves, arsonists, malcontents, communists, college students, political activists, rebels. You get the idea."

Jesus said nothing.

"Jesus, you have to understand that death in the arena is bigger than the death of any one individual gladiator. Death in the arena is a display of power. It is a demonstration that our enemies will be subjugated, and degraded, assaulted and rejected. They will be stripped of their identities and publicly exposed. Humiliated. Reduced to the animalistic subhuman. The more gruesome the death, the more powerful the display."[36]

Jesus maintained his silence.

---

35. Jesus may have been quoting Luther's Small Catechism, or maybe Luther was quoting Jesus. This narrative has become so asynchronous that I can't tell who is quoting whom anymore.

36. Herod may have been a petty tyrant, but apparently he was a forward thinker. This idea was eventually approved by the Roman Senate in 176 CE.

A Life Known and Unknowable

"Fine!" Herod fumed. "Answer some questions for me then: What's written in Most Secret Operation Order No. 173?" Jesus said nothing. "I'll tell you, Jesus. Most Secret Operation Order No. 173 ordered the bombing of Hamburg. Can you tell me why?" Still nothing from Jesus. "No. No, I guess you couldn't. But it was a good and righteous decision. In war one does what must be done, Jesus. Even the killing of civilians. So stop with your pink-bellied nonviolence."

"Here's another question for you: Have you seen the Mysterious Trio? Ritter, Tod, and Teufel? I have; they're very good. They put on a tremendous show." Not a word from Jesus. Not a flicker of acknowledgement. Not a motion or a glance.

"My enemies, Jesus, would hurt the scriptures if they were given a chance. They'd damage the *Torah*, you know? I know it. You know it. Are you one of my enemies, Jesus?" Silence filled the space between them. "No one's done more for the Jewish people than me, right? Right?" Silence.

"Do you think Seth, Adam and Eve's third son, resented being a replacement for their murdered favorite son? Do you think he resented being a placeholder? I think about things like that, Jesus. What about you?"

Jesus said nothing.

"Jesus, you're going to have to answer my questions eventually. So tell me: What *does* Athens have to do with Jerusalem? I'm tired of their interference." But not a single, solitary word from Jesus. He sat silently in the offered chair.

"Jesus, can you hear me? Are you *non compos mentis*? If you won't answer my questions, Jesus, will you do something for me? I've heard reports from my spies and my agents that you are credited with all sorts of miracles. Signs and wonders, I'm told. Now I don't know if I believe in all that supernatural, hocus-pocus, *in hoc est corpus* stuff. But I'm willing to believe. I'd like to believe. Can you do something like that for me? Heal a leper? Give new vision to tired, blind eyes?"

Jesus didn't speak, didn't move. No response. Nothing.

"Nothing, Jesus? You know what I will do with you, so why do you continue this stubbornness?" But still there was nothing.

There was nothing that Herod in his raging could hear, but Jesus whispered a few words to himself. "I've been to the border of the wild frontier and not crossed over. Not yet, but soon. There is a plan, but I prefer the unplanned miracle."

Herod Antipas stood and shouted for his soldiers and the Herodian men of war promptly escorted Jesus to a windowless room where they beat and pummeled him. Mercilessly. When they finished with him they draped a fine vestment of crushed red velvet over his shoulders. "Send him back to Pilate," Herod waved. "I've had enough of the mute." The tetrarch sat back at his desk to resume work at his typewriter, but he'd lost his train of thought. "The mute stole all my words," he shouted to the empty room. "The mute stole all my words!"

And with that back and forth prisoner transfer, the tetrarch Herod and the prefect Pilate became new friends. Where there was enmity, there was love. Where there was injury, pardon. Where there was discord, unity. They met in darkness and in despair, the principled man of a rebellious city and the rebellious man of a principled city, and found common dreams between them. By wine, by salted fire, and innocent death they sealed their newfound affection.

31. Too Great a Discord

Particles stirred up by intense electrical and magnetic fields move in predetermined directions. Jesus is dragged here, dragged there, and swung back and forth between the poles of clamoring crowds and snarling foes. It is too great a volume, too great a discord for anything but nervous aberration. His hands and face are swollen, his eyes are radiation burns beneath a bloodied brow.

Pilate, standing on his balcony, reassembled the pieces of the chaos from scattered parts and scattered posts, "Chief priests, rulers, and screaming people," he addressed them below in the street. "You brought me this man. You've brought him to me twice. You brought him back to me with claims you still can't substantiate. 'Perversion of the youth of the nation', you said and, 'unrest wherever he goes,' but your charges don't hold water. And your water won't hold a charge. I've examined him myself. You were here. I found nothing. We found nothing. We sent him to Herod Antipas who, being either crafty or craven, sent him right back to us. There's nothing of death here. Nothing for death here. Behold nothing. See nothing. There is nothing in this man."

"But," he said as they began to grumble. "I will chastise him. I'll have him beaten to make you happy. Will that make you happy? This Jesus that you have brought me—twice now—is a difficult man. We may have to grind him down a bit." He turned to the soldiers standing at the edge of the room. "Flog him." He turned back to the angry agents of chaos in his antechamber. "We'll chastise him and release him. It's part of our catch and release policy."

"No," they shouted. "That's not what we want."

"You don't want him flogged?"

"No. Well, yes. We want him flogged, of course. Of course we want him flogged. But we don't want him flogged and released. If you must release anyone, release Barabbas," they demanded.

"Barabbas? Release the insurrectionist? You want me to release the murderer? If I release Barabbas, they'll be screaming in Rome that I'm soft on crime. They'll have my head and I'll have to throw myself into the Tiber."

They shouted at him from the streets below. "Lock him up! Lock him up! Crucify him!"

Pilate tried once more. "Is he an usurper? An assassin? Has he, like the gore beaked vultures among you, exploited the death of anyone? Is he a necromantic? A pederast? What has he done? I'll flog him, as I said, but then I will let him go."

The shouts below neared riotous, but still he hesitated. The prefect turned to the manacled man bleeding on his marble floor and said, "Is there anything else?"

Jesus looked up, "Do you want to ask me a question?"

Surprised, Pilate said, "Me?"

"Yes. You. Do you want to ask me a question about the nature of truth?"

"No," said the tired Prefect. "I think that must be some other me. Statistically approximate to me, perhaps, but not quite me." Then he acquiesced to their demands; he released the murderer and condemned the man from Galilee.

Is it too late for me to embrace some sort of Nietzschean nihilism? Maybe not. Nietzsche was in his thirties when he came to his. And I'm told that the number of men (like myself) in their forties who commit suicide is on the rise in this country. In some church traditions (apocryphal perhaps, but does it matter?) we are told that Pontius Pilate committed suicide rather than be sent into ignominious exile. We're told that he flung himself into the Tiber, but the waters of the river were so agitated by his abhorrent presence that the people of Rome were forced to drag his bloated corpse out and transport it to a mysterious and occult cave near a remote lake in

Switzerland where it remains hidden and guarded by a dragon with great flapping wings to this day.

So we'll have a drink for Pilate, and another for nihilism. We're going to need it.

32. Death by Direct Current

It was then that the famed American inventor, Thomas Alva Edison, inventor of the phonograph, the electric light, the carbon fiber telephone transmitter, the motion picture camera and many other useful and labor saving devices spoke up. "Your majesty, if I may have a word." Pilate motioned to the guards to wait a moment. "Might I suggest that crucifixion is not the answer? What if there is a better way?" Edison asked.

"You would spare his life?" Pilate replied, his voice stern with incredulity. "This criminal? Everyone agrees that he must be destroyed, and you would have me spare his life?"

Edison trembled, his voice faltered. "No. No. Of course not, your majesty, but . . ."

"Prefect, please," said Pilate. "There is only one Caesar, and only he holds such title." Pilate, of course, harbored his own private aspirations to godhead. All men do, and especially those in positions of power. But it was not politic to speak of them publicly.

"Of course, Prefect. No. I do not suggest that he be pardoned, merely that the means of his execution should be something more humane. We are civilized men, are we not, and far above the barbarous methods used by our forebears? So let us forswear such cruelties and move forward into the new age of humanity opened to us by technological innovation."

"You have something in mind?"

"Electrocution, my lord."

"I have heard of such thing," the governor of Judea mused. "A representative from Westinghouse spoke to one of my advisors earlier about this."

Edison reacted visibly to the mention of his alternating current rival. "No, my Lord," he said forcibly. He paused to reconsider his tone before continuing. "Death by direct current. It is quicker and more efficient. It is more . . . direct, if I may be allowed such gallows humor. But I can see that you still have questions. May I show you a film perhaps? A film of my own making depicting the electrocution of the assassin Leon Czolgosz with panorama of the Auburn Prison."

Pilate considered the possibilities. "Your suggestion intrigues me." He looked at the condemned man flanked by his guards for several seconds before speaking again. "Your suggestion intrigues me, but no. Let him be lifted up on the cross as I have ordered."

33. The Task Must Be Done

A BBC film crew setting up alongside the road with their tripods, and cameras, and lights, and microphones captures it all—the starving sun disappearing behind gathering storm clouds and the dark spiraling vortices of sand in the wind, the super saturated red cloaks of the Roman soldiers flapping and burning against steel-grey skies, and the white stones of the walls.

They are filming as a man, a black man—tall and thin—is yanked from the crowd and compelled by uniformed officers to carry the condemned man's cross beam. Do not be fooled: this is no act of generous compassion for the suffering of the bleeding man on his knees in the dirt. It is pragmatic expediency. The task must be done. The crossbeam must be carried up the hill, simple as that. And this man will serve as well as anyone to get it there.

The small black man is driven up the hill with lashes on his back and a large burden upon his shoulders. This is the Roman power to motivate and to dominate. This is their power to command and to control. The task must be done. Important men are waiting. A graveyard is there at no great distance, with its maw open in anticipation. The grave is always waiting.

The camera records it all. The BBC crew continues filming right up until the moment when the Roman guards shut them down, smashing the lights with their batons and knocking the camera to the ground. The journalists are arrested and dragged off to some obscure cell of a forgotten dungeon. The execution will not be televised.

34. Days of Spoiled Milk and Spider Silk

Great multitudes of people followed him on the *Via Dolorosa*—and women. They came wailing and lamenting, shrieking into the increasing inky sky. "Weep not for me," he said to these daughters of Jerusalem. "*Dulcis amica dei, lacrymis inflectere nostus.* Weep instead for yourselves. Weep for your children, but do not weep for me. There are days, and not far off, when you will praise and bless the barren, when you'll hail the empty womb. A day will come, and soon, when you'll call the unsuckled pap a beautiful thing."

"Those will be days of spoiled milk and spider silk. Days of death on the ground and destruction in the sky. In the air, the noise of weapons. In the air, the sound of war. It will be days and months of tribulation with no delivery. Labor pains and no birth."

"In those days you can expect the Institute for Defensive Studies to provide an analysis report demonstrating that war would be less expensive than diplomacy and they leaders will embrace it.[37] They will say that 'in order to shorten the war it will be necessary to expand it.' They will say, 'to save the village we have to destroy it.' They will say that 'war is peace.' They'll say whatever is necessary. That's when you'll call for the mountains to fall, and for the hills to entomb and inhume you. The dead eat very little, Sweet Friend of God, but they *will* eat."

35. Two Other Malefactors at Calvary

A thought experiment, a hypothetical: Let's replace Gestas and Dismas on their crosses next to Jesus with Sacco and Vanzetti, one on the right and one on the left. Why not when one malefactor looks like another? They're all foreigners, right? They're all criminals. They're all interchangeable and replaceable. What's another dead shoemaker or fishmonger matter, anyway? There they are, Sacco and Vanzetti, on either side of Jesus, shouting against the rain and thunder, against the screaming crowd. They are the howling condemned and their screams are pure agony. But no one listens to the howling of the condemned.

We must have a firm hand here. We must have law and order because we will have peace. And this is how it's done—at the point of the sword, on the nails of the cross. Mandatory sentences reduce crime, and the death penalty really *is* a deterrent. We tell ourselves these things.

Sometimes we may even believe them.

---

37. But why should those days be different from any others? The Institute for Defensive Studies is always prepared to write that report and the leaders are always ready for the next war.

36. Vain and Barbarous Men

Here and now, late though it is, the execution will take place, beneath tortured skies and contrary winds. Vain and barbarous laws are enforced by vain and barbarous men. All the tributaries of injustice have flowed into this delta of evil. The water ways are flooded. Blood vessels break. This is how antichrists conquer—not with lawless anarchy but firm oratory and strict laws.

"Father forgive them," he says from the cross. "They do not understand what they are doing."

First Question: Who are "they"? Jews? Romans? Does it matter? The infidels and libertines down in Washington will have their way; it doesn't matter who the trigger-men are. No one in the power structure will give a damn. Remember this.

Figure 32–They don't give a damn.

Second Question: Did he say it? I am aware that many of the early manuscripts do not contain this prayer but I'm not overly concerned. Whether it was spoken from the cross by Jesus or it was piously inserted by a later copyist this short prayer is the beating heart of the living, breathing gospel and it reflects, if not Christ's actual-factual words, then the early Christians understanding of Christ's life expressed in a simple prayer. And I will let it guide me, because I am one of the miserable malefactors. One of the infidels. One of the libertines. I am one.

37. Take My Spirit, I Can't Breathe

The people stood watching, the leaders too, deriding him. Riding him. They mocked and scoffed from the ground below his cross. "Let him do for himself what he said he could do for others," they said. The soldiers there mocked him too, offering him vinegar to drink. But this was no act of kindness; this sour wine. They wanted him suffering from thirst as much as anything else. They hung a placard above him, a polyglot accusation, in Latin, Greek, and Hebrew: "This is the King of the Jews."

Truth is where you find it, even in mockery.

One of the malefactors (was it Gestas or Sacco?) mocks him too. "Save yourself" he shouts, "And us." The other condemned (Vanzetti or Dismas?) condemned his associate. "We are justly condemned for what we've done, but this man has done nothing wrong.[38]

"Blow it out your ass," said the first, and went back to angrily dying.

But the second continued, "Remember me in your kingly power, Jesus."

"Today you'll be with me in the walled gardens of paradise sitting by running streams of living water," Jesus told him just before he expired. Some of the people cheered when the condemned man died. "Don't cheer," Jesus told them. "Don't cheer."

"He was a murderer, Jesus. He killed three people."

"Don't cheer. It's just one more futile death heaped up with all the other pointless deaths. It won't bring back the dead. Don't cheer."

"Oh shut and die already," they shouted back at him.

Figure 33–I can't breathe.

---

38. Yeah, yeah, yeah. Our Sacco and Vanzetti thought experiment fails a bit here, doesn't it? Sacco and Vanzetti both maintained their innocence right up to their executions. Even at the end Bartolomeo Vanzetti raged, "I am innocent . . . no death sentence, no judge, no governor, no reactionary state of Massachusetts can change the innocent into a murderer." But, no worries. Hypotheticals are limited. That's understood.

By the sixth hour all was darkness on the earth. Was it an eclipse? No. Not astronomically possible during full moon Passover. And this is more than the physical occlusion of the sun. This is spiritual darkness in the light of day. It is the collision of the tick, tick, tick of past, present, future *chronos*-clock time with the qualitative, unmeasurable *kairos*-time which is unmarked and unpreserved, which can only be experience. It can only be felt. The eternity of four-dimensional time and space is spread out against the sky, etherized upon the table, ready to die with him. The sun is dark, shadowing the earth during daylight, turning festivals into mourning and songs into lamentations. The veil of the temple which is both heaven and earth, is torn in two—an expression of grief and sorrow.[39]

Sticks and stones and a thousand devil bones—these things hurt and break and kill. Yet he was lifted up on the tree of martyrdom to vivify the dead. It is a birth of blood and spirit. Blot out the mountains to make the earth a barren waste. We have killed him. What a waste.

Jesus cried out with a loud voice, "Father, take my spirit. I can't breathe!"

38. The Effusion of Blood and Horror

Figure 34–The blood of yesterday's slaughters.

---

39. A suitable expression of grief and sorrow except for, curiously, the high priest, the one chosen from among his brothers to wear the holy garments of the chief priest, was forbidden from rending his garments in sorrow.

Commander "Lance" Longinus stood beneath darkening skies—skies like the smoke of chemical fire, like the smoke of the charnel house. As Centurion he was the sharpened sword, the cleansing fire, and on occasion the calming water of noble Rome, the intrusion of the great empire into this gross and inferior wasteland. He stood beneath the crosses, looking up at dying men as he led the drive towards their deaths. He was the strong arm and the strong legs of the empire. He was the strong Imperial foot on the ground of Palestine, standing in for the weak minds of Rome.

All the blood of yesterday's slaughters, all the blood of future wars and decimations were spilt there in the dirt and dust. Enthusiastic rioters exploded with passion—which is to say pain, for passion is pain and pain is passion. Everything hurts. Everything burns. Everyone dies. The crowds, the followers, the women shrieking, screaming, crying. They beat their breast and wail against the effusion of blood and horror and the merciless sky. Death came before the downing of the sun, but not much before.

Yet this man, this leader of men, this servant of Caesar and of Mars, saw in that death something more. He watched him die and was moved toward life. "Certainly this was a just man," he said. This simple declaration, this deep declaration gave glory to God—with or without a prior understanding. Righteousness is where you find it, and there he found it upon the skull-worn hill.

As the sun declined into occulted splendor, Death demanded its shameful ransom. The clouds were split. The sky was rent, and stinging rain poured down upon their heads, blood and water in sad abundance, rain and ruin enough for everyone. The crowd dispersed. There was nothing more to see here.

Joseph of Arimathea, a member of the Sanhedrin and author of the dissenting minority report refusing to condemn the Galilean prophet, went in the gathering gloaming, to beg for the body of Jesus from Pilate. Joseph was a good man, and just. And with the permission of the state, he took the body of the murdered teacher down from the rugged cross beams, carefully removed the iron nails from his mangled extremities without wiping away the blood and gore. There was no time for niceties; Joseph raced against the setting sun. The day of preparation was burning away, the Sabbath was about to fall. He wrapped the corpse in simple linen. Later there would be time for the cerements dipped in melted wax and for the oils and spices of death, but not just then. He carried the body away and laid it in an unused sepulcher within the nearby graveyard.

The women who followed him from Galilee, those several women whom he had cured of their vexatious spirits and of their infirmities, who'd followed him along the sorrowful way, now followed again, watching from a distance as his body was laid to unsettled rest. They beheld the spectacle of his execution and the hurried haste of his burial. They beheld the sepulcher and noted how and where his body was laid. Then they went back to prepare the burial spices and ointments, and to take their rest through an unsettled Sabbath.

There are graves in strange places, sepulchers filled floor to ceiling with smiling skulls inside churches. There are sepulchers and sarcophagi beneath rivers with difficult names, and there are sky burials in the upraised stones of Tibetan mountains as well as burials in the abyss of the sea. But here was an unused tomb, newly hewn from pale and dolorous dolomite. Heaven was there but still silent and still unseen.

Let all the earth keep silent.

Figure–35 Be silent.

The Argument

My Own Idiosyncratic Predilections, Peccadillos and Obvious Heresies

*L*OREM IPSUM, BLATHER AND bother. Why am I writing this? Why do I do anything? The world is roiling and boiling over into chaos. The world is burning itself down, and I am, like you and everyone else I know, choking on the bitter ashes. And what am I doing during the collapse? Retelling a story that you already know. And I'm distorting it all. Twisting it, as my enemies might say. Ruining it. Perverting it with my own idiosyncratic predilections, peccadillos and my obvious heresies.

Maybe they're right. I don't know.

I'm a creature of doubt and dust, bone-inflamed and swollen, screaming before the sun. I am a creature of unintentional and unintelligible noise walking the streets in ill-fitting shoes. As much as anyone else, I am a distortion of what I was, of what I might have been. I am a damaged package undelivered. I remain unacknowledged and unnecessary.

So why am I writing this?

Maybe it's because I'm tired and frustrated at work. I've worked an excessive amount of overtime in the last year and I still have a four month back log of work I cannot finish. I've worked more than thirty Saturdays and it's only September. I'm exhausted all the time. My forty-six year old knees ache constantly and the bone spur in my toe has my entire foot screaming every day at the end of my shift. My neck and my shoulders are stiff, tightening up on me to the point that I'm afraid I won't be able to move when I wake up tomorrow. *If* I wake up tomorrow.

But maybe that's not all of it. Is it because for over a year my wife wouldn't sleep with me, wouldn't touch me, wouldn't make anything more than small talk with me and wouldn't let me touch her or look at her. She denied that there was a problem and refused to explain. Then she announced, one day into the New Year, that she was filing for divorce. Maybe I'm tired and frustrated but I'm broken too. I pretend that I can handle this and that I can go on. I pretend because I don't know what else to do.

My stomach is constantly churning, lurching—rebelling against me. And whether I eat or don't, I have burning indigestion. It's heartburn for the brokenhearted. I am collapsing like a burnt out star. Heartburn or no, gravitational collapse is cold.

I've struggled and fought and clawed and begged to stay here where I've been for long years of even longer nights, and for what? It was lies and withheld truth the entire time. "Not all of it was a lie," she told me, "not everything." But so what? I couldn't tell the difference, and she wouldn't explain.

I dream that I am being interrogated for the words of sermons I wrote in my previous career as a minister. Those words were good words and I stand by them, but I've lost them all. I dream restless dreams of futile fights against overwhelming Nazi hordes in silver shirts and I awaken to find that I've flung my books upon the floor. What does it mean? Nothing. Nothing, and nothing more. They're only oneiric illusions. Only words. Desperate, flailing words.

But words, *The Word*, was there in the beginning and words are all I have.

Figure 36–Words are all I have.

The Argument

So I write. Words. I write word after word after word. And marvel of marvels: some of them are even in the proper order! (Though it's only fifty-fifty if I've spelled them correctly.) I write by way of accumulation, by aggregate. I'm an oyster coating my irritants with layer after layer of nacreous words.

But I write. It's either that or drink, I suppose. And I'm doing that too. Maybe too much of that.

Without words there is no voice, no speech. There is only a void. An inexpressible, ontological black-hole stretching into eternity. *Lorem Ipsum*, blather and bother. Why bother? I can't say, but it feels important that I keep writing. If for no other reason than to keep myself occupied and amused. To keep myself sane when everything is scattered to schizophrenic shit. I write words—and in writing words, perhaps I am becoming the *imago dei* which is The Word.

Perhaps.

Lorem Ipsum and all that.

VII

Post Fluxae Carnis Scandala

1. They Burned within Themselves

THE FIRST DAY OF the week, early, before early, the women who'd followed him from Galilee, now followed him to the tomb once again. The myrrhbearers carried with them the articles of their office: unguents, and ointments, spices and spikenard. And they also brought candles and flowers and the waxed cerements for their Lord in his tomb as well as plaster for making an impression of his face, from which they would create a death mask likeness of their master. They went with a feeling, a desire, and a hope. These are not much, it's true, but these three do remain even after the sharp edge of grief has dulled.

But, upon arriving at the tomb, they found the sealing stone rolled away. The entrance was open. Rats and snakes and centipedes were streaming out as the women made their way inside the tomb. They found it empty and they were much perplexed.

Suddenly a shining man in brilliant clothes[1] appeared before them. "Why do you search for life within death? Is this some sort of paradox? Finding light in the darkness? Whatever it is, he is not here. He is risen. Alive."

A second angel followed with oxygen which is more fuel for the fire—though oxygen itself does not burn.[2] "Remember what he told you in

---

1. Or was it a brilliant man in shining clothes? It all happened so fast . . .

2. I only recently learned this myself. We've been told for years and years and years that oxygen is flammable, but it's not true. Oxygen feeds fires, yes, and causes flammable substances to ignite at lower temperatures and to burn hotter and faster, but oxygen does not itself burn. You can test this yourself at home with a simple electrolysis experiment:

Galilee?" the second angel said to the women. "He knew that he would be delivered into wicked hands, that he would be crucified. He told you this. And that he would be raised."

And they remembered. Much perplexed and sore afraid as they were, they remembered all that he'd told them and they burned within themselves. Suddenly the shadows were shining and brilliant. The tomb was empty even of the rats and snakes and centipedes. But the women were filled. They raced back to tell the others what they hadn't found.

2. Idle Tales from Irregular Women

The eleven were listening to news reports that morning as they hid themselves fearing reprisal raids and warrantless arrests. ". . . it may be an occupation of your lands," said the incorporeal voice through tinny speakers of a cheap transistor radio. "But you can be assured that it will be a beneficent occupation. You may feel that your civil liberties are being curtailed but remember that it is a gentle hand that holds the reins. We will hold these territories and these lands until there is a fully established peace. We are here for your security. This is S.P.Q.Radio. Have a happy and blessed Passover."

Andrew dashed the radio to the ground, shattering it and sending shards of plastic and diodes and dials to every corner of the room. "They didn't even mention him," he shouted through his tears and his fear. "They didn't even mention him! After everything that happened, they didn't even mention him."

Mary and the other women burst through the door just then, all sweating and shouting, words over words, overlapping one over the other to tell the story of what they had and what they hadn't seen that morning. And to the eleven men assembled that morning it seemed like nothing more than idle tales from irregular women.

Three monks, dressed unconvincingly as women, with wimples and veils, carrying ampules and an alabaster box stepped in from the wings to assist. "Perhaps and peradventure thyse goodly brothers canst enlyten us together," one of the three *ad similitudinem mulierum* monks said to the remaining disciples in a ridiculous falsetto voice. "Rather the wyrds of the *torah* be burned than entrusted to a wyamn. Doubtless we should not be

---

separate the hydrogen from the oxygen in a glass of water into two separate containers (two separate containers is important—the combination of gasses will be highly explosive). The hydrogen will burn, but the oxygen will not.

muche stered of hur testimony, yea, but must as listen gravely to hur report, though she be a wyman."

The crossdressing monks then began a pantomime performance of Mary's encounter in the garden with sweeping gestures and overdramatic expressions and strange accents. "She didst loke upon his blesse countenaunce and didst clysp him into hur embryce, but he, byinge not yet ascended, didst say unto hur, '*noli me tangir!*'"

"What the hell?" Mary Magdalen exclaimed with her hands on her hips, arms akimbo. "I'm standing right here!" "I don't need you, any of you. I don't need any man to speak for me. I know who I am, and I know what I saw. I can tell my own story, thank you."

3. Many Wonderful Things

Rotate the disk one time.

"My God, woman!" Peter exclaimed and jumped up from where he was seated. "What glass-darkly enigma is this? What mystery?" He ran to the tomb, stepped down into the tomb.

Rotate the disk counterclockwise and ask him, "What do you see?"

"Many wonderful things. Or nothing at all, except the linen burial cloths." What mystery invisible to the unaided eye. Invisible but not accidental or random. He went away by himself wondering within himself what had happened here.

Rotate the disk one more time.

4. Step over Step

That same morning two of them, Cleopas and his traveling companion, made the step over step, step over step, seven mile trek from Jerusalem to the village of Emmaus through a deserted land of rocks, and craters, and canyons. It was a hostile world, a dead world of desert mesquite and sword-sharp yucca spines. Spines like daggers. It was a dead land of scorpions, toxic centipedes, venom dealing rattlesnakes. A land of fire ants and frenzied dancing tarantulas. A dead land itself in need of a resurrection.

And Jesus surprised them on the road as they spoke to each other. "What is it you're discussing? What is happening here?" He asked them. They saw him but did not see. Their eyes were dulled, blinded by the light and understanding was withheld from them.

Post Fluxae Carnis Scandala

Cleopas' companion (some say it was Mary, his wife) replied, "Are you a stranger here? The only one unaware?"

"We speak of Jesus of Nazareth, and his death," said Cleopas.

"And who was he?" Jesus asked.

"He was, we thought, a prophet, mighty in word and strong in creed and in deed. We thought him a prophet before God and in the sight of the people. But now? Maybe this following of our conscience was all just a mad quest. Was it a fool's paradise? Was it just a castle in Spain? We came to the city with a feeling, a desire, a hope. These are not much, I know," Cleopas said to him. "But even these have been taken from us and I'm just trying to retain my goddamned idealism."

Mary continued, "The chief of our priests and our rulers had him assassinated. We had hoped that he would be the One. We had hoped that he'd be the one to redeem our land. But now? Now we wonder if we should add his name to our calendar of martyred saints. It is the third day since his death."

Cleopas picked up the story again, "Some of our women," he glanced at his wife carefully, "have made an astonishing claim—that the tomb, his tomb, has been emptied. They saw no body, but had a vision of angels who say that he is alive."

"And certain of us," said Mary with a critical side-eye to her husband, "found the tomb just as the women said."

"Fools," he said to them both. "Slow hearted fools. Slow to believe. Slow to receive all the words that the prophets gave you. Surely all this was necessary, wasn't it? The Christ had to suffer before glory. That's how it always goes. First the suffering, then the glory. You can't have glory without suffering." Then, beginning with Moses, he walked them (step over step) through all the words of the prophets until they reached the village of Emmaus.

It was late in the evening but he made as if to go further on up the road. "Stay with us," they begged him. "Abide with us for fast falls the eventide." So he did. He joined them at their house for the dinner meal. And sitting at the table with them he took the bread and broke it and gave thanks before offering it to them.

Their dulled, closed eyes were opened then. The scales fell away and they knew him. They saw, and they understood. Then he was gone from their eyes. He was gone from their eyes but not their heart. "Our hearts were all fire and flame while he was with us."

They jumped up, that very hour, that very moment and started back—step over step, step over step, seven miles (now uphill) back to Jerusalem. Up they went, racing through a land reopened, a landscape reinvigorated, to find the others and to tell all that they had seen.

5. *Space and Time Are Unsealed*

While they were still speaking in the fading light of light at the world's end, he suddenly appeared in the room among them saying, *"Pax vobiscum."* The voice of eagles, cymbals, bells and trumpets within the noise and light, and colors of gold resplendent in the room among them. The soul of the world was there with them under one peace and clemency, and they were terrified. "A ghost!" they cried. "A phantasm! A spook!" They were sore afraid. "It is a demon among us!"

"Why are you troubled?" he said to them. "Why are you afraid? Fear not." The admonition to 'fear not' comes in times of terror. Always. "Fear not. Take courage for we are standing between sharp despair and booming joy. Fear not! Why do thoughts rise in your heart and questions in your mind?"

"Jesus! Is that real?" they asked. "Are you real?"

"See now my wounded hands, my pierced feet. Handle my hands, finger my wounds. Explore this corporeal reality, this solid, unsoiled flesh. Every detail is important; I have bones and flesh just as you have flesh and bones. I am not a bodiless demon of ectoplasm. I am no spirit of fogs and vapors."

But they believed it not for joy. For fear and for wonder. For shame and embarrassment, yes it's true, but for joy. For joy! There were changes, yes. Not in eyes but in mind. There were changes in time and space. Stars are temporary. Stars burn out and fade away. Like everything and everyone, stars die. But draw the boundaries wider now. Electrons, protons, neutrons. Energy. Energy, space and time are unsealed.

"Have you anything here to eat?" he asks them. They give him broiled fish and honeycomb, and he eats it. He is resurrected and real. Risen and reliable. The incorruptible made hypostatic union with frail flesh in this shared meal, this alternate Eucharist among friends. Take this and see. Behold! Here is the fairest of experiences. This is mystery. Here was Einstein's cradle of true art and science. Wonder! Here is the mysterious, without which there is only the darkness of a snuffed out candle.

6. He Opened their Minds to Understanding

Taking a breath and tipping them a wink he said, "Here are the words I gave you when I was with you before, all the things that had to be fulfilled. Here is the culmination of everything—law, prophet, and psalm." And he opened their minds to understanding.

"The Christ should suffer," he said, "I told you this. The Christ should suffer, for what else is a Messiah for? And on the third day, rise."

"Take two things with you into all the world: Repentance and Remission. These are the things, and you are witnesses to them. Preach them everywhere, beginning here at home, in Jerusalem. You'll take with you the promise and blessing of the Father, but wait here until you receive an investment of power."

Here is the dissolution of dust reversed and the curse of earth undone. Here is breath returned and body with soul reunited. "I am the destroyer of death, trampling Hades underfoot," he tells them. "I have triumphed over the Enemy for I am the Christ in present immortality."[3]

7. Now They Would Rise

He led them out to Bethany and the Mount of Olives to give them the uplifted hands of his farewell and final blessing. And as he blessed them he was departed from them.[4] Gone. Away.

They worshipped him and returned to Jerusalem with great and growing joy. And they were continually in the temple, praising him and parsing his words. Slowly, regularly, exercising day by day, gradually increasing in strength and numbers, spinning faster and faster. Wisdom made foolish and the foolish made bright in the golden light of a new dawning age. Now they would shrink and swallow and whistle into the wind. Now they would rise. "*Il n'est pas certain que tout soit incertain,*" wrote Blaise Pascal. "It is not certain that everything is uncertain." But this is sure: they would rise. And they did, like fissiparous photons of reflected glory, they would rise. What is the distance between faith and risk? It does not matter. They would rise.

---

3. St. Melito of Sardis, *On Pascha*

4. It's not necessary—but not completely irrelevant—to this narrative that the escape velocity for the planet Earth is 11.19 kilometers per second or just over seven miles per second. At an acceleration of ten gravities, that speed can be reached within two minutes. Do with that what you will.

The Final Argument

I'm Not Much But I'm All I Have

THE LAWS OF PHYSICS being what they are, I should have seen the approach of that dark-star disaster that was my divorce. Divorce was the sound before the light, or rather, the silence before the sight. But, now, in the fading of light of the world as I knew it, there is the new light of a burning heart. I am slow to see. Like the disciples, I am slow to see and to understand. Suffering comes before glory.

I shall always have the memory of her. But memories are dead things and I am alive again. Or I'm trying to live again, anyway. What can I say about my life after the divorce? A quote from one of my favorite science-fiction authors comes to mind: "I'm not much, but I'm all that I have."[1] I'm moving on and starting over. Some days I think I'm doing okay, but it's not true. I'm still a wreck, still a blubbering mess. Let me assure you, sobbing in a truck stop bathroom in the middle of Nebraska is not a good look. I'm not well, but I'm trying.

I don't know what genre this novel fits into. Or if novel is even the correct term. Maybe it's something of a science-fiction burlesque, a work intended, at least in part, to make you laugh with caricature and ludicrous action. It's also a literary schizophrenia, I suppose. It would be a mark of mental illness if I were to talk to myself while riding on the cross-town bus, but if I do it in the narrative, why then it is art. It's literature.

I don't know. I'm trying.

"A time is coming," said Saint Anthony of the Desert, "A time is coming when men will go mad, and when they see someone who is not mad, they will attack him, saying, 'You are not like us,'" That time is now. And

---

1. Dick, *Martian Time Slip*, 209.

that time has always been now. For what it's worth: I believe in Christ, poor and crucified. I believe in Christ resurrected. And like Saint Anselm, I believe it so that I may understand.

Let that be enough. Amen.

April 2020—May 2022

As the philosopher Blaise Pascal once said, "I might have written a shorter book, but I didn't have the time."

jCarter

Appendix 1

An Excerpt from Dr. Tarrec's Field Guide to Demonic Encounters

In my many years of astrological research and alchemical studies I have often encountered representatives of the infernal realms—demonic forces that, had I not been better prepared, would have flayed my very soul. These evil spirits infuse the esoteric world. They are energetic beings stimulating both mystical and chemical reactions. Many incautious practitioners of the alchemical arts have lost their lives (and their souls) because they failed to heed the many warnings, because they failed to notice when they had lost control. There are numerous early warning signs. Watch for them, lest you become one of the demon possessed.

Here are 27 indicators to watch for. If you notice any of these signs you should take action immediately to bind any malicious spiritual entities that may be taking an interest in you:

1. Do you smell strange odors?
2. Are your irises purple in color? Are they larger than normal? Are they evenly sized?
3. Do you have a violent reaction to pictures of Padre Pio?
4. Does your bladder leak when you are in close proximity to a crucifix?
5. Can you levitate yourself or others?
6. Have you ever attended a conference with Bob Larson?
7. Have you ever been abducted by a UFO or been contacted by an EBE?

APPENDIX 1

8. Have you stood in the center of a crossroads at midnight?
9. Are you now, or have you ever been a member of The Brotherhood of Games?
10. Have you ever played Dungeons and Dragons? Have you ever participated in LARP?
11. Have you ever been struck by lightning? Martin Luther was once nearly struck by lightning. Do you think that you are like Martin Luther in any way?
12. Do you experience periodic trances?
13. Do you contradict yourself more than three times a day?
14. Do you feel compelled to wash your hands after coming in contact with a religious person?
15. Does your skin burn when touched by iron? By silver?
16. Have you ever read from the *Naturum De Montum* or from *The Necronomicon*?
17. Have you, or a member of your family, participated in a cattle mutilation?
18. Do you have somnambulistic episodes lasting more than 4 hours?
19. Have you experienced a vision of impossible colours?
20. Do you keep a radioactive meteorite hidden in your basement?
21. Have you consumed the blood of a dead man?
22. Are you restless or irritable at either the Vernal or Autumnal Equinoxes?
23. Have you ever attempted to transmute lead into gold or vice versa?
24. Have you used juju to affect the outcome of professional sporting events?
25. Do you know the identity and location of *Fantômas*?
26. Are there people living under your stairs?
27. Have you visited the City of the Dead Man in Hamunaptra, India?

Appendix 2

Unwritten Notes #132-140

#132 "The future is God," he told me, "she's *the could have been* and *the possibly*, the great *maybe*, the cosmic universal potential, the sum-total-of-all-impending probabilities."

But this I could not understand. Or was it that I would not understand it? It's a noetic toss up and the coin is still in the air.

"You're free to disagree with me," he said.

"Really?" I wondered at him.

"Oh, who knows?" he shrugged back at me. "The singer sings and the song goes on," he said. I wondered if he was attempting a Jackie Mason impersonation.

#133 The state news-media of North Korea has finally admitted that the nation's founder, Kim Il Sung, did not, in fact, have the ability to teleport using the 'flower folded space' technique but the Tetrarch of Galilee and Perea, Herod Antipas refused to concede any such admissions. He still stood in the moonlight upon the high towers of his palace seeking immortality and a body of fire. He never held the crown or the title of King, and this forever rankled him.

#134 An arduous journey will not revive the dead. but don't let that stop you from travelling. Take that vacation. Book that cruise. Step out your front door and see where you wind up.

#135 Though I'm only 47 (nearing 48), I've lived at least that long, and I'll go on living till something better comes along.

#136 If I preach peace—and I do—it's because I know I've been a beast to you.

#137 God, my Mother, gave birth to me and I was born again.

APPENDIX 2

#138 Many of my friends say the word "Liberal" as if it were a swear, a vulgarity, but Psalm 37: 25-26 (NRSV) says the liberal are righteous. But I'm not really a liberal either. I'm more of a leftist.

#139 I am. You are. We were. There's no proximate cause for the tears, no precipitating event. But here we are at the end nevertheless.

#140 I have pages and pages of unwritten notes, hundreds—thousands of these unfinished confessions.

BIBLIOGRAPHY

Athanasius. *De Incarnatiore.*
Balzac, Honore. *Physiologie du Mariage.* 1829.
Bradbury, Ray. *Fahrenheit 451.* New York, NY: Balentine, 1953.
Carter, Jeff. *The Last Persection.* Eugene, OR: Resource Publications, 2021.
———. *There Once Was a Prophet from Judah: Biblical Limericks for Fun and Prophet.* Eugene, OR: Resource Publications, 2018.
Cazzo, Rubin. Colonel. *USDARP Annual Report - 2019.* Washington D.C.: U.S. Defense Advanced Research Projects, 2020.
Chesteron, G.K. *Orthodoxy.* New York: Dodd, Mead & Co, 1908.
Cohen, Leonard. "Suzanne." *Songs of Leonard Cohen.* Columbia, 1967.
Dick, Philip K. *Martian Time Slip.* New York, NY: Ballentine, 1964.
Dimaso, Chris. *Zombies or Robots: Capitalist Alternatives.* Knob Noster, MO: Red and Black Books, 1967.
Dylan, Bob. "Highway 61 Revisited." *Highway 61 Revisited.* Columbia, 1965.
Eco, Umberto. *Kant and the Platypus: Essays on Language and Cognition.* Translated by Alastair McEwen. New York, NY: Harcourt Brace & Company, 1997.
Falso, Uomo. *The Hammer and the Battle Axe: Two Judases, One Nation.* Translated by Lo Estraneo. Rome, 2012.
Fanon, Frantz. *The Wretched of the Earth.* Translated by Richard Philcox. New York, NY: Grove, 2004.
Głowa, Gadająca. *Nero Fiddled, Trump Golfed: Imperial Response to Crisis.* Philadelphia, PA: Wonk Talk Books, 2020.
Gogh, Vincent Van. *The Letter of Vincent Van Gogh.* Edited by Mark Roskill. New York, NY: Atheneum, 1977.
Goldstein, Jonathan A. *1 Maccabees: A New Translation with Introduction and Commentary.* Garden City, NY: Doubleday and Company, Inc., 1976.
Ignatius. *Epistle to the Romans* . n.d.
Johnson, James Weldon. *God's Trombones: Seven Negro Sermons in Verse.* New York, NY: Penguin, 1927.
Kierkegaard, Soren. *Journals and Papers Vol. 1 A-E* . Edited by Howard V. Hong and Edna H. Hong. Bloomington , IN: Indiana University Press, 1967.
King, Stephen. *On Writing: A Memoir of the Craft.* New York, NY: Scribner, 2000.
LaTido, Doremi Fasso. *Where Gwthaints Fear to Gather: Apocalyptic Nightmares in Public Places.* French Lick, IN: Obsurity Pages, 1983.
Marx, Karl. *Wage Labour and Capital.* 1847.

Bibliography

Melanchthon, Philip. *An Underground Depression: Unpublished Essays*. Edited by Diego Occidentis. Bucksnort, TN, 2018.

Mortis, Timothy. *Reasons for Suspicion: The Leftist Roots of the Gospel*. Appelton, WI: John Birch's Books, 1957.

Mowers, Dave. *You Shall Cast Out Demons: A Field Guide to Exorcisms and Expulsions*. 3rd. Conception Junction , MO: Glossolalia Press, 1994.

Muir, Jane. *Of Men and Numbers*. New York, NY: Dover Publications, Inc., 1996.

Mulier-Sitienti, Judith. *Eschatonic Waters: 100 Easy Cocktail Recipes for the End of the World*. New York, NY: Party Times Press, 1999.

Nietzche, Friedrich. *Beyond Good and Evil: A Prelude to a Philosophy of the Future*. 1886.

Nietzsche, Friedrich. *Der Antichrist*. 1895.

Orfila, Seminandis. *The Seed and the Field*. Paris: Alexandrian Esoterica , 1637.

Ovis, Numus. *Mo' Money, Mere Mammon*. Brookyln, NY: Putative Press, 2013.

Pauli, Wolfgang. *Atom and Archetype: The Pauli/Jung Letters*. Princeton University Press, 2014.

Pia, Mya O. *Il Guernico Gospel*. Boston, MA: Squint Eyed Publishing, 1945.

Pseudo-Erronius. "Augurs or Daggers? The Capitoline Dilemma." *S.P.Q.R. Intelligence Weekly*, September 20, 27.

Report of the Security Council- Space Elevator. New York: The United Nations, 2147.

Schiller, Friedrich. "Spruch des Confucius." *Musen-Almanach*, 1796.

Stoker, Chris. *To Train an Octopus: Discipleship in Strange Times*. Shawangunk, NY: Niche Ministries Press, 2014.

Tachyon, Hanina ben. *Targum Absurdum and Other Writings of Rabbi Hanina ben Tachyon*. Edited by Gabriel Swersie. Gravity , IA: Quantum Press, 2001.

Tarrec, P L. *Dr. Tarrec's Field Guide to Demonic Encounters*. Indianapolis, IN: Irrelevant Press, 1976.

———. "Pyscho-Killers and Loving Saviors." *Marginalia Quarterly*, August 1965.

———. *The Toxic Avenger Goes to Bethlehem: Christological Themes in Troma Films*. Indianapolis, IN: Irrelevant Press, 1996.

Thompson, Craig. *How To Destroy a Prophet*. Dix, NE: Antagonist Press, 2014.

Wise, Michael, et al. *Dead Sea Scrolls: A New Translation*. San Francisco, CA: HarperSanFrancisco, 1996.

www.ingramcontent.com/pod-product-compliance
Lightning Source LLC
Chambersburg PA
CBHW062012220426
43662CB00010B/1304